T0301484

Women's Entrepreneurship and Culture

IN ASSOCIATION WITH THE DIANA INTERNATIONAL PROJECT

Titles include:

Women Entrepreneurs and the Global Environment for Growth
A Research Perspective
Edited by Candida G. Brush, Anne de Bruin, Elizabeth J. Gatewood and Colette Henry

Global Women's Entrepreneurship Research
Diverse Settings, Questions and Approaches
Edited by Karen D. Hughes and Jennifer E. Jennings

Women's Entrepreneurship in the 21st Century
An International Multi-Level Research Analysis
Edited by Kate V. Lewis, Colette Henry, Elizabeth J. Gatewood and John Watson

Women's Entrepreneurship in Global and Local Contexts
Edited by Cristina Díaz-García, Candida G. Brush, Elizabeth J. Gatewood and Friederike Welter

Entrepreneurial Ecosystems and Growth of Women's Entrepreneurship
A Comparative Analysis
Edited by Tatiana S. Manolova, Candida G. Brush, Linda F. Edelman, Alicia Robb and Friederike Welter

High-growth Women's Entrepreneurship
Programs, Policies and Practices
Edited by Amanda Bullough, Diana M. Hechavarría, Candida G. Brush and Linda F. Edelman

Women's Entrepreneurship and Culture
Socio-cultural Context, Traditional Family Roles and Self-determination
Edited by Ulrike Guelich, Amanda Bullough, Tatiana S. Manolova and Leon Schjoedt

Women's Entrepreneurship and Culture

Socio-cultural Context, Traditional Family Roles and Self-determination

Edited by

Ulrike Guelich

Assistant Professor, GEM (Global Entrepreneurship Monitor) Thailand Team Leader, Bangkok University School of Entrepreneurship and Management, Thailand

Amanda Bullough

Associate Professor, Management and Global Leadership; Co-founder and Research Director, Women's Leadership Initiative; Principal Co-investigator, GLOBE Project: GLOBE 2020, University of Delaware, USA

Tatiana S. Manolova

Professor of Management, Bentley University, USA

Leon Schjoedt

Visiting Research Scholar, Babson College, USA

IN ASSOCIATION WITH THE DIANA INTERNATIONAL PROJECT

Edward Elgar
PUBLISHING

Cheltenham, UK • Northampton, MA, USA

Published by
Edward Elgar Publishing Limited
The Lypiatts
15 Lansdown Road
Cheltenham
Glos GL50 2JA
UK

Edward Elgar Publishing, Inc.
William Pratt House
9 Dewey Court
Northampton
Massachusetts 01060
USA

A catalogue record for this book
is available from the British Library

Library of Congress Control Number: 2021938657

This book is available electronically in the **Elgar**online
Business subject collection
http://dx.doi.org/10.4337/9781789905045

ISBN 978 1 78990 503 8 (cased)
ISBN 978 1 78990 504 5 (eBook)

Printed and bound by CPI Group (UK) Ltd, Croydon, CR0 4YY

Contents

Figures

Tables

Contributors

Upasna A. Agarwal is an Associate Professor in Organization Behavior and Human Resource Management at the National Institute of Industrial Engineering (NITIE), Mumbai, India. She has an MBA and Master's in Labor Law from Symbiosis, Pune, and a PhD from the Indian Institute of Technology, Bombay, India. She has corporate and teaching experience of over a decade and a half. Upasna's areas of interest are leadership, work engagement, psychological contract, diversity and inclusion, and toxic work behaviour and entrepreneurship.

Pervaiz K. Ahmed is Professor of Management at Monash University, Malaysia. He is the Head of School (Business), Director of Global Asia in the 21st Century (GA21), and also Director of Entrepreneurship and Innovation Hub (eiHub). Prior to joining Monash University Malaysia, he held a variety of senior academic positions at universities in England. He has worked with industry and advised numerous blue chip companies and government agencies. He has extensive experience serving on the editorial boards of journals. He has published more than 100 research papers in top tiered international journals. He is also the author of four books, with publishers Butterworth-Heinemann and Prentice Hall. Professor Ahmed continues to be an active researcher and speaks regularly at international symposia and conventions.

Zahra Arasti is an Associate Professor of Entrepreneurship at the University of Tehran, Iran. Her research and teaching spans women's entrepreneurship, social entrepreneurship, and entrepreneurship education programmes. She publishes in premier journals, in English, French and Persian. Dr Arasti has a PhD in Management Science from Toulon University and a DEA in Industrial Engineering from the Grenoble Institute of Technology, France and a BS in Industrial Engineering from Sharif University of Technology, Iran.

Wee Chan Au is a Lecturer in the Department of Management at Monash University Malaysia. After a career in industry, she obtained her PhD from Monash University. Her research interests lie in the area of Human Resource Management, Organisational Behavior and Entrepreneurship. She has published her research work in international journals and presented at international conferences. She has been actively working on national and industry-related projects commissioned by the Economic Planning Unit (under the Prime

Minister's Office) Malaysia, Malaysian Plastics and Machinery Association (MPMA), and Certified Practising Accountants (CPA) Australia. She has secured research grants from the Ministry of Higher Education Malaysia, and The Newton Fund British Council Grant.

Mário Augusto is a Full Professor at the Faculty of Economics, University of Coimbra, Portugal, where he has been teaching courses on the field of finance and supervises several MS and PhD students. He is researcher at the Centre for Business and Economics Research at the University of Coimbra (CeBER). His publications include several dozen articles in peer-reviewed international journals, as well as proceedings of scientific meetings, and also several books.

Jasmine Banu (MS and PhD) is Research Scholar, Department of Management Studies, Indian Institute of Technology Madras, India. Her research interest primarily focuses on women entrepreneurs' work–life balance, wellbeing, growth and sustainability. She has more than ten years' experience in the IT industry. She has a Bachelor's of Engineering (Computer Science) and a Post-Graduate Diploma in Business Administration (HRM).

Rupashree Baral is an Associate Professor in the Department of Management Studies, Indian Institute of Technology Madras, India with a PhD from IIT Bombay, India. She has more than ten years' experience in teaching and research. Her key interest lies in teaching, research, training and consulting in the areas of work–life balance, women in management and entrepreneurship, employer branding, corporate social responsibility, knowledge sharing and hiding behaviour, and technology and human interface.

Bettina Lynda Bastian is Associate Professor of Entrepreneurship and Innovation Management at the Holy Spirit University of Kaslik, Lebanon. Her research addresses the intersections of gender, culture, governance, policy and organization associated with entrepreneurship and innovation. Dr. Bastian also specializes in the role of entrepreneurship and innovation for development, performing policy-focused research with international organizations and professional women's organizations, as well as state governments in the Middle East. She is active in the Lebanese entrepreneurship ecosystem, where she has been organizing seminars and workshops especially for women entrepreneurs, and intervening at numerous conferences and panels as speaker.

Amanda Bullough is an Associate Professor of Management and Co-founder and Research Director of the Women's Leadership Initiative at the University of Delaware, USA. She is also a Principal Co-Investigator on the GLOBE Project: GLOBE 2020. Her research and teaching span global leadership, organizational behaviour, women and gender, cross-cultural management, international business, entrepreneurship and professional development, to undergraduate and graduate students and executives. She publishes in premier journals such as the *Journal of Management, Academy of Management Perspectives, Entrepreneurship Theory and Practice, Leadership Quarterly*, and others, and has presented at countless international business and management conferences. Dr Bullough has also consulted for high-profile organizations like the World Bank, the OECD, Goldman Sachs, and the Global Business School Network (GBSN). She has travelled and worked in approximately 40 countries. Bullough has a PhD in Management & International Business and an MA in International Studies, from Florida International University, and a BS in Marketing from the University of South Florida, USA.

Regina Frank is Senior Lecturer in Entrepreneurship and Innovation at Leicester Castle Business School, De Montfort University (DMU), UK. Dr Frank has a distinctively international personal, educational and professional background which also informs her positionality in research. In academia, Dr Frank has always particularly enjoyed interdisciplinary work. Today, her primary research interests include social innovation and entrepreneurship for poverty alleviation and empowerment, for and with marginalized communities, and in emerging markets; and education for sustainable development. Current projects range from critical perspectives on entrepreneurship (research), women entrepreneurship, entrepreneurship education to art and entrepreneurship for social inclusion.

Ulrike Guelich is Assistant Professor at the School of Entrepreneurship and Management at Bangkok University in Thailand. She is Global Entrepreneurship Monitor (GEM) Thailand team leader. She holds a PhD in Entrepreneurship and MBAs from the University of Maryland, USA and from Zurich, Switzerland. Dr Ulrike Guelich contributed to several national and international reports on entrepreneurial activities, attitudes and aspirations, such as for GEM, ILO, UNDP and UNESCAP. Her 25 years of entrepreneurship experience include years as business owner in a manufacturing family business in the fourth generation and leading an IT start-up as supplier to the automotive industry. Ulrike's research interests evolve around women entrepreneurship, the use of entrepreneurial networks and their influence on innovation in entrepreneurial activities.

Stephen Hill is Emeritus Professor at Sohar University, Oman, and works closely with USEK, Lebanon, the UK LebanonTechHub and GEM Global. His recent publications focus on entrepreneurship, including the *Global Entrepreneurship Monitor (GEM) Global Report 2019/2020* and successive *GEM National Reports for Lebanon* (2015–19). Earlier books include *Managerial Economics*; *Time, Work and Organisation* (with K. Starkey, J. Hassard and P. Blyton); *The Regional Distribution of Foreign Manufacturing*

Investment in the UK (with M. Munday); and *Input–Output Tables for Wales* (with A. Roberts); amongst others.

Bridget N. Irene is an Assistant Professor in Enterprise and Entrepreneurship at the International Centre for Transformational Entrepreneurship, Coventry University, UK. Her scholarly interests range widely, encompassing entrepreneurship and focusing on the culturally instantiated facets of the debate on gender entrepreneurship, entrepreneurial competencies, family businesses, entrepreneurship education, and the informal economy. Her PhD research contributes to the already established discourse on gendering entrepreneurship and provides explicit feminist perspectives highlighting the inadvertent reinforcement of women's subordination to men in the context of the entrepreneurial endeavours.

Nancy C. Jurik is Professor Emerita of Justice & Social Inquiry in the School of Social Transformation, Arizona State University, USA. Her publications focus on gender, work organization and entrepreneurship. Her books include *Doing Justice, Doing Gender: Women in Legal and Criminal Justice Occupations* (Sage, 2007), *Bootstrap Dreams: U.S. Microenterprise Development in an Era of Welfare Reform* (Cornell University Press, 2005), and *Provocateur for Justice: Jane Tennison and Policing in "Prime Suspect"* (University of Illinois Press, 2012). She is a 2019–2020 Fulbright Research Scholar.

Bernadette Mandawa-Bray is a Lecturer in Enterprise and a member of the Centre for Entrepreneurship and Innovation at the Leicester Castle Business School, De Montfort University, Leicester, UK. She is a Fellow of the Higher Education Academy and a recipient of the Commonwealth Scholarship and Kofi Annan Fellowship, respectively. Her PhD investigates performance in women-owned MSMEs in developing countries, with a focus on entrepreneurial competencies and entrepreneurial orientation. Her research interests include women entrepreneurship, small business performance, entrepreneurial characteristics, and women's leadership.

Tatiana S. Manolova (DBA, Boston University) is a Professor of Management at Bentley University, USA. Research interests include strategic management (competitive strategies for new and small companies), international entrepreneurship and management in emerging economies. Tatiana is the author of over 70 scholarly articles and book chapters, has co-authored two books, and was the lead editor of a compendium of research on women in entrepreneurial ecosystems published in 2017 by Edward Elgar Publishing. She is a Senior Editor for the *International Journal of Emerging Markets*, a Consulting Editor for the *International Small Business Journal* and the *International Journal of Management Reviews*, and serves on the editorial boards of *Entrepreneurship*

Theory and Practice, Journal of Business Venturing and *Small Business Economics.*

Magdalena Markowska (PhD, Jönköping University) is Assistant Professor at Jönköping International Business School (JIBS), Sweden. She teaches entrepreneurship courses, sustainable venture development, professional portfolio development and project management. Her current research interests include entrepreneurial identity, entrepreneurial careers as well as issues of contextualizing entrepreneurship. Magdalena has published in peer-reviewed journals: *Small Business Economics, Entrepreneurship and Regional Development, International Journal of Innovation and Entrepreneurship* and *Journal of Small Business and Enterprise Development* as well as in edited books, and has co-edited a book entitled *Contextualizing Entrepreneurship in Emerging Economies and Developing Countries* with Marcela Ramirez Pasillas and Ethel Brundin.

Beverly Dawn Metcalfe is Professor of Women, Leadership and Development at ESA (Grand Ecole), Lebanon and has held a number of research positions in academic institutions in the UK, Lebanon and elsewhere. Her research highlights the intersections between culture, women's studies and leadership, usually in a Middle East context. Her many publications include books, journal articles and policy advice. Dr Metcalfe is very active on ResearchGate, and has worked hard to inspire and guide young scholars. Her book on *Leadership Development in the Middle East* is the core text for most undergraduate leadership courses in the GCC.

William K. Murithi is a Lecturer in Entrepreneurship and a member of the Centre for Entrepreneurship and Innovation at the Leicester Castle Business School, De Montfort University, UK. His PhD investigates strategic behaviours of family and non-family businesses in developing economies. He has presented at international conferences and published in leading journals. His research interests include entrepreneurship, strategic management, family business, regional development, and socio-cultural and institutional context within developing economies.

Sabrina Nourin is a Research Associate at the Center for Entrepreneurship Development at BRAC University, Bangladesh and at the School of Business, Monash University Malaysia. Sabrina has more than 11 years' work experience in managing supply chains in Bangladesh. She started her career at Avery Dennison Bangladesh and subsequently worked in Sanofi Bangladesh, Banglalink Digital Telecommunication Ltd and Berger Paints Bangladesh Ltd. In 2017, she completed her postgraduate research diploma at Monash University Malaysia, where she researched women entrepreneurship in Bangladesh under the supervision of Dr Wee Chan Au and Professor Pervaiz

K. Ahmed. Her research focuses on the experiences and challenges faced by women entrepreneurs in their entrepreneurial journeys. Prior to her research experience, she completed her Master's and Bachelor's degrees in Business Administration from BRAC University Bangladesh.

Mansi Rastogi is associated with Department of Management Studies, NIT Silchar. She obtained her PhD degree from Department of Management Studies, Indian Institute of Technology Roorkee as a UGC sponsored fellow. As a bright millennial researcher, she has published her work in many top SCI, SSCI, and ABDC journals. Her research interests include work-family interface, positive psychology, and women entrepreneurship.

Laleh Sadeghi holds a Master's degree in Entrepreneurship Education and Promotion from the Faculty of Entrepreneurship, University of Tehran, Iran. She is interested in research in the field of women's entrepreneurship, so she has been studying and researching in this field for some time.

Maryam Saeedian holds a Master's degree in Entrepreneurship from the Faculty of Entrepreneurship, University of Tehran, Iran. She is interested in research in the field of women's entrepreneurship.

Leon Schjoedt, PhD, is a visiting scholar at Babson College, USA. His research focuses on entrepreneurial behaviour – the intersection between entrepreneurship and organizational behaviour. He has presented his research at numerous academic meetings, including the annual meeting for the Academy of Management and Babson College Entrepreneurship Research Conference. Leon's research has appeared in 125 publications, including *Entrepreneurship Theory and Practice*, *Journal of High Technology Management Research*, *International Journal of Entrepreneurial Behaviour & Research* and *Small Business Economics*. His research has been featured in *The Wall Street Journal*. Leon is an award-winning reviewer and serves as editor of *Small Business Economics*.

Tigist Tesfaye Abebe (MBA) is a PhD student at the Addis Ababa University, Ethiopia. Her main research interest is on how mumpreneurs start business and balance both family and business in the Ethiopian context. She has a Master's degree in Business Administration in Marketing Management and a BA in Business Management. She worked as a lecturer at Hawassa University, Ethiopia between 2009 and 2018. Outside of work, Tigist is a mother to three young daughters.

Pedro Torres is Professor of Marketing and Strategy at the University of Coimbra and research member at the Centre for Business and Economics Research (CeBER), Portugal. He holds a PhD in Business Management from the University of Coimbra and he received an MBA from the Católica–Lisbon

University. He is currently the coordinator of the MBA for Executives and President of the Association for University Extension (APEU). His research has been presented at international conferences and has been published in refereed journals.

Dongling Zhang is an Assistant Professor of Criminology in the Department of Global Languages, Cultures & Societies at Webster University in the United States. He obtained his PhD degree in Justice Studies from Arizona State University. His research primarily focuses on university entrepreneurship education, microenterprise development programs in urban China and women's massive entry into entrepreneurship in post-1978 China. He is currently working on a new research project on China's partnership with the United Nations Development Program to promote women's entrepreneurship.

1. Introduction to women's entrepreneurship and culture: socio-cultural dynamics, role-influenced behaviors and constraint negotiation

Ulrike Guelich, Amanda Bullough, Tatiana S. Manolova and Leon Schjoedt

INTRODUCTION

Women's entrepreneurship is pivotal for both national economic development and societal advancement, as it provides employment opportunities and promotes self-reliance (Elam et al., 2019; UN Women, 2020; Venkatesh et al., 2017; World Bank, 2012). Gender equality and the empowerment of women are an effective way to combat poverty, hunger and disease and to stimulate sustainable economic development (Neimanis and Tortisyn, 2003). While it is generally recognized that the competitiveness of a country relies on the active involvement of women in education, business, politics, and research and development, existing gender stereotypical beliefs and practices, deeply ingrained in the socio-cultural context of a nation, can be a challenging constraint (Shukla and Arntzen, 2013). Indeeed, gender and culture dynamically interact, shaping gender role expectations and identities, and the economic and social environment in which women's entrepreneurship is embedded (Bullough et al., forthcoming).

According to the Global Entrepreneurship Monitor (GEM) Report on Women's Entrepreneurship 2018/2019 in 59 economies around the globe, around 231 million women were involved in entrepreneurial activities, either as start-ups or established business owners (Elam et al., 2019). Although women are increasingly engaged in entrepreneurship, their ownership still lags that of men (Pandey and Amezcua, 2020). While it is acknowledged that there is no single ideal context for entrepreneurship (Welter et al., 2017), socially supportive cultures enable both higher rates of entrepreneurial activity and the quality of women's entrepreneurship (Stephan and Uhlaner, 2010). While culture affects the rate and quality of women's entrepreneurial activities, women's entrepreneurial activities, in turn, shape societal norms, values and acceptance of women's business leadership roles. Succinctly put, culture shapes women's entrepreneurship and women's entrepreneurship shapes culture.

To better appreciate culture as an antecedent and a consequence of women's entrepreneurship, we begin by introducing the concept of culture. Culture may be viewed as a "rich complex of meanings, beliefs, practices, symbols, norms, and values prevalent among people in a society" (Schwartz, 2006, p. 138). It is manifested in artifacts, rituals and symbols and operates at multiple levels. At the deepest level, basic and invisible assumptions are taken for granted (Leung et al., 2005). Culture may also be considered as the "underlying system of values peculiar to a specific group or society" (Pinillos and Reyes, 2011, p. 25) and is one of six elements of an entrepreneurship ecosystem, besides finance, support systems, human capital, markets and policy (Walsh and Winsor, 2019). Culture operates at the organizational and at the small group (team) levels. In all, culture forms a context in which people function on a daily basis and, for entrepreneurs, a context that may facilitate or hinder entrepreneurs' actions in new venture creation and management.

Culture evolves over time on an ad hoc basis or by decision. If repeated actions or decisions are made by people who are in formal leadership positions, or are informal leaders and interpreted as desirable by a set of followers, those actions or decisions may become part of a culture. This means that the founders' personal values, espoused through actions and decisions, can mold the culture in the new venture over time (Ford et al., 2008; Selznick, 2011). As such, the espoused culture based on the personal values of the entrepreneur is instilled into the venture through a hierarchical process (Payne and Joyner, 2006). Cultural values are broad and encompassing, while entrepreneurship is a rather specific behavior. However, entrepreneurship constitutes value-based leadership if used by design (Stephan and Pathak, 2016). This shows that entrepreneurs' actions affect the culture of the new venture. The entrepreneurs' actions may also impact the culture beyond the new venture as direct and indirect stakeholders may consider the actions and decisions of the entrepreneur to be socially desirable.

Gender norms can be viewed as essential aspects of culture. Differences in women's entrepreneurship across societies and entrepreneurial activities can be explained by multifaceted explanations. Many gender-specific barriers and constraints relate to cultural values, norms and customs (Anambane and Adom, 2018; Baughn et al., 2006; Khandelwal and Sehgal, 2018). As just one example, large and voluminous images of a country's father figure, as seen in societies like North Korea and Thailand, inculcate a culture of respect for and value of a male figurehead. And yet, gender role expectations, gender egalitarianism and the socio-cultural context in the ecosystem are under-researched cultural factors in women's entrepreneurship (Bullough et al., forthcoming). The goal of this book, therefore, is to foster a discussion among researchers, government agencies and related organizations on how culture enables or limits women's entrepreneurship.

We chose the topic for three reasons: first, discussions about the right ecosystems for women's entrepreneurship are gathering importance. Social and cultural norms are one of the important framework conditions for an entrepreneurial ecosystem, besides finance, government policies and programs, research and development transfer, physical and commercial infrastructure and market conditions (Elam et al., 2019). Private organizations who advise government policy makers encourage the development of stronger entrepreneurial ecosystems. Although business degrees alone are not the only pathway to business success for female entrepreneurs, institutions of higher education have increasingly integrated entrepreneurship education targeted at women into their strategic plans (Prill, 2019). Yet, gender inequalities remain deeply ingrained in every society, with women lacking access to decent work, facing occupational segregation and gender wage gaps (UN Women, 2020). In addition, in many cultures, women are often denied access to basic education and health care and are under-represented in political and economic decision-making processes (UN Women, 2020). Women across the globe are confronted with gendered cultural environments within diverse determinants of the entrepreneurial ecosystem that either foster or hinder the opportunity for women entrepreneurs and business owners to build and grow their businesses (Acs et al., 2016). Importantly, as the leaders of the Global Leadership and Organizational Behavior Effectiveness (GLOBE) project hypothesize, while the role of economic barriers in international business exchange have come down, cultural barriers for entrepreneurs and leaders may increase, because internationalization exposes the different values of the different cultures, making it more difficult to navigate across cultures (House et al., 2004).

Second, the roles and expectations, especially related to gender, vary significantly depending on the cultural context. The cultural context affects both male and female entrepreneurs by exerting pressures to behave in accordance with cultural norms (Welter and Smallbone, 2011). In general, cultural norms limit women's potential to pursue entrepreneurship more than men's (Masbout and Van Staveren, 2010). More specifically, in highly patriarchal, or conservative, cultures, two social realms exist: the outside and inside realms. The "outside realm" is where men are seen as breadwinners who work outside the home and control interactions between the family and the outside world (Schuler et al., 1996); while the "inside realm" is populated by women who depend on men to take care of them. In these cultures, women are often restricted to indoor activities; hence, they are hidden away from the outside world (Ali,

2013; Ali et al., 2017). As a result, women's entrepreneurial or employment pursuits are limited, as the norms for women pertain to activities in the inside realm such as household management and child and elder caring. In these conservative cultures, women entrepreneurs are seen as non-conforming because they act against cultural norms by venturing out of the inside realm to pursue activities in the outside realm. By breaking into the outside realm to pursue new venture creation or business ownership, women entrepreneurs may be sanctioned by the cultural barriers such as lack of or limited family support, and limited access to funding and to networks (Tlaiss, 2015). In contrast, an egalitarian culture where men and women may share the activities in the inside and outside realms is conducive of women's entrepreneurship. According to the GLOBE study, societies with higher gender egalitarianism minimize role differences between genders (House et al., 2004). In such cultures women are welcomed, even encouraged, to pursue work outside the family domain. The benefits of the egalitarian culture, with its cultural norms of both men and women in the outside realm, cannot be understated. Extending GLOBE's work on gender egalitalitarianism by incorporating collectivism, and building on the notion of inside–outside realms, Bullough et al. (2017) demonstrated how women's entrepreneurship interacts with the family-level in-group differently, and more strongly, than it does with the societal-institutional level of collectivism. Women's participation in the outside realm is widely acknowledged as an important factor in economic growth (Brush et al., 2018; Bullough et al., 2017; De Bruin et al., 2006; Hechavarria et al., 2019).

Third, the concept of balancing norms associated with male-dominated family cultures and Western neoliberal values of entrepreneurship (Bruni et al., 2005) shows how economic and cultural contexts lead to struggles of individual women with these structural inequalities (e.g., Villares-Varela and Essers, 2019; Xheneti et al., 2019). As entrepreneurs tend to shape their living and working contexts, women also try to navigate the socio-cultural environment in order to engage in entrepreneurship.

With this volume, we not only contribute a gender perspective to cultural factors but also show how women in developing countries are able to carefully find a way around limitations. Governmental support to empower women to choose entrepreneurship as their career goal is not always successful and might lead to necessity-driven entrepreneurs within patriarchal cultural settings (Zhang et al., 2006). Women thus need to find their way within a cultural context to develop what they perceive as the best path to business success. In light of this, in this edited volume we sought chapters that fit within the overarching theme of women's entrepreneurship and culture with respect to the socio-cultural context, family roles and self-determination as influencers of women's entrepreneurship in different geographical and cultural conditions.

Specifically, we sought chapters which offered valuable and novel perspectives on the contextual embeddedness of women's entrepreneurship and culture to create a better understanding of how, why and where gender plays a role in various cultural contexts. Our call for chapter proposals requested papers that covered the following factors:

- key cultural and societal settings, with a particular focus on women's entrepreneurship and culture;
- interactions between and among cultures and societies;
- cross-cultural similarities and differences;
- the impact of culture on women's entrepreneurship and the impact on culture on women's entrepreneurship.

In response to our call for chapter proposals, we received 36 submissions. After we reviewed all these submissions, 16 were solicited for full chapter contributions that were reviewed using a double-blind review process. Working with an editor and a set of reviewers, eight chapters met our expectations for inclusion in this book. Our final selection comprises both conceptual and empirical papers, employs a mixture of methodological approaches and adopts a range of perspectives on gender and culture. While each chapter offers its own unique viewpoint, collectively, the chapters offer a contemporary view of the socio-cultural embeddedness of women's entrepreneurship.

The eight chapters in this book fall into three main themes: (1) socio-cultural context as the base of women's entrepreneurship; (2) emancipation from traditional family roles; and (3) targeted policies and programs versus engrained women's rights leading to self-determination. These main themes are displayed in Figure 1.1. The figure also shows minor themes that overlap among the major context.

In the following three sections, we consider each of the main themes by introducing the topic and each of the chapters within the main theme with brief summaries of the authors' work.

THE EFFECTS OF A SOCIETY'S CULTURE ON THE EMBEDDEDNESS OF WOMEN'S ENTREPRENEURSHIP

Society and culture are highly influential contextual factors for women's entrepreneurship (Bastian et al., 2019). Examining culture across national boundaries is often complicated because of differences among values, languages and meanings that may cause ambiguity (Gunnell, 2016). Culture comprises the values that a society is built upon. This indicates that a cross-cultural entrepreneurship study is challenged by the effects of culture on meanings and values as seen in some cultures where entrepreneurship is seen as a last resort option

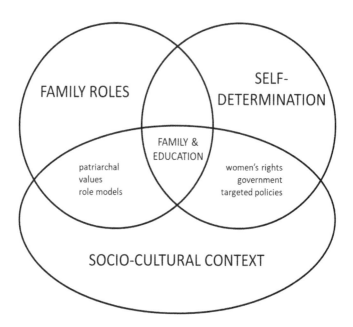

Figure 1.1   The interplay of socio-cultural context with family roles and self-determination

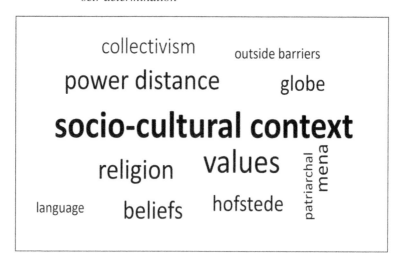

Figure 1.2   Socio-cultural context

for employment while in others it may be seen as a revered opportunity for employment.

Research on women's entrepreneurship in developing countries, specifically those with patriarchal societies, identifies barriers, struggles and difficulties for women entrepreneurs (e.g. Al-Dajani and Marlow, 2013; Itani et al., 2011; Naguib and Jamali, 2015). Despite this research, there are a multitude of research opportunities to provide a more nuanced and deeper understanding of socio-cultural influence on women entrepreneurs. This may be within and between socio-cultural contexts.

In Chapters 2 and 3, under the theme "The effects of a society's culture on the embeddedness of women's entrepreneurship", Bastian, Metcalfe and Hill and Au, Nourin and Ahmed utilize the two large research studies on culture and entrepreneurship: Geert Hofstede's six cultural dimensions and the Global Leadership and Organizational Behavior Effectiveness (GLOBE) study. In Chapters 2 and 4, Bastian et al. and Torres and Augusto respectively also explore the context of patriarchal societies and their impact on women entrepreneurs, questioning if women entrepreneurs might be able to break the glass ceiling in a patriarchal society context.

The chapters utilizing Hofstede's cultural dimensions investigate the influence of the six dimensions on patriarchal societies and regional differences and institutional collectivism in comparison to in-group collectivism, displaying the effects of a society's culture on its values and how these values then relate to actual behavior (Hofstede 2015).

In Chapter 2, Bastian, Metcalfe and Hill investigate the MENA (Middle East and Northern Africa) region, where many countries exhibit some of the largest gender inequalities worldwide (World Economic Forum, 2018). This chapter compares the differences in entrepreneurship for both genders between the Mediterranean geographic territory and the Arab Gulf territory and explores how gendered cultural and governance factors contribute to different entrepreneurial outcomes and experiences in the region.

Bastian et al. categorized 15 countries of the MENA region into two "blocks" and highlight substantial gendered differences in entrepreneurial activities within Mediterranean countries and Gulf countries over the last decade, with the Gulf countries in MENA having achieved near gender parity in entrepreneurship by 2018, fueled, amongst other things, by gender quotas implemented by the governments. In general, men in the largely patriarchal MENA societies (Hofstede, 1992) are regarded as decisive, whereas women are seen as intuitive and relationship-focused (Omair, 2008), thus less powerful and influential (Zamberi Ahmad, 2011). One focus of Bastian et al. is therefore related to work–family balance as one of the greatest challenges for women entrepreneurs across the MENA region (e.g. Erogul and McCrohan, 2008), constraining women entrepreneurs, who are expected to combine family obligations and responsibilities in their roles as mother, daughter or daughter-in-law with their entrepreneurial endeavors.

Bangladesh (Chapter 3) with its strong patriarchal societal orientation and a Muslim majority of 90 percent of the population, determines the context of this chapter, with Au, Nourin and Ahmed exploring the role of agency on women entrepreneurs, embedded within the three sections of gender, religion and socio-economic class. Au et al. discuss how and if entrepreneurship can help women in Bangladesh build agency and if women can act as agents for change. The findings contrast sharply with the idealized and romanticized view of entrepreneurship as the "Holy Grail of elevation and emancipation" (Verduijn and Essers, 2013, p. 100) as entrepreneurial activities of women are often only possible at high personal costs, specifically with regard to psychological and physical well-being. Whereas many studies focus on women entrepreneurs' success stories and see them not restricted by socio-cultural context factors (Khan et al., 2007; Weik, 2011), Au et al. point out the risks and costs for the individual women, ingrained in a societal context that limits their entrepreneurial activities.

In addition to utilizing the GLOBE study, Torres and Augusto in Chapter 4 also draw on World Bank data and study the 20 countries of Argentina, Australia, Austria, Czech Republic, Denmark, Finland, France, Greece, Hungary, Ireland, Italy, Japan, the Netherlands, New Zealand, Poland, Portugal, Slovenia, Spain, Sweden and the United States. To shed light on the role of self-protective leadership ideals, Torres and Augusto identify combinations of cultural practices and culturally-endorsed leadership ideals, leading to higher levels of women's self-employment. By using qualitative comparative analysis, the authors point out that different combinations of factors such as uncertainty avoidance, institutional and in-group collectivism and self-protective leadership ideals can lead to different outcomes, depending on the cultural context. In addition, configurations of different combinations of factors contribute to clarify the role of collectivism with regard to women's entrepreneurship, suggesting that the importance of collectivism is overestimated because its presence or absence appeared to be irrelevant for the entrepreneurial activities of women entrepreneurs.

WOMEN'S EMANCIPATION FROM TRADITIONAL FAMILY ROLES

Theme 2 narrows the contextualized view of women's entrepreneurship to entrepreneurial activity in a *particular* context (Brush et al., 2009; 2017; Welter, 2011), that of the family. In many emerging economies, women entrepreneurs tend to operate their businesses as part of the informal economy (ILO, 2009; UNESCAP 2017). These businesses are also often smaller, grow

Figure 1.3   Family–work balance

more slowly and are less profitable (Bardasi et al., 2011; Hallward-Driemeier, 2013). Gender norms and societal values influence what a woman can do or cannot do and thus shape women's entrepreneurial activities (Jamali, 2009). Depending on how context and entrepreneurship intertwine, they influence entrepreneurship dynamics and either enable or constrain particular role-influenced behaviors (Markowska and Lopez-Vega, 2018). Family context consigns women and men to cultural norms and values (Bullough et al., 2017; Nelson and Constantinidis, 2017) and can be seen as the closest and possibly strongest network. Thus, new venture creation is influenced by an individual's family-related roles and responsibilities (Jennings and Brush, 2013).

In Chapters 5 and 6, Markowska and Tesfaye Abebe, and Irene, Murithi, Frank and Mandawa-Bray, respectively, display the importance of women entrepreneurship and their role for the economic development of African countries, looking at interfaces between women entrepreneurship, economic empowerment and breaking free from familial roles, thus emancipating from their situations. Both chapters highlight the importance of non-economic factors that could lead to autonomy and freedom for women entrepreneurship, increasing feelings of motivation and personal achievement in women. In Chapter 7, Banu, Baral, Agarwal and Rastogi add an Asian component to the same context where a patriarchal society and caste systems in India limit women's entry into entrepreneurship without familial support.

Specifically, Markowska and Tesfaye Abebe examine which cultural constraints limit the attractiveness of entrepreneurship as a career choice for well-educated women in Ethiopia, where gender inequality and female subordination are largely present despite government efforts to encourage more women into entrepreneurship (Amine and Staub, 2009; Kalantaridis and Fletcher, 2012), and how to overcome these cultural challenges. Markowska and Tesfaye Abebe identify three major constraints for Ethiopian women to legitimate their entrepreneurial endeavors: (1) women entrepreneurs experienced problems convincing family and friends that entrepreneurship was a legitimate career path for them, especially as they were well educated: while families can accept the necessity for informal entrepreneurship among poor and less well-educated women, they disapprove of entrepreneurship by educated women; (2) families objected to the type of business; and (3) women were censured for prioritizing business over the role of mother.

In Chapter 6, Irene, Murithi, Frank and Mandawa-Bray present entrepreneurship as a socio-economic dilemma between the traditional role of women in South Africa and the interface of women entrepreneurship, economic empowerment and emancipation, analyzing interviews with 152 South African women entrepreneurs. The findings of Irene et al. demonstrate the resilience of women entrepreneurs, choosing entrepreneurship not only as a way out of poverty but also as a way out of a life of subordination, dependence on men and obscurity by family. Thus, entrepreneurship is able to eliminate perceived barriers for women, especially barriers that hinder them from fully participating in economic and social activities. As a result, non-economic factors such as autonomy and freedom in entrepreneurial activities help women feel motivation and achievement.

In Chapter 7, Banu, Baral, Agarwal and Rastogi investigate the impact of society and culture on the decision of women to enter entrepreneurship and on their business performance through interviews with 20 female Indian small business entrepreneurs. The combination of family, community, cultural and religious norms of India have intentionally or unintentionally influenced Indian society, limiting a girl's literacy, education and occupational mobility (Senapati and Ojha, 2019), contributing to a female to male entrepreneurship ratio of 0.7, with only seven women entrepreneurs compared to ten men entrepreneurs (Bosma and Kelley, 2019). Banu, Baral, Agarwal and Rastogi applied Geert Hofstede's cultural dimensions to the Indian context to develop an in-depth understanding of women's career choices towards entrepreneurship. Culture was found to be highly influential for business growth and success of women entrepreneurs in India, especially since male family support is needed for women to start and run their businesses due to the strong family orientation of the Indian culture, a pervasive gender inequality, the dominance of masculinity, and widened power distance in the society.

CULTURE AND SELF-DETERMINATION IN WOMEN'S ENTREPRENEURSHIP

Figure 1.4   *Self-determination*

The concept of balancing norms associated with male-dominated family cultures and Western neoliberal values of entrepreneurship shows how economic and cultural contexts lead to struggles of individual women with structural inequalities. This work–life imbalance creates barriers for women starting and running businesses. Thus, women have found ways to combine work and personal lives (Ruderman et al., 2002). Women in male-dominated family cultures might decide to choose self-determination to enter entrepreneurship, be it in negotiating within the cultural context or navigating limitations by finding the least offensive approach within cultural constraints. On the other hand, also balancing work and personal responsibilities, family businesses are the most prevalent form of businesses in the world (Lien et al., 2016; Oudah et al., 2018), accounting for more than half of the GDP, 60 percent of new employment, and 65 percent of wages paid (Pieper et al., 2013). A specific form, but not a new phenomenon, of family businesses is entrepreneurial couples, firms owned and managed by a couple (Othman et al., 2016). Their number is increasing at a higher rate than other types of businesses (Othman et al., 2016; Wu et al., 2010), with advantages for the economies because of higher productivity (Dahl et al., 2015); however, on the down side, few of them survive in the long term (Nicholson, 2008).

To balance the different norms and limitations of both purely women-led or co-preneurial businesses, Zhang and Jurik (Chapter 8) and Arasti, Sadeghi and Saeedian (Chapter 9) suggest that policies are needed to overcome the socio-cultural challenges of women to increase the feasibility of creating women's entrepreneurship in different formations. Both chapters investigate women entrepreneurship in an Asian context. In Chapter 8, Zhang and Jurik explore how women in patriarchal China simultaneously construct businesses and gender in the context of country and family. Supported by the Chinese government's promotion for women's self-employment, the term "she economy" evolved, acknowledging women's contributions to economic development through both self-employment and consumption (Ren, 2019). While most women entrepreneurs in China run necessity-driven microenterprises with little to no employees and limited start-up capital (Chan and Lin, 2014; Wang, 2017), younger, college-educated women prioritized work and self-employment over family, leading to postponing marriage and motherhood. The authors suggest that the Chinese government's interest in promoting women's entrepreneurship develops from the strategy to make use of women entrepreneurs' productive potential for economic growth rather than promoting gender equality.

In Chapter 9, Arasti, Sadeghi and Saeedian provide a study on co-preneurship as a gendered process in Iran, where prevailing gender ideologies are rooted in social norms and a patriarchal culture. The authors investigate the socio-cultural context of women in co-preneurial businesses by interviewing 14 female heads of small early-stage businesses in the service sector in Tehran, Iran and applying institutional theory. The findings extend existing knowledge about family businesses by shedding light on the under-studied field of co-preneurial businesses in the context of a culture where women's entrepreneurship is constrained by societal norms which prefer women to work with their family in the workplace rather than with external people.

With these considerations of the eight chapters that constitute the remainder of this book complete, we turn to how the chapters in combination, that is, this book as a whole provide new insights in women's entrepreneurship and culture to advance the literature on women's entrepreneurship.

CONCLUDING COMMENTS

Our objective with this edited volume was to assemble contributions that offer valuable and novel perspectives on the socio-cultural embeddedness of women's entrepreneurship in order to better understand the interplay between women's entrepreneurship and culture. Collectively, the studies included in this volume provide a rich portrayal of the multi-faceted interactions between gender and culture in different economic, social and institutional contexts around the world. While cultural norms and espoused traditions still present numerous hurdles to women's entrepreneurial initiatives, it is also evident that women's entrepreneurial agency can lead to wider social acceptance and support for women's economic participation and leadership. Through self-determination, which often challenges the traditional family roles, women entrepreneurs can shape and structure the socio-cultural context and thus be a powerful force for change.

With the studies included in this volume, we make a substantial contribution to advancing knowledge about women's entrepreneurship and culture. Future work can provide additional insights into this complex interaction through several avenues of research with regard to the topics.

The studies display a significant heterogeneity in cultural contexts. More detailed research has to target how women's entrepreneurship is, or is not, embedded in the political and institutional environment. Gender parity in entrepreneurship in certain cultural contexts cannot be compared to those in others, as state-promoted gender equality, for example in patriarchal countries, might result in different entrepreneurial outcomes for women than a gender parity embedded in the day-to-day culture of a country.

As the studies reveal, constraints of certain women entrepreneurs stem from the interplay of gender, religion and social class and go beyond merely economic pressures. Thus, more insights are needed to understand the social struggles of women entrepreneurs for legitimized acceptance and gender equality to be able to build on opportunities in entrepreneurship. Future studies should try to shed light on how policy-makers, aiming to promote and thus embed women's entrepreneurship into their cultures, can do so by changing societal culture as cultural practices are difficult to change. In this regard, research exploring different dimensions and norms of culture and their impact on changing the beliefs about equality in women's entrepreneurship could contribute to quality entrepreneurship not only on a communal, regional or country level but also in rural versus urban settings and in the family context. In addition, future studies could investigate how a more sensitive government influence towards the socio-cultural dimensions of women's experiences could lead to successful self-determination of women entrepreneurs, instead of necessity-driven entrepreneurship.

As many studies have local or regional perspectives, and thus cannot be generalized even across a single country, further studies of women's entrepreneurship across different patriarchal societies or regions could deliver a larger picture and contribute towards more generalizable entrepreneurship theory-building of women's entrepreneurship and culture.

In conclusion, insights on the influencers of the socio-cultural context, of traditional family roles and self-determination on women's entrepreneurship, can lead to a better understanding of necessary measures, leading not only to higher rates of women's entrepreneurship but also to increased quality of their enterprises. A unified effort for initiatives supporting women in different cultural contexts, combined with targeted policies and cultural education of communities, could help remove barriers to an increase of women's representation in business. There are still significant gaps to be filled in this area. We hope that with the studies included in this volume, we give an overview of some less-researched countries and research fields to enhance the knowledge about women's entrepreneurship and culture and their embeddedness in the socio-cultural context.

REFERENCES

Acs, Z., T. Åstebro, D. Audretsch and D.T. Robinson (2016), 'Public policy to promote entrepreneurship: A call to arms'. *Small Business Economics*, 47 (1), 35–51.

Al-Dajani, H. and S. Marlow (2013), 'Empowerment and entrepreneurship: A theoretical framework'. *International Journal of Entrepreneurial Behavior & Research*, 19 (5), 503–24.

Ali, F. (2013), 'A multi-level perspective on equal employment opportunity for women in Pakistan'. *Equality, Diversity and Inclusion: An International Journal*, 32 (3), 289–309.

Ali, F., A. Malik, V. Pereira and A.A. Ariss (2017), 'A relational understanding of work–life balance of Muslim migrant women in the West: Future research agenda'. *International Journal of Human Resource Management*, 28 (8), 1163–81.

Amine, L.S. and K.M. Staub (2009), 'Women entrepreneurs in sub-Saharan Africa: An institutional theory analysis from a social marketing point of view'. *Entrepreneurship & Regional Development*, 21 (2), 183–211.

Bardasi, E., S. Sabarwal and K. Terrell (2011), 'How do female entrepreneurs perform? Evidence from three developing regions'. *Small Business Economics*, 37 (4), 417.

Bastian, B.L., B.D. Metcalfe and M.R. Zali (2019), 'Gender inequality: Entrepreneurship development in the MENA region', *Sustainability*, 11 (22), 6472.

Bosma, N. and D. Kelly (2019), 'The Global Entrepreneurship Monitor 2018/2019 Global Report', accessed 5 August 2020 at https://www.gemconsortium.org/report/gem-2018-2019-global-report.

Bruni, A., S. Gherardi and B. Poggio (2005), *Gender and Entrepreneurship: An Ethnographical Approach*, New York, NY: Routledge.

Brush, C., A. de Bruin and F. Welter (2009), 'A gender-aware framework for women's entrepreneurship'. *International Journal of Gender and Entrepreneurship*, 1 (1), 8–24.

Brush, C., A. Ali, D. Kelley and P. Greene (2017), 'The influence of human capital factors and context on women's entrepreneurship: Which matters more?'. *Journal of Business Venturing Insights*, 8, 105–13.

Brush, C., L.F. Edelman, T. Manolova and F. Welter (2018), 'A gendered look at entrepreneurship ecosystems'. *Small Business Economics*, 52 (3), 393–408.

Bullough, A., M. Renko and D. Abdelzaher (2017), 'Women's business ownership: Operating within the context of institutional and in-group collectivism'. *Journal of Management*, 43 (7), 2037–64.

Bullough, A., U. Guelich, T.S. Manolova and L. Schjoedt (forthcoming), 'Women's entrepreneurship and culture: Gender role expectations and identities, societal culture, and the entrepreneurial environment'. *Small Business Economics Journal.*

Chan, S. and J. Lin (2014), 'Financing of micro and small enterprises in China: An exploratory study'. *Structural Change*, 22, 431–46.

Dahl, M.S., M. Van Praag and P. Thompson (2015), 'Entrepreneurial couples'. In *Academy of Management Proceedings* (Vol. 2015, No. 1, p. 14776). Briarcliff Manor, NY: Academy of Management.

De Bruin, A., C.G. Brush and F. Welter (2006), 'Introduction to the special issue: Towards building cumulative knowledge on women's entrepreneurship'. *Entrepreneurship Theory and Practice*, 30 (5), 585–93.

Elam, A.B., C.G. Brush, P.G. Greene, B. Baumer, M. Dean and R. Heavlow (2019), 'Global Entrepreneurship Monitor 2018/2019 Women's Entrepreneurship Report'. Babson College, Smith College, and the Global Entrepreneurship Research Association (GERA). Accessed 23 February 2020 at https://www.gemconsortium.org/report/gem-20182019-womens-entrepreneurship-report.

Erogul, M.S. and D. McCrohan (2008), 'Preliminary investigation of Emirati women entrepreneurs in the UAE'. *African Journal of Business Management*, 2 (10), 177–85.

Ford, J.D., L.W. Ford and A. D'Amelio (2008), 'Resistance to change: The rest of the story'. *Academy of Management Review*, 33 (2), 362–77.

Gunnell, M. (2016), 'A comparison of the GLOBE and Geert Hofstede findings and their implications for global business leaders'. Accessed 3 November 2020 at https://www.linkedin.com/pulse/comparison-findings-globe-geert-hostede-implications-global-gunnell/.

Hallward-Driemeier, M. (2013), *Enterprising Women: Expanding Economic Opportunities in Africa*. Washington, DC: World Bank Publications.

Hechavarria, D., A. Bullough, C. Brush and L. Edelman (2019), 'High growth women's entrepreneurship: Fueling social and economic development'. *Journal of Small Business Management*, 57 (1), 5–13.

Hofstede, G. (1992), 'Cultural dimensions in people management: The socialization perspective'. In V. Pucik, N.M. Tichy and C.K. Barnett (eds), *Globalizing Management: Creating and Leading the Competitive Organization*, New York, NY: Wiley & Sons.

Hofstede, G. (2015), 'Culture's causes: The next challenge'. *Cross Cultural Management: An International Journal*, 22 (4), 545–69.

House, R.J., P.J. Hanges, M. Javidan, P. Dorfman and V. Gupta (2004), *Culture, Leadership, and Organizations: The GLOBE Study of 62 Societies*. Thousand Oaks, CA: Sage.

ILO (2009), 'The informal economy in Africa: Promoting transition to formality: Challenges and strategies'. Geneva: International Labour Organisation.

Itani, H., Y.M. Sidani and I. Baalbaki (2011), 'United Arab Emirates female entrepreneurs: Motivations and frustrations'. *Equality, Diversity and Inclusion: An International Journal*, 30 (5), 409–24.

Jamali, D. (2009), 'Constraints and opportunities facing women entrepreneurs in developing countries'. *Gender in Management: An International Journal*, 24 (4), 232–51.

Jennings, J.E. and C.G. Brush (2013), 'Research on women entrepreneurs: Challenges to (and from) the broader entrepreneurship literature?'. *Academy of Management Annals*, 7 (1), 663–715.

Kalantaridis, C. and D. Fletcher (2012), 'Entrepreneurship and institutional change: A research agenda'. *Entrepreneurship & Regional Development*, 24 (3–4), 199–214.

Khan, F.R., K.A. Munir and H. Willmott (2007), 'A dark side of institutional entrepreneurship: Soccer balls, child labour and postcolonial impoverishment'. *Organization Studies*, 28 (7), 1055–77.

Leung, K., R.S. Bhagat, N.R. Buchan, M. Erez and C.B. Gibson (2005), 'Culture and international business: Recent advances and their implications for future research'. *Journal of International Business Studies*, 36 (4), 357–78.

Lien, Y.C., C.C. Teng and S. Li (2016), 'Institutional reforms and the effects of family control on corporate governance'. *Family Business Review*, 29 (2), 174–88.

Markowska, M. and H. Lopez-Vega (2018), 'Entrepreneurial storying: Winepreneurs as crafters of regional identity stories'. *The International Journal of Entrepreneurship and Innovation*, 19 (4), 282–97.

Masbout, R. and I. Van Staveren (2010), 'Disentangling bargaining power from individual and household level to institutions: Evidence on women's position in Ethiopia'. *World Development*, 38 (5), 783–96.

Naguib, R. and D. Jamali (2015), 'Female entrepreneurship in the UAE: A multi-level integrative lens'. *Gender in Management: An International Journal*, 30 (2), 135–61.

Neimanis, A. and A. Tortisyn (2003), 'NHDR occasional paper 2: Gender thematic guidance note'. Accessed 5 July 2020 at http://hdr.undp.org/sites/default/files/nhdr_gender_gn.pdf.

Nelson, T. and C. Constantinidis (2017), 'Sex and gender in family business succession research: A review and forward agenda from a social construction perspective'. *Family Business Review*, 30 (3), 219–41.

Nicholson, N. (2008), 'Evolutionary psychology and family business: A new synthesis for theory, research, and practice'. *Family Business Review*, 21 (1), 103–18.

Omair, K. (2008), 'Women in management in the Arab context'. *Education, Business and Society: Contemporary Middle Eastern Issues*, 1 (2), 107–23.

Othman, N., S. Mohamed and S. Suradi (2016), 'Motivating factors of couple involvement in copreneurship businesses in Malaysia'. *International Journal of Social, Behavioral, Educational, Economic, Business and Industrial Engineering*, 10 (1), 256–9.

Oudah, M., F. Jabeen and C. Dixon (2018), 'Determinants linked to family business sustainability in the UAE: An AHP approach'. *Sustainability*, 10 (1), 246.

Pandey, S. and A.S. Amezcua (2020), 'Women's business ownership and women's entrepreneurship through the lens of US federal policies'. *Small Business Economics*, 54 (4), 1123–52.

Payne, D. and B.E. Joyner (2006), 'Successful U.S. entrepreneurs: Identifying ethical decision-making and social responsibility behaviors'. *Journal of Business Ethics*, 65, 203–17.

Pieper, T.M., J.H. Astrachan and G.E. Manners (2013), 'Conflict in family business: Common metaphors and suggestions for intervention'. *Family Relations*, 62 (3), 490–500.

Pinillos, M.J. and L. Reyes (2011), 'Relationship between individualist collectivist culture and entrepreneurial activity: Evidence from Global Entrepreneurship Monitor data'. *Small Business Economics*, 37 (1), 23–37.

Prill, O. (2019), 'Soft skills and university support foster female entrepreneurs'. Accessed 20 October 2020 at https://www.timeshighereducation.com/blog/soft-skills-and-university-support-foster-female-entrepreneurs.

Ren, X. (2019), 'She economy makes rapid strides', *China Daily*. Accessed 1 November 2019 at www.chinadaily.com.cn/a/201903/08/WS5c81a82da3106c65c34ed6bf.html.

Ruderman, M.N., P.J. Ohlott, K. Panzer and S.N. King (2002), 'Benefits for multiple roles for managerial women'. *Academy of Management Journal*, 45 (2), 369–86.

Schuler, S.R., S.M. Hashemi, A.P. Riley and S. Akhter (1996), 'Credit programs, patriarchy and men's violence against women in rural Bangladesh'. *Social Science & Medicine*, 43 (12), 1729–42.

Schwartz, S.H. (2006), 'A theory of cultural value orientations: Explication and applications'. *Comparative Sociology*, 5 (2), 137–82.

Selznick, P. (2011), *Leadership in Administration: A Sociological Interpretation*. New Orleans, LA: Quid Pro Books.

Senapati, A.K. and K. Ojha (2019), 'Socio-economic empowerment of women through micro-entrepreneurship: Evidence from Odisha, India'. *International Journal of Rural Management*, 15 (2), 159–84.

Shukla, M. and A.B. Arntzen (2013), 'Gender diversity in management and leadership: A new competitive advantage?'. Paper presented at the International Conference on Management, Leadership and Governance ICMLG 2013, Bangkok University, 8 February.

Stephan, U. and S. Pathak (2016), 'Beyond cultural values? Cultural leadership ideals and entrepreneurship'. *Journal of Business Venturing*, 31 (5), 505–23.

Stephan, U. and L.M. Uhlaner (2010), 'Performance-based vs socially supportive culture: A cross-national study of descriptive norms and entrepreneurship'. *Journal of International Business Studies*, 41 (8), 1347–64.

Tlaiss, H.A. (2015), 'How Islamic business ethics impact women entrepreneurs: Insights from four Arab Middle Eastern countries'. *Journal of Business Ethics*, 129 (4), 859–77.

UNESCAP (2017), 'Fostering women's entrepreneurship in ASEAN: Transforming prospects, transforming societies'. Bangkok: ESCAP.

UN Women (2020), 'United Nations entity for gender equality and the empowerment of women'. Accessed 15 October 2020 at https://www.un.org/womenwatch/daw/daw/index.html.

Venkatesh, V., J.D.Shaw, T.A. Sykes, S.F. Wamba and M.W. Macharia (2017), 'Networks, technology, and entrepreneurship: A field quasi-experiment among women in rural India'. *Academy of Management Journal*, 60, 1709–40.

Verduijn, K. and C. Essers (2013), 'Questioning dominant entrepreneurship assumptions: The case of female ethnic minority entrepreneurs'. *Entrepreneurship & Regional Development*, 25 (7–8), 612–30.

Villares-Varela, M. and C. Essers (2019), 'Women in the migrant economy: A positional approach to contextualize gendered transnational trajectories'. *Entrepreneurship & Regional Development*, 31 (3–4), 213–25.

Walsh, J. and B. Winsor (2019), 'Socio-cultural barriers to developing a regional entrepreneurial ecosystem'. *Journal of Enterprising Communities: People and Places in the Global Economy*, 13 (3), 263–82.

Wang, D. (2017), 'Chinese women's fortune report of 2017'. Accessed 16 April 2020 at http://i8.hexunimg.cn/hxsps/2017/whitepaper.pdf.

Weik, E. (2011), 'Institutional entrepreneurship and agency'. *Journal for the Theory of Social Behaviour*, 41 (4), 466–81.

Welter, F. (2011), 'Contextualising entrepreneurship: Conceptual challenges and ways forward'. *Entrepreneurship Theory and Practice*, 35 (1), 165–84.

Welter, F. and D. Smallbone (2011), 'Institutional perspectives on entrepreneurial behavior in challenging environments'. *Journal of Small Business Management*, 49 (1), 107–25.

Welter, F., T. Baker, D.B. Audretsch and W.B. Gartner (2017), 'Everyday entrepreneurship – A call for entrepreneurship research to embrace entrepreneurial diversity'. *Entrepreneurship Theory and Practice*, 41 (3), 311–21.

World Bank (2012), 'World Development Report 2012: Gender equality and development'. Accessed 1 July 2019 at https://openknowledge.worldbank.org/handle/10986/4391.

World Economic Forum (WEF) (2018), *The Global Gender Gap Report 2018*. Accessed 28 July 2020 at http://www3.weforum.org/docs/WEF_GGGR_2018.pdf.

Wu, M., C.C. Chang and W.L. Zhuang (2010), 'Relationships of work–family conflict with business and marriage outcomes in Taiwanese copreneurial women'. *The International Journal of Human Resource Management*, 21 (5), 742–53.

Xheneti, M., S. Karki and A. Madden (2019), 'Negotiating business and family demands within a patriarchal society: The case of women entrepreneurs in the Nepalese context'. *Entrepreneurship & Regional Development*, 31 (3–4), 259–87.

Zamberi Ahmad, S. (2011), 'Evidence of the characteristics of women entrepreneurs in the Kingdom of Saudi Arabia: An empirical investigation'. *International Journal of Gender and Entrepreneurship*, 3 (2), 123–43.

Zhang, J., L.X. Zhang, S. Rozelle and S. Boucher (2006), 'Self-employment with Chinese-characteristics: The forgotten engine of rural China's growth'. *Contemporary Economic Policy*, 24 (3), 446–58.

PART I

The effects of a society's culture on the
embeddedness of women's entrepreneurship

2. Gender, culture and entrepreneurship in the Middle East and North Africa (MENA)

Bettina Lynda Bastian, Stephen Hill and Beverly Dawn Metcalfe

INTRODUCTION

The Arab Spring has had profound impacts on economic and social development in the MENA region. Investigations of conflict resolution, together with critiques of globalization, have stimulated international research that explores cultural similarity and variance in business practices and management philosophies. One key reason for widespread protest has been concerns about employment and future employment creation (El Azhary, 2016). As a consequence, the nurturing of entrepreneurial capacity, especially for women, has remained a central thread of economic development policy across the region. Recent research has reviewed empirical evidence to assess the changing nature of female entrepreneurship in the Middle East and North Africa (MENA), and has shown that whilst average levels of female entrepreneurship overall have hardly changed over the last decade, there has been much more convergence of female to male entrepreneurship levels in MENA Gulf countries than in those MENA countries closer to the Mediterranean (Barakat et al., 2018) (see Table 2.1 below). This chapter will critique this evidence, and will explore how cultural and social changes in different MENA states have been contributory factors in the differing experiences of female entrepreneurs in the region. This work seeks to contribute to scholarship that stresses the need to unravel the 'contextual embeddedness' of entrepreneurship, in order to unveil the socio-cultural and geo-political dynamics of entrepreneurial conceptualizations and policy (Bastian et al., 2019).

While MENA countries have much in common in terms of language, religion and shared origins, there are significant socio-cultural and political variations across the region, including: diverse forms of patriarchal relations; variations in gendered labor force participation; variations regarding structural changes in economies; variations as to women's advance in the polity; differences in how entrepreneurship is regarded; and others. Considering such social and cultural change provides a greater understanding of entrepreneurship development processes, together with contributing to broader debates of women's rights and empowerment in the region (Syed and Metcalfe, 2017). A key factor that is often ignored in entrepreneurial research is the diverse range of governance machineries and institutional frameworks that have evolved to evaluate and monitor women's development (Metcalfe, 2011). This highlights the importance of governance 'structures', operations and policy development, alongside social and 'cultural' change. All of these factors may influence the propensity of women to start their own business, both in absolute levels and in relation to male entrepreneurship. The Gulf countries have developed national gender and development programs to support women's advance, including quotas for women (ranging between 30 and 40 percent) in government in Saudi Arabia, Kuwait, Bahrain, Qatar and UAE. This is significant as these states have higher numbers of women in government than the USA, UK and Australia. These initiatives are aligned with the Sustainable Development Goals (SDG). These are greater advances than in those countries that experienced revolutions and social unrest (Egypt, Morocco, Tunisia). Women's role and status have worsened under Sissi as quota gains achieved under Mubarak, which had provided female-only seats, attaining 64 out of the 493 Assembly seats just one month before the revolution, are reversed. The women's movements in Tunisia and Morocco have made gains in family and personal status law, but there have been limited opportunities to gain access to decision-making roles.

This chapter is structured as follows: the first section gives an overview of the region and its culture. The subsequent section considers statistics regarding entrepreneurship levels for women and men in the MENA region. These are then combined in an analysis, which leads to conclusions and final remarks.

THE MIDDLE EAST AND NORTH AFRICAN REGION (MENA) AND GENDERED CULTURE AND GOVERNANCE

The MENA region is located in North Africa, Asia Minor and in the Persian and Arab Gulf. Altogether it comprises 22 countries and about 440 million inhabitants (World Bank, 2018). The region is rich in natural resources (hydrocarbons, metals and minerals), mainly in Algeria and in the Gulf, and varies significantly in terms of wealth levels. The International Monetary Fund (IMF) (2014) showed that total country GDP levels range between US$ 1.5 billion in developing countries and US$ 777 billion in highly developed countries, mainly in the Gulf. Independent of the economic discrepancies within the region, many MENA countries exhibit some of the highest gender inequalities worldwide: according to the World Economic Forum (2018) the region has closed around 60 percent of its gender gap, with a gap of 40 percent remaining. However, all countries in the region are signatory to the UN 2030 agenda and the Sustainable Development Goals.

MENA societies are largely patriarchal (Hofstede, 1992), where men are viewed as decisive and women are considered as intuitive and relationship focused (Omair, 2008), as well as less powerful and influential than men (Zamberi Ahmad, 2011). Some have argued that policy developments for men and women are premised on these 'different' identity signifiers (World Bank, 2012; WEF, 2018), leading to a social organization of Arab life which reflects the following:

- The centrality of the family, rather than the individual, as the main unit in society;
- Recognition of the man as the sole breadwinner of the family;
- A code of modesty that rests on family dignity and the reputation of the woman;
- An unequal balance of power in the private sphere that is anchored in family laws. (Metcalfe, 2011, from Esposito, 2005; UNDP, 2010)

Underlying the importance of this organization is religion, notably Islam, with a strong and defining impact on women's role and status and therefore having been argued to impact entrepreneurial motivations and behavior (Erogul and McCrohan, 2008; Zamberi Ahmad, 2011). The 'Islamic gender regime' (Metcalfe, 2006) positions the family as the central identity marker in society, with ascribed roles for men and women, with women viewed as the homemaker and mother, and men as the breadwinner (Tlaiss, 2013). Within the Arab Middle East patriarchal relations create hierarchies between men and women, so that in most institutions men hold higher-level positions. Gendering is also evident in everyday behaviors, and in the interactions between men and women. There are cultural expectations that perpetuate gender discrimination (Melki and Mallat, 2016), which in turn create barriers that hinder women in their career advancement (Tlaiss, 2013). Women who do run businesses experience a lack of capital access at different venture stages (Zamberi Ahmad, 2011), and little access to bank loans and funding from financial institutions (Bahramitash and Esfahani, 2014; Weeks, 2009). Moreover, gendered regimes construct inequalities in the labor market with regard to female workforce participation, resulting in a segregated labor market, whereby the majority of women work in three sectors: health, education and social services (Afiouni and Karam, 2017). Additionally, employment laws in some jurisdictions are guided by Sharia and urf (custom), and only allow women to work in a moral work environment (Alotaibi et al., 2017). Finally, cultural norms around the dignity of the woman require that her sexuality be protected (Moghadam, 2005), restraining her personal mobility and requiring women to obtain permission from male guardians (e.g. father, husband, brother, and others) to travel abroad from some Gulf States (Zamberi Ahmad, 2011).

Culture and Women Entrepreneurship in the MENA

Previous research has addressed and explored the intersections between contexts constrained by gendered cultural norms as well as practices, and women entrepreneurship in MENA countries (Bastian et al., 2018). Islam as the predominant religion in the region, as well as Christian faith, have a strong defining influence on expectations regarding women's role in society (Dechant and Lamky, 2005; Erogul and McCrohan, 2008; Sidani, 2005; Zamberi Ahmad, 2011): typically, they are assigned the role of caregivers and mothers above all other occupations (Sidani, 2005; Tlaiss and Kauser, 2011). On the other hand, recent research also shows that, for example, Islam provides varied interpretations regarding the status of women, and most often local gendered traditions and cultural practices tend to affect women's roles much more (Tlaiss and McAdam, 2020). Yet gendered cultural expectations represent substantial barriers for women to advance with their entrepreneurial ambitions, and to develop their ventures in numerous countries (Tlaiss, 2013). This is valid for the MENA Mediterranean as well as the MENA Gulf region: women entrepreneurs for the most part lack access to critical resources, such as financial capital during all venture stages (Sakir Erogul, 2014; Zamberi Ahmad, 2011); research on Jordan reveals that women typically cannot provide sufficient collateral to secure credits (Al Dajani and Marlow, 2010). Less than a third of women had received bank loans or support from financial institutions, as research on Tunisia, Lebanon, Jordan, Bahrain and the UAE revealed (Weeks, 2009). Research in different countries of the MENA region reveals that women perceive the lack of skilled workers (Bahramitash and Esfahani, 2014; Goby and Erogul, 2011; Weeks, 2009; Zamberi Ahmad, 2010), expensive bureaucratic processes (Weeks, 2009; Zamberi Ahmad, 2010), lack of managerial skills (Welsh et al., 2014), and limited access to training (Weeks, 2009; Welsh et al., 2014; Zeidan and Bahrami, 2011), as major constraints regarding the development of their entrepreneurial ventures. Women entrepreneurs across the region tend to rely on private networks (family and friends) to compensate for their lack of resources (Bastian and Tucci, 2017; Bastian and Zali, 2016b), which is in line with the specific collectivist cultural context of MENA societies (Erogul and McCrohan, 2008; Weeks, 2009; Zamberi Ahmad, 2011). The merit of individuals most often derives from their personal relationships and connections (Rosen, 2000), and trust and cooperation rely on reciprocity, reputation and repeated interactions between members of small and personalized groups (Rosen, 2000).

In the Gulf region the male guardianship system entrusts male family members with the power to take critical decisions for women. Even though some of the restrictions have been lifted in recent times and women in Saudi Arabia and in the UAE are now permitted unprecedented mobility and work protection (Abousleiman, 2020), substantial restrictions for the female pursuit of professional and entrepreneurial careers remain prevalent. In Saudi Arabia, women still need male legal intermediaries in order to proceed with some business transactions (Welsh et al., 2014), and in many Gulf states women rely on their husbands with regard to essential social connections for their business (Erogul and McCrohan, 2008). A lack of spousal support has been shown to potentially jeopardize the success of female ventures.

This is especially the case since work–family balance remains one of the greatest challenges for women entrepreneurs across the region, as research on Bahrain (Al Ghazali et al., 2013), the UAE (Erogul and McCrohan, 2008; Itani et al., 2011), the Kingdom of Saudi Arabia (KSA) (Welsh et al., 2014; Zamberi Ahmad, 2011), Jordan (Al Dajani and Marlow, 2010), Lebanon (Jamali, 2009) and Morocco (Gray and Finley-Hervey, 2005) convincingly shows. Women are expected to combine their family obligations with their entrepreneurial roles without compromising on their responsibilities as mother, daughter or daughter-in-law. In fact, family obligations have been cited as one of the main reasons why women have been unable to sustain their business in Jordan (Al Dajani and Marlow, 2010). Women apply different coping strategies, for example hiring domestic helpers, efficient time management strategies (Karam and Afiouni, 2014), lobbying for greater support of the family, or networking strategies (Al Dajani and Marlow, 2010; Itani et al., 2011). Previous research reveals how women in different countries constantly negotiate their entrepreneurial roles with family obligations as well as gendered role expectations (Al Dajani and Marlow, 2010), illustrating how gendered social norms substantially challenge female venturing in countries of the MENA Gulf and the MENA Mediterranean alike.

ENTREPRENEURSHIP IN THE MENA REGION

This section uses and analyzes data from the Global Entrepreneurship Monitor (GEM) that describes female and male entrepreneurship activities and behavior in the region. GEM is an on-going research collaboration to define and measure levels of entrepreneurial activity according to a common methodology, so that comparisons can be made between countries as well as enabling the evolution of entrepreneurship to be traced for the same country over time. Each country participating in GEM implements an Adult Population Survey of a representative sample of at least 2000 adults, using the standard GEM questionnaire. For the present research, GEM data from 15 MENA countries is considered: Algeria, Egypt, Iran, Israel, Jordan, Lebanon, Libya, Morocco, Qatar, Saudi Arabia, Syria, Tunisia, United Arab Emirates (UAE), West Bank & Gaza, and Yemen. Data was collected over the decade from 2009 to 2018. However, there was little continuity in this data collection, as countries drop in and out of participation in GEM, meaning that GEM data for MENA in some years is more representative than for other years. The key indicator for GEM is the level of Total early-stage Entrepreneurial Activity or TEA, measured as the proportion of the adult population actively engaged in starting or running a new business. Table 2.1 shows the level of TEA for those MENA countries participating in GEM in the period. The year 2009 saw a high level of participation in GEM because of International Development Bank sponsorship.

These statistics refer to the absolute and relative entrepreneurship levels in MENA countries over the past decade. For the purpose of this analysis, the economies in the region can be categorized countries into two 'blocks', Gulf or Mediterranean, that display a certain level of homogeneity and resemblance when it comes to female entrepreneurial activities. Here, MENA Gulf is defined as the four countries of Qatar, Saudi Arabia, the United Arab Emirates (UAE) plus Yemen, leaving MENA Mediterranean as the catch-all term for the other 11 countries within the MENA region. The rationale for this is that the Gulf Cooperation Council (GCC) countries tend to be resource-rich, whereas the other remaining countries are largely resource poor and have far lower levels of development in GDP terms. Results will show that there has been much more convergence in female to male entrepreneurship levels in MENA Gulf countries than in MENA Mediterranean countries.

The penultimate row of Table 2.1 shows the percentage of the total MENA population represented by those countries participating in GEM in that year. Then in 2009, 83 percent of the MENA population was represented in GEM, compared to just under 20 percent in 2014. Clearly, more confidence can be attached to GEM data as representative of MENA in 2009 than in 2014.

It is interesting to note that, despite the 'Arab Spring' and a decade of change, the proportion of adults starting or running a new business in MENA was virtually the same in 2018 as it had been in 2009, although that population-weighted average rate had fluctuated between a low of 6.8 percent (2010) and a high of 16 percent in (poorly-represented) 2014.

Tables 2.2 and 2.3 show the levels of Total early-stage Entrepreneurial Activity (TEA) for each gender over the same period. For men, the population-weighted MENA average level of TEA (TEAm) had varied from a low of 11.5 percent in 2015 to a high of 16.1 percent in 2017. Interestingly, the level of male TEA in 2018 was virtually the same as it had been in 2009.

Table 2.1   *Rates of Total early-stage Entrepreneurial Activity (TEA, %*
                   adults), by country, MENA 2009–2016

	2009	2010	2011	2012	2013	2014	2015	2016	2017	2018
MENA Med										
Algeria	16.68		9.26	8.75	4.89					
Egypt		7.02		7.82			7.39	14.30	13.25	9.84
Iran	12.08	12.31	14.54	10.79	12.32	16.02	12.93	12.79	13.32	14.24
Israel	6.07	5.02		6.53	10.04		11.82	11.31	12.78	8.98
Jordan	10.24							8.20		
Lebanon	14.98						30.15	21.15	24.13	24.08
Libya					11.15					
Morocco	15.74						4.44	5.56	8.76	6.65
Syria	8.46									
Tunisia	9.43	6.12		4.78			10.13			
West Bank[a]	8.59	10.37		9.84						
MENA Gulf										
Qatar						16.38		7.85	7.43	8.52
Saudi Arabia	4.66	9.40						11.44	11.45	12.09
UAE	13.25		6.19					5.66	8.97	10.72
Yemen	24.01									
MENA Participation (%)	83.5	53.7	30.8	55.5	32.5	19.2	64.7	83.6	61.8	59.9
MENA average	10.11	6.80	12.33	8.95	9.93	16.03	8.30	9.24	12.68	10.20

Note: [a] Includes Gaza Strip: 2012 estimate is listed in GEM as Palestine.

The population-weighted MENA average level of female Total early-stage Entrepreneurial Activity (TEAf) in 2018 was also very close to the level in 2009, but had fluctuated from 4.5 percent in 2010, to 10.5 percent in 2014, although noting the caveat about poor GEM representation in MENA in that year.

More interesting, however, and more salient to this chapter, is the relative gender gap, or the ratio of male to female levels of TEA, shown for these MENA countries in Table 2.4. The simplest interpretation of these figures is that, as long as the total number of adult men is reasonably close to the total number of adult women, they show the ratio of male to female start-ups. Then, for example, in 2018 in Egypt there were more than two and a half male start-ups for every female one, compared to virtually identical proportions of men and women starting and running businesses in Qatar in that year. It is interesting to contrast the relative position in 2009 to that of 2018. In Lebanon,

Table 2.2   *Male Total early-stage Entrepreneurial Activity (TEAm, % men), MENA 2009–2018*

	2009	2010	2011	2012	2013	2014	2015	2016	2017	2018
MENA Med										
Algeria	19.94		10.76	12.08	6.43					
Egypt		9.54		13.09			11.06	20.91	18.82	14.12
Iran	16.22	16.43	19.56	15.66	18.07	21.45	17.5	16.6	16.1	12.94
Israel	8.01	6.71		7.62	13.66		14.41	13.27	14.82	
Jordan	15.79							12.76		
Lebanon	20.18						35.66	26.24	28.82	31.28
Libya					14.76					
Morocco	19.89						6.1	6.7	12.9	9.16
Syria	13.64									
Tunisia	13.74	8.22		6.75			14.98			
West Bank	13.59	13.62		16.01						
MENA Gulf										
Qatar						19.29		8.09	7.44	8.56
Saudi Arabia	7.93	12.05						12.85	12.39	14.75
UAE	15.69		6.91					6.58	9.29	10.97
Yemen	29.02									
MENA TEAm %	13.53	12.26	15.97	13.33	14.21	21.39	11.49	11.62	16.12	13.4
MENA Represent %	83.5	53.7	30.8	55.5	32.5	19.2	64.7	83.6	61.8	59.9

for example, the ratio of male to female start-ups had fallen from 2.0 to 1.8, in Iran from 2.5 to 2.0, but in Morocco had increased from 1.7 to 2.2, and in Egypt from 2.2 (2010) to 2.6 in 2018. But it is those countries in MENA from the Gulf that deserve closest attention. In the UAE this ratio had fallen from 2.5 to 1.1, in Saudi Arabia from a massive 11.2 to 1.7, and in Qatar from 1.9 (2014) to 1.0 in 2018. It is these observations that had led to this research, including the search for cultural explanations.

There are substantial differences between 2009 and 2018 in Table 2.4. The population-weighted average MENA ratio of male to female start-ups has fallen from 3.3 to 2.2, driven largely by those falls in ratios in the Gulf countries. It is in comparing the MENA Gulf countries to the MENA Mediterranean countries that this examination of evidence now turns. Before that, however, the question of how representative of the Gulf and Mediterranean countries is the GEM data is considered.

Table 2.3   Female Total early-stage Entrepreneurial Activity (TEAf, % women), MENA 2009–2018

	2009	2010	2011	2012	2013	2014	2015	2016	2017	2018
MENA Med										
Algeria	13.37		5.56	5.37	3.31					
Egypt		4.41		2.39			3.67	7.48	7.51	5.35
Iran	6.48	4.14	4.6	5.58	6.49	10.47	8.46	8.93	10.48	6.45
Israel	4.17	3.37		5.46	6.55		9.3	9.36	10.74	
Jordan	4.52							3.26		
Lebanon	10.2						24.58	16.07	19.8	17.44
Libya					7.21					
Morocco	11.78						2.85	4.46	4.74	4.26
Syria	3.13									
Tunisia	5.08	4.08		2.87			5.33			
MENA Gulf										
Qatar						10.32		6.8	7.39	8.36
Saudi Arabia	0.71	5.87						9.74	10.33	8.5
UAE	6.26		4.32					3.7	8.28	10.14
West Bank	3.35	6.95		3.42						
Yemen	18.84									
MENA TEAf	6.51	4.5	4.87	4.24	5.59	10.47	5.13	6.01	8.51	6.41
MENA Represent %	83.5	53.7	30.8	55.5	32.5	19.2	64.7	83.6	61.8	59.9

According to World Bank data, between 2009 and 2018, the population of MENA increased from 380 m to 444 m. Using the earlier definition of the MENA Gulf countries as Saudi Arabia, Kuwait, Oman, Bahrain, the UAE and Yemen, over the same period the combined MENA Gulf population increased from 66 m to 83 m. Finally, given that MENA Mediterranean is here defined as MENA minus the Gulf, this region saw its population increase from 314 m to 361 m between 2009 and 2018.

Given the data on which MENA countries participated in GEM since 2009, and their respective populations, it is a relatively small step to calculate the proportion of both MENA Gulf and MENA Mediterranean represented in GEM since 2009, with results shown in Figure 2.1.

Representation in GEM for MENA Gulf was greater than 40 percent in the years 2009–2010, and 2016–2018, and it is on these five years that attention is focused, regarding the intervening years as unrepresentative. For MENA Mediterranean (a much larger total population), GEM representation was more than a third of the total population in 2009–2010, 2012 and from 2015 to 2018.

Table 2.4   *Ratio of male to female start-ups, MENA 2009–2021*

Tm/Tf	2009	2010	2011	2012	2013	2014	2015	2016	2017	2018
MENA Med										
Algeria	1.49		1.94	2.25	1.94					
Egypt		2.16		5.48			3.01	2.79	2.51	2.64
Iran	2.50	3.97	4.25	2.81	2.78	2.05	2.07	1.86	1.54	2.00
Israel	1.92	1.99		1.40	2.09		1.55	1.42	1.38	
Jordan	3.49							3.91		
Lebanon	1.98						1.45	1.63	1.46	1.79
Libya					2.05					
Morocco	1.69						2.14	1.50	2.72	2.15
Syria	4.36									
Tunisia	2.71	2.01		2.35			2.81			
MENA Gulf										
Qatar						1.87		1.19	1.01	1.02
Saudi Arabia	11.16	2.05						1.32	1.20	1.74
UAE	2.51		1.60					1.78	1.12	1.08
West Bank	4.06	1.96		4.68						
Yemen	1.54									
Sum										
MENA Tm/Tf	3.28	2.77	3.36	3.72	2.46	2.04	2.46	2.11	1.97	2.17
MENA Represent %	66.61	53.93	30.51	55.83	31.49	19.19	54.42	63.95	61.66	59.76

For each of these representative years, population-weighted average values of male Total early-stage Entrepreneurial Activity and female early-stage Entrepreneurial Activity were calculated for both MENA Gulf and MENA Mediterranean, with results for the gender difference shown in Figure 2.2.

Figure 2.2 shows a clear pattern: the absolute gender gap was more or less the same in both parts of MENA in 2009, at around 8 percentage points, while in 2010, the gender gap was greater in MENA Gulf than in MENA Mediterranean. By 2015 the situation had completely reversed, with the gender gap in MENA Mediterranean having grown to more than ten percentage points before falling slightly to eight points in 2018. MENA Gulf was very different, the absolute gender gap having fallen to three percentage points in 2016, two points in 2017 and just over four points in 2018.

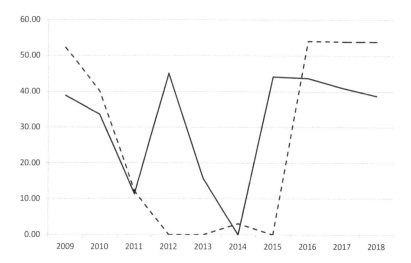

Figure 2.1   Proportions of MENA Gulf (dashed line) and MENA
Mediterranean (solid line) represented in GEM in period
2009–2018 (% adults)

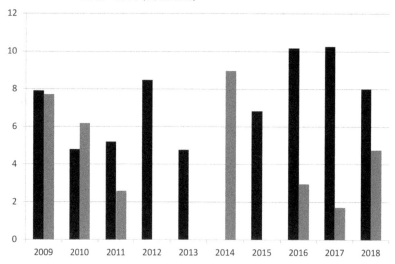

Figure 2.2   The gender gap (male minus female TEA rates) for MENA
Mediterranean (black) and MENA Gulf (grey)

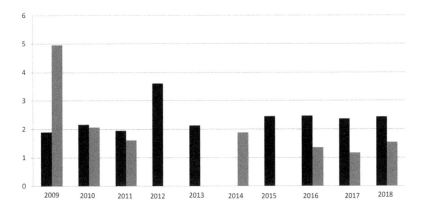

Figure 2.3   *Ratio of male start-ups to female start-ups, MENA for MENA Mediterranean (black) and MENA Gulf (grey)*

These observations are confirmed by the preferred measure of the gender gap, the ratio of male TEA to female TEA, or the ratio of male start-ups to female start-ups, shown in Figure 2.3. Figure 2.3 is quite stark: in 2009 there were almost five male start-ups to every female start-up in MENA Gulf, but this ratio fell to just 1.5 in 2018. By contrast, the ratio of male to female start-ups has remained above 2 to 1 for MENA Mediterranean since 2010.

Cultural Values

It is much more difficult to quantify culture than levels of entrepreneurship. Table 2.5 presents one attempt, using Hofstede's definition of Cultural Dimensions. The table has been arranged with the eight MENA Mediterranean countries for which data is available in the left columns, and the three Gulf Mediterranean countries for which this data is available on the right. Hofstede (2015) measures culture on six dimensions: power distance, which refers to 'the extent to which the less powerful members of organizations and institutions (like the family) accept and expect that power is distributed unequally' (Hofstede, 2015); individualism, which refers to the degree to which individuals within a given society are integrated in groups; masculinity, which refers to the degree to which a society values achievement, heroism, assertiveness and material rewards as expressions for success; uncertainty avoidance, which refers to a society's tolerance for change and ambiguity regarding events that change the status quo; long-term orientation, which refers to their willingness to adapt to change and their pragmatic approach to problem solving with regard to circumstantial developments. Societies high on this dimension are innovation oriented and open to the new, whereas societies low on this dimension value traditions and cultural stability more highly. Finally, indulgence refers to a society that 'allows relatively free gratification of basic and natural human desires related to enjoying life and having fun' (Hofstede, 2015).

There are some clear differences in values between the MENA Mediterranean and MENA Gulf countries. When comparing the averages for eight Mediterranean countries for which this data is available (Egypt, Iran, Israel, Jordan, Lebanon, Libya, Morocco, Syria), with those for the three Gulf countries (Qatar, Saudi Arabia, UAE), there are substantial differences on various levels: the MENA Gulf scores higher on *power distance*, with an average value of 92, compared to the MENA Mediterranean, with an average value of 74.

Moreover, the MENA Gulf scores significantly higher on the dimension of *uncertainty avoidance* (average of 80), compared to the MENA Mediterranean (average of 65).

On the other hand, the MENA Mediterranean has an average value for *individualism* of 48, which is nearly double the average MENA Gulf score of 25.

Both groups are nearly equal regarding their average score on the *masculinity* dimension: MENA Gulf (55) and MENA Mediterranean (52). The dimensions *long-term orientation* and *indulgence* are not considered due to data gaps.

However, these culture variables remain very stable over time. The lack of variance makes it difficult to explicitly identify changes in culture as explanatory in the divergence of relative gender differences in entrepreneurial activity in the two parts of MENA.

The final piece of statistical evidence also comes from the Global Entrepreneurship Monitor (GEM).[1] Each year, alongside the Adult Population Survey, GEM conducts a National Expert Survey (NES), asking at least 35 identified national experts to assess the conditions for entrepreneurial activity in that country across a broad range of dimensions, ranging from access to finance to entrepreneurship education, and from intellectual property rights to social and cultural norms. In 2018 GEM introduced the National Entrepreneurship Context Index (NECI), converting these expert assessments into a single national figure to assess the sufficiency or otherwise of the entrepreneurial environment in that country, on a scale from 0 (totally insufficient) to 10 (totally sufficient). Table 2.6 illustrates the results for the MENA region in 2018. There is a clear distinction between MENA Gulf and MENA Mediterranean, with each of the Mediterranean economies having an NECI score that barely reaches 5, compared to the Gulf countries where two out of three have scores that are substantially greater than 5. There is then evidence that in 2018, the environment for entrepreneurship in the Gulf countries was,

Table 2.5　　*Cultural dimensions of specified MENA countries (2019)*

Cultural Dimension	Egypt	Iran	Israel	Jordan	Lebanon	Libya	Morocco	Syria	Qatar	Saudi	UAE
Power Distance	70	58	13	70	75	80	70	80	93	95	90
Individualism	25	41	54	30	40	38	46	35	25	25	25
Masculinity	45	43	47	45	65	52	53	52	55	60	50
Uncertainty Avoidance	80	59	81	65	50	68	68	60	80	80	80
Long Term Orientation	7	14	38	16	14	23	14	30		36	
Indulgence	4	40		43	25	34	25			52	

Source:　　Hofstede's cultural dimensions. Accessed 28 November 2019 at https://www.hofstede-insights.com/product/compare-countries/.

Table 2.6   *National Entrepreneurship Context Index (NECI) scores and
the relative gender gap, 2018*

	NECI score	TEAm/TEAf
Egypt	4.72	2.64
Iran	4.29	2.00
Lebanon	4.67	1.79
Morocco	4.26	2.15
Turkey	5.05	2.38
Qatar	6.69	1.02
Saudi Arabia	4.40	1.74
United Arab Emirates	5.92	1.08

on average, better than in the Mediterranean countries. It would not be surprising if a more supportive environment for entrepreneurship proves conducive to a narrowing of the relative gender gap. Unfortunately, the NECI data is only available for a single year, so that no conclusions can be reached on whether the environment for entrepreneurship has improved in the Gulf countries relative to the Mediterranean ones.

WHY HAS THE ENTREPRENEURIAL GENDER GAP NARROWED IN MENA GULF BUT NOT IN MENA MEDITERRANEAN?

This analysis, as well as the description of the MENA region, has shown that most countries in the region share cultural similarities, such as Islam as the predominant religion (to an extent where in many countries Sharia law governs state institutions); countries also share a common language, as well as common history and traditions. In fact, in all countries in the region a certain level of gendered environment prevails, which is not pervasive in women entrepreneurship in all MENA countries (Bastian and Zali, 2016a; 2016b; Bastian et al., 2018). Yet this analysis regarding entrepreneurial activities in the regions reveals substantial differences in how the gender gap in entrepreneurship has developed since 2009 in the MENA Mediterranean countries compared to the MENA Gulf countries. The latter display a significant decrease in the gender gap in entrepreneurship levels in the past 10 years, whilst the gender gap has stayed pretty stable in the MENA Mediterranean countries.

Regarding the explicatory power of culture, Sidani (2018) warns that there is a false notion of a 'single monolithic Arab culture' that could sufficiently explain women's participation in the public sphere across the MENA region. Such overgeneralization of culture misses out on the important historic diversity of Arab MENA countries. Mediterranean countries and Gulf countries differ significantly with regard to power distance and individualism: MENA Gulf countries are very high on the first and very low on the second dimension.

In broader assessments of social change following the Arab Spring, the empowerment of women is both unevenly mixed and unevenly spread. The development of family laws and greater access to court mechanisms were significant for women in Tunisia and Morocco. These were welcome changes. However, these initiatives were led from the bottom up, via collectivist Islamic feminisms.

In contrast, the Gulf countries have led bottom-up Islamic Feminist agendas, since cultural characteristics were shown to have a 'causal relevance' for policy design and implementation (Dan, 2017). For example, culturally conservative Gulf countries have done far better in terms of women's integration into the workforce than most other MENA countries – and that despite KSA, where cultural traditions still impose a strict segregation of men and women in public spaces (Sidani, 2018). Such observations suggest that other factors than just cultural ones would affect women's participation in the labor market and in entrepreneurship.

Entrepreneurship has been promoted across the region as a means for economic development through international organizations such as the World Bank and United Nations (entrepreneurship is an intrinsic element of the UN 2030 agenda). For the past two decades, entrepreneurship has been used as a means to accompany other economic policy reforms proposed by international organizations. For example, the Arab Human Development Report anticipates youth entrepreneurship playing a central role in job creation and professional opportunity generation for youth, and the possibility to integrate them into the labor force (UNDP, 2016). According to the World Bank (2014), women's entrepreneurship is pivotal for economic development and diversification of the economy as a whole, and for the inclusion of women in the job market. Also policy advice from private consultancy organizations encourages the states to develop entrepreneurial systems. Higher education institutions have equally integrated 'entrepreneurship education' into their strategic plans, with most of the universities ranked in the first 1000 by the 'Times Higher Education Ranking' (2018), establishing infrastructure conducive to entrepreneurship, such as technology transfer offices, incubator programs, co-working spaces, entrepreneurship courses, and more.

Entrepreneurship Promotion in MENA Gulf Countries

Gulf countries strongly advocate entrepreneurship. Reasons for this can mainly be found in the structural change affecting Gulf economies. Gulf countries have been rentier states, based on their oil economy. This oil wealth has helped government in providing for its citizens, notably through financial subventions and support, and the provision of jobs in the state administration. In fact, in the Gulf monarchies the state has been the primary employer for citizens (Fox et al., 2006; Metcalfe, 2011), and public sector jobs have been the preferable individual choice. Private sector jobs, on the other hand, have been unattractive, so that private companies mainly hire employees from abroad (Shayah and Sun, 2019). This has led to a sharply divided labor market, with Gulf citizens in the subsidized public sector and foreigners in the private sector. However, the depletion of natural resources and relatively low oil prices (2015–16) have restricted state revenues and expenditures quite significantly. This has required serious economic restructuring (Foley, 2010). In this context, the 'top-down promotion of entrepreneurship' (Ennis, 2019) pursues the diversification of economies and intends to trigger economic growth through innovation. In the long run, the rentier logic is not financially sustainable as the state has to grant employment for all its citizens, and provide reasonable infrastructure for foreigners that are in the majority in most states (Hertog, 2019). Unemployment is of great concern for Gulf countries, and entrepreneurship is seen as a way to encourage individuals to start their own business and therefore to individualize the employment challenge (Farzanegan, 2014). For example, Saudi Arabia's Vision 2030 and the National Transformation Plan (NTP) of 2016 both envisage a complete restructuring of the economy based on diversification and a strong knowledge economy. The Kingdom plans to create millions of new jobs through innovation and entrepreneurship, and to raise the participation of women in the workforce from the current level of 22 percent to 30 percent by 2030. The participation of women in the workforce is among the top priorities of the development plan, and women's entrepreneurship, in particular, is appreciated as a tool to develop the economy (Al-Kwifi et al., 2019). Equally, the UAE is pursuing an ambitious Vision 2030 that aims to turn the country into a global economic player for long after oil runs out. Vision 2030 foresees innovation and entrepreneurship as key pillars of the plan, and hence these are national strategic priorities.

Moreover, the UAE is pursuing an ambitious gender strategy that envisages the country to be among the top 25 worldwide in the UNDP gender equality index. In the same vein, Qatar aims to transform itself into an advanced economy based on sustainable development principles as expressed in the Qatar National Vision 2030. These examples show that Gulf countries are strongly promoting and pursuing entrepreneurship and women's entrepreneurship in a top-down fashion, and they are aligned with a global development approach, as expressed in the UN 2030 Sustainable Development agenda, but equally by the World Bank (2007, 2011) and OECD (2014), all of which see entrepreneurship as a catalyst to gender equality.

A key factor that is often ignored in entrepreneurial research is the diverse range of institutional frameworks that have evolved to evaluate and monitor women's development (Metcalfe, 2011). In most of MENA, state institutions are still governed by Islamic Sharia. There are some variations in Islamic schools of thought and interpretation, but this has profound consequences for the formation of governance machineries (Metcalfe, 2011) that represent the architecture of governance institutions that are responsible for managing women's development. In Saudi Arabia, women's development planning, including entrepreneurship planning, was allocated to the Women's Section of the Chamber of Commerce in Jeddah and Riyadh. The UAE has a long tradition of women's organizations established in support of female entrepreneurship and leadership. For example, since 1973 the UAE has had the Women's Organization, since 1974 the Umm Al Moumineen Women's Association, and since 2002 the Emirates Business Women Councils (Shahnawaz, 2015). Women's development planning was also part of the General Women's Society led directly by the wife of Sheik Zayed. In 2015, the Gender Balance Council was formed as a government body (led by Sheikha Manal Bint Rashid Al Maktoum, wife of the Deputy Prime Minister) to promote women's leadership and entrepreneurship. In Qatar, women's entrepreneurial planning comes under the jurisdiction of the Ministry of Foreign Affairs, but the prime responsibility for development lies with the International Family Institute, which has established itself as a leading research body on women's public policy in the Middle East. The ethos of GCC states' women's development planning, however, is positioned within an Islamic economic framework – to provide work opportunities compatible with women's nature and role in society, as well as maternal/child policies. Figure 2.4 illustrates how the interplay between drivers of change and governance institutions promotes women's entrepreneurship. *Drivers* refers to external structural changes as well as the requirements of the international community that necessitate proactive change on behalf of Gulf states. *National Strategic Plans* refers to top-down measures that support entrepreneurship and women's development.

The nature of governance and the structures for managing women's issues help to shape prevailing gender norms as well as local cultural practices and their interpretations (Hilsdon and Rozario, 2006). In sum, the Gulf countries have advocated support for Islamic feminism, and integrated tenets that support women's empowerment (UN Women, 2018; UN Women, 2020). The Gulf countries have strongly advocated women's empowerment agendas. This is significant, as economic, social and democratic change has been aligned with women's groups, and has been directed from government. Women have attained positions in various government decision-making roles, attained via legislative systems (Metcalfe et al., 2020). Research by political theorists has illustrated that greater numbers of women in government systems enhances

Figure 2.4   *A model of institutional framework for entrepreneurship*
                and gender equality in MENA Gulf and Mediterranean
                2009–2018

development issues to support women's education, work, welfare and wellbeing (Metcalfe et al., 2020).

This is a significant transformation as social movement theorists often
stress that a concern for women's development is often not a key aspect of
reform agendas. Gulf countries have shaken this idea and openly advocate the
involvement of women in the home, polity and economy.

As a consequence, governance systems which incorporate women's voices
promote entrepreneurial policies, and are reflected in modified cultural practices and in the identities of men and women. This is not seen as negating
their religiosity in any way. This is a core signifier of their identity. There are
also other social changes happening. A key social change in the GCC is, for
example, that women tend to marry later, and have fewer children, now that
they have health education and are familiar with fertility policies. Moreover,
more women than men, particularly in the Gulf, obtain graduate and post-
graduate degrees (UNDP, 2019; WEF, 2018). These social changes have had
profound implications for women's engagement in social venturing, which has
increased progressive policies (Htun and Weldon, 2012; World Bank, 2012).
Yet women entrepreneurship in the region still emanates from a traditional
patriarchal culture (Khan, 2017), and a significant number of women entrepreneurs are motivated by improving future perspectives for their families.
They have begun to take a proactive role in society and the family, pursuing
motherhood and providing for their families economically (Khan, 2017). In

this context, the strategy of Gulf countries to support women's development through entrepreneurship has recently been criticized as reinforcing existing cultural norms (Ennis, 2019). In this view, policies regarding women's empowerment are 'top-down' prescriptions of a state-defined female emancipation, whereby women's entrepreneurial agency remains firmly attached to the patriarchic society, and where 'only a woman who successfully runs a family, can also be successful as an entrepreneur' (Kaiser et al., 2011 in Ennis, 2019).

It cannot be denied that a key aspect of social and cultural change has been the greater acceptance and promotion of women's decision-making in politics in MENA Gulf. Alongside the use of 'women-only shortlists' and quotas, tackling inequality has, as the description of national development strategies shows, in many cases been addressed by government agencies at senior levels in politics and public administration. As a consequence, women's role in the polity has been legitimized, and economic and social efforts towards inclusive growth and development have been gaining momentum (Bastian et al., 2019).

Entrepreneurship Promotion in MENA Mediterranean Countries

In Mediterranean states women have advanced in politics as well as society, whilst underlying philosophies for gender equality and ideas for venturing seem to have been filtered through gender mainstreaming discourses rather than through specialized national governmental plans. Therefore, many reforms to support the integration of women into labor markets or to promote their participation in the polity have been catalyzed via gender budget reforms from international donor organizations. For example, during the drafting process of the constitution in Tunisia, UN Women collaborated with the Tunisian Association of Democratic Women (ATFD) and other NGOs, as part of the project titled 'Women's March for a Constitution integrating Equality and Citizenship', to ensure that gender equality arguments would receive sufficient attention in the constitution-making process. To enhance this process, in March 2013 UN Women also supported the Centre for Research, Studies, Documentation and Information on Women (CREDIF) in organizing advocacy events, including a high-level debate on integrating the principle of parity into the Constitution. The event gathered members of the National Constituent Assembly (NCA), government policymakers and civil society representatives at a crucial moment in the drafting process (Tamaru and O'Reilly, 2018; UN Women, 2014). The participation of women advocacy organizations in the constitution process was equally built and strengthened (Tamaru and O'Reilly, 2018). Prior to the 2018 elections, UN Women, in collaboration with several civil society organizations, invested in invigorating a politically engaged culture and participatory democracy with women, a supported gender-sensitive election observation, and provided capacity building for gender-sensitive election observers (UN Women, 2018). At the level of parliament, UN Women supported the establishment and implementation of a women's caucus in the Tunisian Assembly of Representatives.

Efforts in MENA Mediterranean countries regarding the promotion of women entrepreneurship appear hapless in comparison to the concerted strategic efforts in the MENA Gulf, since these Mediterranean countries have yet to develop an integrated and multidimensional strategic approach to it (UN, 2017). Moreover, governments have lacked communications that would make it very clear that female entrepreneurship plays a key role in their policies in order to empower women and promote gender equality (UN, 2017). Like Tunisia, most countries made commitments in their constitutions regarding gender equality; all these countries have been signatories to the Millennium Development Goals and the Sustainable Development Goals committed to promote gender equality; and like their peers in the Gulf, they are signatory to the UN Convention of all forms of discrimination against women (CEDAW). Yet their commitment has not translated into significantly greater economic opportunities for women (Džindo, 2014), or any reduction in gender gaps regarding entrepreneurial behavior. These countries have only superficially incorporated the gender component into SME policies, and lack coherent policies in this regard. Contrary to the Gulf States, these countries have yet to develop strategic framework plans that encompass enabled institutions, and especially those that endow focal government institutions with the necessary power and resources (Džindo, 2014; UN, 2017).

CONCLUSION

This present research has analyzed the entrepreneurship activities of men and women in the MENA region and found substantial divergence regarding the gender gap in entrepreneurial activities within Mediterranean countries and Gulf countries over the past decade, with the latter having achieved near gender parity by 2018.[2] Measured cultural differences between the two defined sub-regions have insufficient explanatory power to justify this variance in gender gaps. Instead, this chapter shows that more attention has to be paid to how women's entrepreneurship planning is, or is not, embedded in governance machineries and institutional frameworks. The key difference that has facilitated this change is that Gulf States have introduced gender quotas in government that are even now not countenanced by the UK, USA and Australia. This is both important in its own right (given MENA as home to 400 m+ people), and as a global signifier of women's capabilities and opportunities for gender development. Put simply, countries such as Saudi Arabia, the UAE and Qatar have aligned with women's agendas and significantly engaged in gender policy-making to promote women's working and entrepreneurial development.

These policy approaches have also been criticized as a way to portray an otherwise profoundly patriarchic society as reformist, and to perpetuate gendered structures without substantial reforms regarding gender relations (Ennis, 2019), and many feel that state-led feminisms are co-opting with male political power, rather than liberating or advocating female agency. In this sense, greater gender parity in entrepreneurial behavior cannot always be taken as greater female empowerment and progress regarding gender equality (Bastian et al., 2019). Female empowerment must be linked to sustainable change that challenges existent hierarchies and power structures (Kabeer, 2005).

Nevertheless, the changes in the GCC are transformational. They represent moves to articulate Arabization, and to negate Western notions of imperialism as a marker for economic and social development. The efforts of MENA Gulf also represent a shift in policy approaches compared to other countries in the MENA region and worldwide. In fact, they correspond to contemporary WEF Davos 2020 calls for inclusive agendas for business that could help redistribute vast wealth. The dialogue presented by Klaus Schwab at Davos 2020 was not just about empowering less privileged groups, but in re-imagining opportunities for sharing and eradicating vast inequalities, and the role that MNCs can play in this. Behavioral and attitudinal changes about what inclusive business involves move development agendas beyond sameness and difference debates (Walby, 2009). It remains to be seen how the WEF can influence policy, as the mantra of stakeholder capitalism was not favored with most MNC leaders advocating shareholder capitalism.[3]

If conservative Gulf countries can get close to gender parity in terms of levels of entrepreneurial activity, there is a case for addressing wide (and in some cases, widening) gender gaps in other MENA countries (and beyond). Closing these gaps has the potential to create thousands of new businesses and jobs, as well as elevating incomes and inclusion. This chapter shows that socio-economic factors, coupled with culture, can account for more complex explanations. This debate also suggests that women's social movements are active in the MENA region, and represent diverse drivers in improving women's status in multiple ways, relevant to their own history and culture. This chapter has also shown that women's agency in MENA is growing, and that their voices are getting louder and louder.

NOTES

1. Bosma and Kelley (2019).
2. This is in relation to entrepreneurial activity and venturing, not to all equality measures.

3.   The WEF was formed by Klaus Schwab to provide a forum for global MNCs to aid economic development policies. The WEF have strongly pushed equity agendas, and their annual Global Gender Gap Report is ardently followed. However, the turning back to stakeholder capitalism was not favored by most Global North corporations. This is not the case in MENA, as the GCC are very much advocating a moral Islamic economy (Metcalfe et al., 2020).

REFERENCES

Abousleiman, Issam (2020), 'GCC reforms are changing women's lives', accessed 26 February 2021 at https://www.worldbank.org/en/news/opinion/2020/03/04/gcc-reforms-are-changing-womens-lives.

Afiouni, F. and C. Karam (2017), 'Debunking myths surrounding women's careers in the Arab region: A critical reflexive approach', *Career Guidance and Livelihood Planning across the Mediterranean*, **1**(1), 55–70.

Al-Dajani, H. and S. Marlow (2010), 'Impact of women's home-based enterprise on family dynamics: Evidence from Jordan', *International Small Business Journal*, **28**(5), 470–86.

Al-Ghazali, B.M., R.M. Yusoff and M.A. Sadi (2013), 'Women entrepreneurs in Bahrain: Motivations and barriers', *Jurnal Teknologi*, **64**(2), 139–43.

Al-Kwifi, O.S., T. Tien Khoa, V. Ongsakul and Z.U. Ahmed (2019), 'Determinants of female entrepreneurship success across Saudi Arabia', *Journal of Transnational Management*, 1–27.

Alotaibi, F., R. Cutting and J. Morgan (2017), 'A critical analysis of the literature in women's leadership in Saudi Arabia', *International Journal of Business Administration and Management Research*, **3**(1).

Bahramitash, R. and H.S. Esfahani (2014), 'Gender and entrepreneurship in Iran', *Middle East Critique*, **23**(3), 293–312.

Barakat, H., S. Hill and E. Akhrass (2018), 'Women and entrepreneurship in the contemporary Middle East', *KnE Social Sciences*, **3**(10), 20–29.

Bastian, B.L. and C.L. Tucci (2017), 'Entrepreneurial advice sources and their antecedents', *Journal of Enterprising Communities: People and Places in the Global Economy*, **11**(2), 214–36.

Bastian, B.L. and M.R. Zali (2016a), 'Entrepreneurial motives and their antecedents of men and women in North Africa and the Middle East', *Gender in Management: An International Journal*, **31**(7), 456–87.

Bastian, B. and M.R. Zali (2016b), 'The impact of institutional quality on social networks and performance of entrepreneurs', *Small Enterprise Research*, **23**(2), 151–71.

Bastian, B.L., B.D. Metcalfe and M.R. Zali (2019), 'Gender inequality: Entrepreneurship development in the MENA region', *Sustainability*, **11**(22), 6472.

Bastian, B.L., Y.M. Sidani and Y. El Amine (2018), 'Women entrepreneurship in the Middle East and North Africa: A review of knowledge areas and research gaps', *Gender in Management: An International Journal*, **33**(1), 14–29.

Bosma, N. and D. Kelley (2019), 'Global Entrepreneurship Monitor 2018/2019 Global Report', London: GERA.

Dan, H. (2017), 'Is social progress subject to cultural influences? Arguments for considering cultural characteristics as inputs for social policy design and implementation', *Modelling the New Europe. An On-line Journal*, **22**, 104–22.

Dechant, K. and A.A. Lamky (2005), 'Toward an understanding of Arab women entrepreneurs in Bahrain and Oman', *Journal of Developmental Entrepreneurship*, **10**(2), 123–40.

Džindo, D. (2014), 'Women's entrepreneurship in North Africa: Looking into the Western Balkans' experience', in Sasha Toperich and Andy Mullins (eds), *A New Paradigm: Perspectives on the Changing Mediterranean*, Washington, DC: Center for Transatlantic Relations, accessed 3 February 2020 at https://sashatoperich.com/wp-content/uploads/2016/09/A-New-Paradigm-COMPILED-TEXT.pdf.

El Azhary, S.A. (2016), 'Normative paradigms on constraints on equal rights for women in the Arab World', in M. Shalaby and V. Moghadam (eds), *Empowering Women after the Arab Spring*, New York, NY: Palgrave.

Ennis, C.A. (2019), 'The gendered complexities of promoting female entrepreneurship in the Gulf', *New Political Economy*, **24**(3), 365–84.

Erogul, M.S. and D. McCrohan (2008), 'Preliminary investigation of Emirati women entrepreneurs in the UAE', *African Journal of Business Management*, **2**(10), 177–85.

Esposito, J.L. (2005), *Islam: The Straight Path*, 3rd edn, Oxford: Oxford University Press.

Farzanegan, M.R. (2014), 'Can oil-rich countries encourage entrepreneurship?' *Entrepreneurship & Regional Development*, **26**(9–10), 706–25.

Foley, S. (2010), *The Arab Gulf States: Beyond Oil and Islam*, Boulder, CO: Lynne Rienner.

Fox, J.W., N. Mourtada-Sabbah and M. Al Mutawa (eds) (2006), *Globalization and the Gulf*, Abingdon: Routledge.

Goby, V.P. and M.S. Erogul (2011), 'Female entrepreneurship in the United Arab Emirates: Legislative encouragements and cultural constraints', *Women's Studies International Forum*, **34**(4), 329–34.

Gray, K.R. and J. Finley-Hervey, (2005), 'Women and entrepreneurship in Morocco: Debunking stereotypes and discerning strategies', *The International Entrepreneurship and Management Journal*, **1**(2), 203–17.

Hertog, S. (2019), 'What would the Saudi economy have to look like to be "post rentier"?' *POMEPS Studies*, pp. 29–33.

Hilsdon, A.M. and S. Rozario (2006), 'Special issue on Islam, gender and human rights', *Women's Studies International Forum*, **29**(4), 331–8.

Hofstede, G. (1992), 'Cultural dimensions in people management: The socialization perspective', in V. Pucik, N.M. Tichy and C.K. Barnett (eds), *Globalizing Management: Creating and Leading the Competitive Organization*, New York, NY: Wiley & Sons.

Hofstede, G. (2015), 'Culture's causes: The next challenge', *Cross Cultural Management. An International Journal*, **22**(4), 545–69.

Htun, M. and S.L. Weldon (2012), 'The civic origins of progressive policy change: Combating violence against women in global perspective, 1975–2005', *American Political Science Review*, **106**(3), 548–69.

International Monetary Fund (IMF) (2014), 'Regional Economic Outlook. Middle East and Central Asia', accessed 26 February 2021 at file:///C:/Users/Bettina/Downloads/_mreo1014pdf.pdf.

Itani, H., Y.M. Sidani and I. Baalbaki (2011), 'United Arab Emirates female entrepreneurs: Motivations and frustrations', *Equality, Diversity and Inclusion: An International Journal*, **30**(5), 409–24.

Jamali, D. (2009), 'Constraints and opportunities facing women entrepreneurs in developing countries: A relational perspective', *Gender in Management: An International Journal*, **24**(4), 232–51.

Kabeer, N. (2005), 'Gender equality and women's empowerment: A critical analysis of the third millennium development goals', *Gender and Development*, **13**(1), 13–24.

Karam, C.M. and F. Afiouni (2014), 'Localizing women's experiences in academia: Multilevel factors at play in the Arab Middle East and North Africa', *The International Journal of Human Resource Management*, **25**(4), 500–538.

Khan, M.R. (2017), 'Succeeding in challenging environments: Female technology start-ups evidence from Saudi Arabia', *Academy of Entrepreneurship Journal*, **23**(2), 1–11.

Melki, J.P. and S.E. Mallat (2016), 'Block her entry, keep her down and push her out: Gender discrimination and women journalists in the Arab world', *Journalism Studies*, **17**(1), 57–79.

Metcalfe, B.D. (2006), 'Exploring cultural dimensions of gender and management in the Middle East', *Thunderbird International Business Review*, **48**(1), 93–107.

Metcalfe, B.D. (2011), 'Women, empowerment and development in Arab Gulf States: A critical appraisal of governance, culture and national human resource development (HRD) frameworks', *Human Resource Development International*, **14**(2), 131–48.

Metcalfe, B.D., Y. Makarem and F. Afiouni (2020), 'Macro talent management theorizing: Transnational perspectives of the political economy of talent formation in the Arab Middle East', *The International Journal of Human Resource Management*, **32**(1), 1–36.

Moghadam, V.M. (2005), 'Women's economic participation in the Middle East: What difference has the neoliberal policy turn made?', *Journal of Middle East Women's Studies*, **1**(1), 110–46.

OECD (2014), *Women in Business 2014: Accelerating Entrepreneurship in the Middle East and North Africa Region*, Paris: OECD.

Omair, K. (2008), 'Women in management in the Arab context', *Education Business and Society: Contemporary Middle Eastern Issues*, **1**(2), 107–23.

Rosen, L. (2000), *The Justice of Islam: Comparative Perspectives on Islamic Law and Society*, Oxford: Oxford University Press.

Sakir Erogul, M. (2014), 'Entrepreneurial activity and attitude in the United Arab Emirates', *Innovation*, **16**(2), 195–211.

Shahnawaz, M.R. (2015), 'Preliminary investigation of Emirati women entrepreneurship in the UAE: Motivating factors, challenges and government initiatives', *International Journal of Scientific & Technology Research*, **4**(8), 50–61.

Shayah, M.H. and Z. Sun (2019), 'Employment in the Gulf Cooperation Council (GCC) Countries: Current issues and future trends', in *2nd International Conference on Social Science, Public Health and Education (SSPHE 2018)*. Atlantis Press.

Sidani, Y. (2005), 'Women, work, and Islam in Arab societies', *Women in Management Review*, **20**(7), 498–512.

Sidani, Y.M. (2018), 'Introduction', in *Muslim Women at Work*, Cham: Palgrave Macmillan.

Syed, J. and B.D. Metcalfe (2017), 'Under western eyes: A transnational and postcolonial perspective of gender and HRD', *Human Resource Development International*, **20**(5), 403–14.

Tamaru, N. and M. O'Reilly (2018), 'How women influence constitution making after conflict and unrest', Washington, DC: Inclusive Security.

Tlaiss, H. (2013), 'Entrepreneurial motivations of women: Evidence from the United Arab Emirates', *International Small Business Journal*, **33**(5), 562–81.

Tlaiss, H. and S. Kauser (2011), 'Women in management in Lebanon', in M.J. Davidson and R.J. Burke (eds), *Women in Management Worldwide: Progress and Prospects*, Gower Publishing, pp. 299–315.

Tlaiss, H.A. and M. McAdam (2020), 'Unexpected lives: The intersection of Islam and Arab women's entrepreneurship', *Journal of Business Ethics*, pp. 1–20.

UNDP (2010), *The Real Wealth of Nations: Pathways to Human Development*, New York, NY: United Nations Publications.

UNDP (2016), 'Arab Human Development Report', accessed 1 July 2019 at https:// www.un-ilibrary.org/economic-and-social-development/arab-human-development -report_1db838ae-en.

UNDP (2019), '365 days of a gender journey 2019', accessed 1 July 2019 at https:// www.undp.org/content/dam/lebanon/docs/Women%20Emp/365%20Days%20of %0a%20Gender%20Journey_2019.pdf.

UN Industrial Development Organization (2017), *Promoting Women Empowerment for Inclusive and Sustainable Industrial Development in the Middle East and North Africa Region. A Study on Women Entrepreneurship Development in Egypt, Jordan, Lebanon, Morocco, Palestine and Tunisia*, accessed 1 July 2019 at https://www .unido.org/sites/default/files/files/2019-10/MENA_REPORT_Eng_interactive-1_0 .pdf.

UN Women (2014), 'Tunisia – New Constitution a breakthrough for women's rights', accessed 1 July 2019 at https://wunrn.com/2014/02/tunisia-new-constitution -a-breakthrough-for-womens-rights/.

UN Women (2018), 'Historic leap in Tunisia: Women make up 47% more of local government', accessed 1 July 2019 at https://www.unwomen.org/en/news/stories/ 2018/8/feature-tunisian-women-in-local-elections.

UN Women (2020), 'The world for women and girls. Annual Report 2019–2020', accessed 28 April 2021 at https://www.unwomen.org/en/digital-library/publications/ 2020/06/annual-report-2019-2020.

Walby, S. (2009), *Globalization and Inequalities: Complexity and Contested Modernities*, London: Sage.

Weeks, J.R. (2009), 'Women business owners in the Middle East and North Africa: A five-country research study', *International Journal of Gender and Entrepreneurship*, **1**(1), 77–85.

Welsh, D.H., E. Memili, E. Kaciak and A. Al Sadoon (2014), 'Saudi women entrepreneurs: A growing economic segment', *Journal of Business Research*, **67**(5), 758–62.

World Bank (2007), 'The environment for women's entrepreneurship in the Middle East and North Africa Region', Washington, DC: World Bank, accessed 1 July 2019 at http://web.worldbank.org/WBSITE/EXTERNAL/COUNTRIES/MENAEXT/0 ,,contentMDK:21517656~pagePK:146736~piPK:146830~theSitePK:256299,00 .html.

World Bank (2011), 'Capabilities, opportunities, and participation: Gender equality and development in the Middle East and North Africa region. A companion to the World Development Report 2012', Washington, DC: World Bank, accessed 1 July 2019 at http://siteresources.worldbank.org/INTMENA/Resources/World_Development _Report_2012_Gender_Equality_ Development_Overview_MENA.pdf.

World Bank (2012), 'World Development Report 2012: Gender equality and development', accessed 1 July 2019 at https://openknowledge.worldbank.org/handle/10986/ 4391.

World Bank (2014), 'Voice and agency: Empowering women and girls for shared prosperity', accessed at https://www.worldbank.org/content/dam/Worldbank/document/Gender/ALTERNATE_VOICE_AGENCY_EXECUTIVE_SUMMARY_PRINTING.pdf.

World Bank (2018), 'Middle East and North Africa', accessed 26 February 2021 at https://www.worldbank.org/en/region/mena/overview.

World Economic Forum (WEF) (2018), *The Global Gender Gap Report 2018*, accessed 1 July 2019 at http://www3.weforum.org/docs/WEF_GGGR_2018.pdf.

Zamberi Ahmad, S. (2011), 'Evidence of the characteristics of women entrepreneurs in the Kingdom of Saudi Arabia: An empirical investigation', *International Journal of Gender and Entrepreneurship*, **3**(2), 123–43.

Zeidan, S. and S. Bahrami (2011), 'Women entrepreneurship in GCC: A framework to address challenges and promote participation in a regional context', *International Journal of Business and Social Science*, **2**(14), 100–107.

3. The unfolding process of women's entrepreneurship in a patriarchal society: an exploration of Bangladeshi women entrepreneurs' experiences

Wee Chan Au, Sabrina Nourin and Pervaiz K. Ahmed

INTRODUCTION

The traditional perspective of entrepreneurship as a positive economic activity, in which women's entrepreneurship contributes to a country's economic wellbeing by creating jobs, alleviating poverty, enhancing productivity, and boosting innovativeness, has been widely discussed and documented (Minniti and Naudé, 2010; Welter and Smallbone, 2008). However, an increasing number of researchers have noted that this dominant view of entrepreneurship as an economic activity is one-sided and undermines what entrepreneurship is and does (Kantor, 2002; Steyaert and Katz, 2004). Critical perspectives have called for the study of women's entrepreneurship to probe beyond the economic narrative (Alkhaled and Berglund, 2018; Calás et al., 2009; Datta and Gailey, 2012; Steyaert and Hjorth, 2008). In particular, there is concern over "who and what are represented within the main theoretical frameworks of the literature and who and what are left out" (Calás et al., 2009, p. 553). Our study adds to the literature by exploring what entrepreneurship does to women in a patriarchal society, by exploring women entrepreneurs' lived experiences in Bangladesh.

Our primary research question is: "How do Bangladeshi women entrepreneurs (BWEs) maneuver around socio-cultural barriers in their entrepreneurship journeys?" Taking this research question a step further, we explore if and how entrepreneurial activities among women lead to positive social change in the patriarchal context of Bangladesh. In other words, can women's entrepreneurship create social change in Bangladesh?

The extant literature on women's entrepreneurship in developing-country contexts, especially those with patriarchal societies, has made significant progress in identifying barriers to, struggles of, and difficulties of women entrepreneurs (Al-Dajani and Marlow, 2010; Itani et al., 2011; Naguib and Jamali, 2015). While this line of enquiry has built a solid foundation, there remains considerable scope for further study, particularly research that can develop a more nuanced understanding of the diverse lived experiences of women entrepreneurs. In this study, we build on prior research and further advance the literature by focusing our attention on the experiences of BWEs in dealing with the sociocultural and institutional context that prevails in Bangladesh. In so doing, we elucidate how these women travail on their entrepreneurial journeys and uncover the underlying process these women use in the nurturance and use of agency.

BANGLADESH: THE INSTITUTIONAL CONTEXT

Bangladesh offers an interesting societal context to study women entrepreneurship because of its strong patriarchal nature. As Bangladesh is a Muslim majority country in which 90 percent of the population are Muslims, Islam plays a pivotal role in determining women's rights and obligations (Zaman, 1999). Many have seen Bangladesh as a typical example of patriarchy, where male supremacy is accepted as a natural order of things (Sayem and Nury, 2013; Schuler et al., 1996). In other words, men have priority over women in all situations, while women are powerless in both public and private spheres. For example, Muslim personal laws, following the principles of *Sharia* (Islamic principles and teachings), perpetuate male domination by placing women under the control and authority of men (Zaman, 1999).

In the prevailing environment of high levels of patriarchy in Bangladesh, women's status is low, and women are undervalued (Naved and Persson, 2010; Sayem and Nury, 2013). Consequently, women's subdued social position is widely evidenced. Many women in Bangladesh have no independent sources of income, little or no education and skills, and no socially sanctioned identity outside of the family (Schuler et al., 1996). According to Zaman (1999), the social, economic and political structures in Bangladesh, including property rights, state laws and policies, are discriminatory in nature and they deny women socioeconomic autonomy at every stage of their lives. To make the situation worse, Bangladeshi women are everyday targets of discrimination, exploitation and violence, even within their households (Schuler et al., 1996; Zaman, 1999).

Despite the challenges over the years, women in Bangladesh have attempted to improve their socioeconomic status. The emergence of microfinance, primarily through Grameen Bank and the Bangladesh Rural Advancement

Committee, has encouraged self-employment and entrepreneurial activity among women, especially those from the lower social class, as a means to escape poverty (Jansen and Pippard, 1998). The Bangladeshi government has also taken numerous steps to improve the socioeconomic status of women in Bangladesh. These steps include specifying equal economic rights and opportunities, including a special provision to promote entrepreneurship among women, under Article 28 of the Constitution of the People's Republic of Bangladesh, enacted in 1972 (Alliance for Financial Inclusion, 2017). Furthermore, in line with the Perspective Plan of Bangladesh (2010–21), which is designed to make Bangladesh a middle-income country, the National Women Development Policy 2011 emphasizes empowering women economically through micro, small and medium enterprises (Alliance for Financial Inclusion, 2017). However, the progress of women in business leadership and entrepreneurship remains low in Bangladesh. Bangladesh tops the list in terms of the gender gap, recording a total entrepreneurial activity gap of 16.7 percent, while the global average is slightly above 5 percent (Warnecke, 2013). The humble state of BWEs is also reflected by low access to finance. In 2017, only 15 percent of BWEs had access to finance. Of the total outstanding small and medium enterprise (SME) loan of Tk 140 000 crore (about US\$166 million), only Tk 5000 crore (about US\$6 million) was given to women entrepreneurs (*Daily Star*, 2017).

Women's Entrepreneurship in a Patriarchal Society

As authority figures in the family, men play the role of gatekeepers in patriarchal and Islamic societies (Kazemi, 2000), "safeguarding" women through the creation of an inside–outside dichotomy (Ali, 2013; Ali et al., 2017). On the outside element, men are regarded as providers who work outside of the home and control interactions between the family and the outside world (Schuler et al., 1996). On the inside element, women are presumed to be dependent and to need to be looked after by men. Hence they are restricted to indoors, hidden away from the outside world (Ali, 2013; Ali et al., 2017). This form of dichotomy constrains women's freedom in patriarchal and Islamic societies (Hattab, 2012; Itani et al., 2011). Practices in many Islamic societies assign household roles (inside), especially motherhood, to women as their priority over all other possible (outside) roles, including employment and entrepreneurship. Women involved in entrepreneurial activities are therefore seen to go against the expected "inside" role.

Operating within patriarchal and Islamic societies, women need permission and support from the family to engage in entrepreneurial activities (Al-Dajani and Marlow, 2010; Barragan et al., 2018; Naguib and Jamali, 2015). Doing otherwise, women run the risk of being perceived as deviating from social norms, which risks bringing shame to the family. Accordingly, women entrepreneurs in many Muslim majority countries, such as Saudi Arabia and the Emirates, are highly constrained by a patriarchal culture, which Tlaiss (2015) perceives as an outcome of misinterpretations of Islam's teachings. Lack of family support, limited access to funding, and limited access to networks are some of the common obstacles women entrepreneurs face in these societies (Tlaiss, 2014), where entrepreneurship is still primarily considered as a men's activity.

Many studies have focused attention on the barriers and difficulties of women entrepreneurs operating in patriarchal contexts (e.g., Al-Dajani and Marlow, 2010; Itani et al., 2011; Naguib and Jamali, 2015). Far fewer studies have examined how women entrepreneurs navigate through and within patriarchal conservative societies (Al-Dajani and Marlow, 2010; Barragan et al., 2018). Though few in number, these studies provide initial support for the need to explore and understand more fully the mechanisms women use to navigate the barriers they face. For example, Al-Dajani and Marlow (2010) examined how Palestinian women who operate home-based enterprises in Jordan negotiated the right to be self-employed within the context of conservative family dynamics. Barragan et al. (2018) showed how Emirati female entrepreneurs in the United Arab Emirates engaged in strategic (dis)obedience to navigate the expectations of male gatekeepers of the family in patriarchal and Islamic societies.

Women's Entrepreneurship and Women's Agency

The assumption that entrepreneurs have the agency to act is widely evident in the entrepreneurship literature. Entrepreneurs are perceived as agents pursuing specific interests and acting strategically, as creators of the enterprise institution (Garud et al., 2007; Misangyi et al., 2008; Weik, 2011), and as agents who mobilize resources and mobilize other actors (e.g., Garud et al., 2007; Khan et al., 2007). We raise a concern about the wholesale acceptance of such assumptions and argue that in certain contexts, for example in a country where women are the victims of a patriarchal culture, like Bangladesh as in this study, women entrepreneurs may not possess the agency to act freely or have access to the same level and source of agency as they would in advanced democratic societies.

In this study, we adopt an agency lens to examine the lived experiences of women entrepreneurs in Bangladesh. Individual agency, drawing upon social cognitive theory, operates within a broad social structure and social system, in which "people are producers as well as products of the social system" (Bandura, 2001, p. 1). In other words, it is not possible to understand women entrepreneurs' agency without relating it to the institutional structures in which they operate. Stereotypes, gender role ideologies, and the social acceptability of entrepreneurship as a career among women are all important considerations to understand the experience of women entrepreneurs in a specific country context (Baughn et al., 2006). According to Datta and Gailey (2012), institutional structures, especially sociocultural norms, may hinder women from making their own decisions freely. For instance, operating within a patriarchal context, the culturally embedded male domination and dependency on men limits a woman's agency in pursuing opportunities and personal capabilities (Sen, 1999). Similarly, Klyver et al. (2013) highlighted that while individuals exercise individual autonomy in their (self)-employment choice, such choices are influenced by the unique institutional context to which they belong. In particular, social and institutional forces determine "what individuals will, can and are legitimatized to do" (Klyver et al., 2013, p. 475). Moreover, possessing agency in terms of having leeway and the ability to exercise choice is vital for individuals to overcome institutional pressures (Ali et al., 2017).

According to social cognitive theory, "to be an agent is to influence intentionally one's functioning and life circumstances" (Bandura, 2006, p. 164). In this study, we are interested in understanding the agency of women in Bangladesh and how they exercise it to control the nature and quality of their life. Operating within broad sociostructural influences, one should possess three modes of agency (Bandura, 2001; 2006): (a) individual agency, which assumes that one has direct control over one's own functioning and the conditions that affect the quality of life; (b) proxy agency, where one relies on others to act on one's behalf for desired outcomes; and (c) collective agency, which is achieved through a pooling of resources. One's daily functioning involves a combination of these three forms of agency. In this study, we explore the sources from which BWEs draw and use agency and how its nature shapes their experiences in dealing with the institutional and sociocultural obstacles that prevail in Bangladesh.

RESEARCH DESIGN

In this study, we adopted a phenomenological methodology, which describes the meaning for several individuals of their lived experiences of a concept or a phenomenon and which can reduce individual experiences (with the phenomenon) to a description of the universal essence (Creswell, 2007). The phenomenological approach fits our research, as we seek to understand BWEs' lived experiences in dealing with sociocultural barriers in their entrepreneurship journeys. The phenomenological approach offers an avenue to gain a rich, unique insight into women's entrepreneurial activities and perceptions (Cope, 2005).

Sample

We adopted multiple sampling strategies to recruit participants. We used two selection criteria to ensure that all participants were Muslim and owned at least 50 percent of their businesses. First, we obtained a list of women entrepreneurs ($n = 17$) from the Center for Entrepreneurship Development Unit of the Bangladesh Rural Advancement Committee University. All BWEs on this list had gone through the Young Entrepreneurship Development Program, part of the University of Oklahoma fellowship program, in 2016. We contacted them all, and seven agreed to share their experiences with us. Second, we contacted BWEs listed on the SME Women Entrepreneurs Directory ($n = 65$) published by the SME Foundation Bangladesh. After multiple email exchanges and follow-up phone calls, 17 of the BWEs accepted our invitation to participate in the study. Next, the second author visited a number of commercial complexes within Dhaka and the surrounding suburbs to invite women shop-owners to participate. Five BWEs agreed to share their stories. We also used snowball sampling by asking the study participants to forward our invitation to other BWEs they knew. We managed to interview another five women entrepreneurs through snowballing. In total, we managed to capture the narratives of 34 Bangladeshi Muslim women entrepreneurs.

Demographics

Our participants owned a variety of businesses, mostly retail ($n = 14$) and services ($n = 14$), with a few in manufacturing ($n = 7$). They all owned micro, small and medium-sized businesses, with the number of employees ranging from sole owners to 40 employees. The oldest business was established in 1995 and the most recent in 2015. In terms of individual characteristics, the age range of BWEs lay between 22 and 65 years. In terms of marital status, 21 were married, six single, two widows, one separated, and five divorced. Education ranged from illiterate to a Master's degree. For social class, we felt it was inappropriate to ask respondents directly. Following Dy et al. (2017), we used reflective indicators from participants and observational indicators from the interviewer to infer information about their socioeconomic class. These indicators include family background, income, education and employment history, job title in previous jobs (if applicable), and personal and business networks. Accordingly, we identified that 17 participants came from lower to middle class, and 18 came from higher social class backgrounds.

Data Collection

We adopted a semi-structured interview technique to collect data. The inter-view focused on three areas: motivations of business initiation, experiences (both positive and negative) in entrepreneurship journeys, and factors that enabled or constrained their businesses. The second author, who speaks Bengali, Bangladesh's native language, conducted the interviews. She con-ducted 31 interviews in Bengali and three in English. On average, the inter-views lasted one hour. We digitally recorded and transcribed the interviews verbatim, coded them using NVivo10, and analyzed them thematically. We transcribed and translated interviews in Bengali into English. To ensure accu-racy in translation, we randomly selected transcripts for verification by a third party who is fluent in both English and Bengali. We conducted this verification step to ensure our translation was accurate. We collected demographic infor-mation with a short checklist at the end of each interview.

DATA ANALYSIS

Our analysis was guided by Colaizzi's (1978) recommended procedures. Before data coding, we immersed ourselves in the data by reading all the transcripts repeatedly and individually. We read them by batch in a group and we held weekly meetings to discuss the commonalities and differences in each BWE's narrative. Through this process, we acquired feelings and an overview of the data. Next, we proceeded to data coding using NVivo. Based on earlier group discussions, the first author coded and analyzed the dataset, pulling out significant statements from the transcripts and parking them under respective categories (tentative themes). After coding every five transcripts, the group met and discussed the identified significant statements and meaning of each category. In this process, new categories emerged, and some repetitive catego-ries collapsed and merged. We also discussed the potential of subcategories. Eventually, our analyses yielded four key themes on how BWEs gain and use agency during the process of dealing with institutional and sociocultural barriers. To ensure the trustworthiness of the study, we took the following steps suggested by Lincoln and Guba (1985): (a) for member checks, we sent transcripts to participants who agreed to verify them; and (b) the interviewer updated a reflective journal upon completion of each interview, and all of us did this upon completing the reading of each transcript to document our thought processes.

Table 3.1   Summary of findings

Borrowing:	Consolidating:	Leveraging:	Sustaining:
Situational Agency Proxies	Coping Stratagems	Discovering Oneself	Transitioning to Collective Agency
• Family standing/network • Male (support)	• Enduring the negative • Avoiding and deflecting the negative • Confronting the negative	• Finding independence • Finding self-worth/ esteem • Finding confidence and strength	• Enabling, guiding, and providing opportunities to other women • Promoting and inspiring women • Changing attitudes and promoting women's rights and agency

FINDINGS

This section presents findings that critically examine how BWEs acquire and use agency to navigate sociocultural barriers in their entrepreneurship journeys. Through our analysis of BWE accounts of establishing enterprises and running them in Bangladesh, we identified four major themes that capture the key stages in the way BWEs gain and use agency. These stages are: borrowing, consolidating, leveraging, and sustaining. Table 3.1 summarizes our findings.

Theme 1: Borrowing – Situational Agency Proxies

In the early part of their entrepreneurial journey, particularly at the start-up stage, BWEs find themselves in highly vulnerable positions, exposed to the vagaries and constraints of a strong patriarchal society. In this setting, BWEs, lacking sufficient agency themselves, resort to borrowing agency from situational others around them to counter the social and cultural barriers they face. The BWEs widely practice borrowing, in terms of relying on situational agency proxies, in the early stages of their entrepreneurship journeys. BWEs rely heavily on family standing and family networks, and the support of men to tackle sociocultural barriers. We briefly elaborate the subthemes, along with supporting quotations from the interview transcripts, below.

Family standing and family networks
BWEs, especially those from the middle to higher social class backgrounds, tap their personal networks to overcome the sociocultural hurdles they face. BWE25 shared how she tactfully makes sure her male business counterparts

treat her respectfully by drawing reference to her immediate and extended family network.

> Whenever I go for a meeting, I try to work out how I am connected to these men … I will see if any of my cousins went to university with him. Do I know his wife? Do I know his wife's friend? If I can make a reference, then I am no longer an object. I am a human being. Then it would be easier to communicate. Then he won't mess with me. Best still, if I know his family, brother, or uncle. Then, he will be nice to me. [BWE25]

Male (support)

Most BWEs identified having a male presence as particularly helpful to overcome the sociocultural norms that prevail in Bangladesh, such as "A decent Bangladeshi Muslim woman should not engage actively in activities outside the household." Accordingly, many BWEs involve their husband, father or even son in their business. Occasionally, this involvement is informal, but often BWEs must involve men formally to navigate the negative cultural and institutional norms towards women. Men are involved as investors, advisors, or business partners, and BWEs tap on their agency to build a proxy base of agency for themselves. BWE6, who runs a children's apparel shop, first involved her husband and later her son to establish and expand the business. Without their assistance, she noted, it would have been almost impossible for her to succeed in Bangladesh. She noted:

> The reality is, if you don't get support from the family, then your journey will be very hard. Male support is a must. It can be husband or father or brother. As a woman, if you get a man's support, then your journey will be easier. [BWE6]

BWEs from the lower social class background often operate their businesses within the confines of even more conservative communities than those in the broader societal context. In this type of environment, the presence of a male family member is a critical buffer in dealing with community resistance to a woman's presence in business enterprise. Additionally, men are used to play a "security guard" function, since an unaccompanied woman runs the risk of abuse and even physical attack. BWE1 shared the role of her husband in her retail business below:

> When I go away from Dhaka to source clothing, he [my husband] must always accompany me. If he did not accompany me, I would not be able to sustain this business. He has given me a lot of support, from the start to now.

In the case of BWEs who are from middle to higher social class backgrounds, the presence of male family members often offers more than just security support. Men, including extended family members, tend to be resourceful in providing financial capital, social capital, and even business expertise relevant to the BWEs' business. BWE15 shared how her male relative helped her to initiate the business:

> My relative advised me to start outsourcing [business]. He encouraged me to set up the enterprise in Bangladesh, and he would find some clients for me from the UK. That's how I started. We started with accounting BPO (Business Process Outsourcing), outsourcing the whole accounting solution.

A number of BWEs choose to recruit male employees to cope with the sociocultural resistance they encounter in their daily business operation. For example, BWE 25, who owns a cruise ship, hired a male cruise manager to manage crew members, who are all men.

> They [ship's crew members] cannot deal with a female leader. They just cannot. They cannot accept it. So I have a male manager to manage these people. For instance, if I asked someone nicely to clean the table, the table would never be cleaned. But if my male manager asks, and even verbally abuses them, they are ok, and they will do it. So the best way to manage these people is through a male voice.

Theme 2: Consolidating – Coping Stratagems

Following the initial stage of sourcing agency from proxies, BWEs still need to establish their own agency. Our analysis suggests that this occurs when BWEs begin the process of building a self-derived agency by consolidating upon the initially borrowed agency from male proxies. We observe that this transition involves considerable struggle and pain on the part of the BWEs. Our analysis identifies that during the consolidating process, BWEs deploy a number of coping stratagems to help them to maneuver through Bangladesh's institutional and sociocultural barriers. We identify three coping strategies: (a) enduring the negative; (b) avoiding and deflecting the negative; and (c) confronting the negative.

Enduring the negative

Several BWEs shared that little can be done with the sociocultural barriers rooted deep within the patriarchal culture of Bangladesh. They simply put up with the difficult constraining circumstances as best they can. Analysis of their narratives reveals that while most of them demonstrate sturdiness and persistence when facing bullying and unfairness, the enduring strategies they adopt are slightly different, depending on the nature of their agency. BWEs who are fairly well educated and who possess working experience demonstrate a higher sense of control and confidence in coping with impediments. They deploy a passive-yet-active enduring strategy, in which they ignore negativity because they are confident that they can break through these barriers and succeed in the future.

> I was daring and enthusiastic … I was full of courage. I told myself "as long as what I am doing is good, then I should not care about what others say." Of course, I felt terrible, but I ignored them. I blocked all these negative things by working. I worked days and nights. I just filled it up with work, no time to think about all those nasty comments. I told myself, I will respond to these negative words with my accomplishment in business one day. [BWE24]

Other BWEs, especially those coming from lower social class backgrounds, with low levels of education and little work experience, tend to deal with sociocultural impediments in a more submissive manner. Just to survive and feed the family, these BWEs feel they have to tolerate bullying and harassment, and live in the desperate hope that the situation will become better by itself. BWE13, who came from a very humble background, shared how she swallowed all the soreness because she felt unable to do anything when she was facing taunts and threats at her business premises:

> There were few guys; they would stand in front of my store. They would scare me and shout many bad and vulgar things. I kept telling myself "I am here to earn a living. I am not doing anything wrong." I prayed that they would leave me alone one day. Slowly, they stopped disturbing me. I had to pass through this "hurdle". Once I was over it, I am ok … So, I never wear good clothes or accessories [to attract attention]. I always tried to keep a low profile. I even made myself look dirty so that nobody would pay attention to me. I just concentrated on my business. This is how I saved myself and this business.

Avoiding and deflecting the negative
Avoiding and deflecting the negative is another stratagem BWEs adopted during the consolidating stage. To safeguard themselves from sociocultural discrimination, some BWEs choose to deal only with groups that do not demonstrate hostile or discriminatory behavior. As much as they can, these BWEs try to avoid contact with groups or institutions that consider them inferior and subordinate to men. BWEs working with international supply chains highlight that dealing with international clients is generally more pleasant than dealing with domestic clients. Analysis of the narratives suggests that BWEs who are more experienced, knowledgeable and confident, owing to their education and expertise, tend to exercise agency in selecting who they would like to make business deals with and who they would wish to avoid. A case in point is BWE30, who owns an IT company:

> We focus on international clients. I will bid [tender], and if I deserve it, I get the job. They don't bother about me being [a] woman; only [the] quality of work matters.

Previously, I visited some local companies to get contracts. These local men had very negative views about me being a woman. They thought to be a woman, I am not capable of this [technical] job. To make things worse, my team is 100% women. There is a strong stereotype; IT is a male sector. After a number of experiences and incidents, I decided not to get jobs from the local market. Now, we have a firm stance on this; we won't deal with local companies.

Confronting the negative

Some BWEs used confronting the negative as another mechanism. Unlike some BWEs who felt powerless in the face of constant harassment, a few BWEs, particularly those coming from families with high social standing, fought back on their right to be acknowledged as entrepreneurs on their own merits.

> Once, I went to an iron factory to buy some rods. My husband was not with me; he was not well. The owner was shocked to learn that I am doing a hardware business. He told me to stop it because it's a man's business. I told him, "My husband and my family do not have any problem with it. What's your problem?" He still disapproved of it, making lots of excuses. Eventually, I told him, "Forget it, I am not buying from you." This is how I dealt with this sort of people. [BWE14]

Theme 3: Leveraging – Discovering Oneself

BWEs move into the stage of leveraging agency once they become more stable in their entrepreneurship journey. At this stage, they start to discover themselves as people endowed with agency. The process of discovering agency comes about when BWEs begin to discover independence, self-worth, confidence, and even empowerment through their entrepreneurial activities.

Finding independence

Entrepreneurial activity helps many BWEs to find independence, and through this to discover their own agency. This is especially the case for those from the lower social class, who have spent a lifetime dependent on men due not only to social norms, but also financial insecurity. Entrepreneurship not only brings about financial independence, but also facilitates greater independence in the daily lives of BWEs.

> When I first started, I was very young. I missed a lot of opportunities. I was not con-fident. My family didn't support me. After marriage, my husband helped me a lot, but it was not possible for him to be with me all the time. Slowly, I have built more confidence. Now, I am not afraid to go far anymore. I went to Islampur by myself, which is far from here. I can interact with people easily now. [BWE1]

> Now I am self-sufficient. I am earning by myself. It's a different type of strength and courage. When I was merely a housewife, I didn't have this strength and courage. It

is also a matter of social prestige. Customers, other women, neighbors often praise me, especially when I kept the business going [after my husband passed away]. This is my biggest achievement. [BWE4]

Finding self-worth/esteem

Our analysis shows that the BWEs find self-worth and esteem through their entrepreneurship activities. The realization of self-worth typically starts inside the home, and over time it extends outwards to wider business and social spheres. For quite a number of BWEs, entrepreneurship helps to nurture greater agency within the household and uplifts their social status at home. BWE15, who has a Master's degree, shared how her husband and family started to value her opinions as she expanded her business.

> In Bangladesh, [the] man is the head of the family. But not in my family, not anymore. It is not the case anymore. Now, I am making [the] most of the decisions. I live with my in-laws; they too take my opinions seriously. Now, they rely on me for any [decision]. They ask me for my opinion. Even my brother-in-law seeks my advice. This is not happening with my other sisters-in-law. I have now achieved a respectable position in my family.

Finding confidence and strength

Most BWEs identified that they find confidence and strength through entrepreneurship. Entrepreneurship contributes to their personal agency by developing their social skills and self-efficacy. This is most striking among BWEs from lower social class backgrounds, given they have been denied access to education and employment opportunities in their earlier lives. BWE12 shared how entrepreneurship has transformed her into a different (better) person.

> This business makes me brave and confident. I can interact with people easily now. I was not sociable previously, [I was] by myself most of the time, just like the other girls in our community. Now, not only am I communicating with people comfortably, [but] I am [also] going to banks, different offices and even the police station, which was unthinkable to me before I started this business. I [have] gain[ed] courage through my business.

Theme 4: Sustaining – Transitioning to Collective Agency

In the sustaining stage, the BWEs transition from individual agency to collective agency. After engaging in entrepreneurship and struggling against high odds to create agency for themselves within the confines of Bangladesh's hostile patriarchal society, some BWEs start to contribute to the creation of a collective agency for women through a range of care activities directed to help others, particularly other women in Bangladesh.

Enabling, guiding, and providing opportunities to other women
Our findings show that success in entrepreneurship allows BWEs to help
and guide other women. Acknowledging limited opportunities for women
in Bangladesh to secure decent employment, a number of BWEs execute
women-friendly business models. For example, BWE30, who owns an IT
support business, which is a male-dominant industry in Bangladesh, only
recruits women in her company, and BWE28's business partners (suppliers)
for her online catering business are mostly women who had to opt out of
employment after marriage or childbirth. By offering jobs, providing earning
power, and giving training and development opportunities to their "fellow
sisters" within the enterprises that they run, BWEs can contribute to the nurturance and development of women's collective agency in Bangladesh.

Several BWEs highlight that despite some progress in Bangladesh, women
still have a weak voice as single individual women entrepreneurs in tackling
the deeply embedded sociocultural barriers in Bangladesh. Faced with such
circumstances, BWE29 highlighted the importance of BWEs joining forces
and coming together in battling what would otherwise be a lonely, painful and
challenging entrepreneurship journey. Whether by creating women's networks
within a specific industry, creating general support groups, or coming together
to fight for women's rights, many BWEs felt compelled to develop collective
agency after they realized they possessed individual agency.

> If more women join this industry, then women's voices in the ABC [Name of
> the industry association] will be heard. In ABC meetings, whenever I voiced my
> opinion, others [men] were not interested. They never gave me space [to voice
> my opinion]. … If more women come on board, I believe acceptance of women's
> opinion[s] will become higher. [BWE25]

> I pull one woman to another woman, I connect them, and I connect myself with
> them. Even though it's not the same industry, I find that I learn from what they are
> doing. It's good to be connected. We talk about our problems. It's a community …
> I am in the core team. We try to pull women entrepreneurs together. If we all come
> together, we may be able to [create a] change, to push for [better] policies and things
> like that. [BWE 29]

Promoting and inspiring women
Over time, as they become successful, a number of BWEs discover that they
have become inspirational figures for other women in Bangladesh to venture
into business. BWE21, who runs a beauty salon, and BWE22 who owns an
agriculture business, shared how their presence has encouraged many more
women to step forward and initiate similar businesses ventures.

> Being an Islamic country, people are rigid about women's employment and entre-
> preneurship. But things are changing slowly. When another woman and I started our

businesses in this complex, we were the first businesswomen here. Following us, many other women opened their shops here. [BWE21]

Previously, all I had seen here were men. But once I started this firm, many women came to visit. They used to say "If she can run a business, why can't we?" Following me, many of them [the women] also started their business[es here]. [BEW22]

Changing attitudes and promoting women's rights and agency
The presence and success of BWEs in their businesses have forced numerous community members to recognize, even if grudgingly at first, the positive contribution women can make to Bangladesh's economy and society. The success of BWEs challenges a number of the prevailing norms in Bangladesh, such as the cultural belief that the role of a woman is to be nothing other than a wife and a mother (Sayem and Nury, 2013). A number of the BWEs shared that their success story had inspired relatives and acquaintances to allow their daughters to enroll for higher education. By doing so, they were gradually changing a number of societal attitudes toward girls.

One of my relatives told me that he wants his daughter to complete her education so that she can be like me. Because I am balancing all my roles, that's why they are motivated to educate their daughter. [BWE15]

In our society, people [used to] think that women are getting educated for marriage. At a small scale, I think I changed this perception. They can see that [with education] I can earn. I am self-sufficient. [BWE26]

The presence and persistence of these BWEs is slowly eroding the negative stereotypes of women. Acceptance of women owning and operating a business is rising gradually. It usually starts by changing proximal attitudes of family members, and after that, this change begins to radiate outwards into the broader community.

When they [the in-law's family] noticed that I am successful at what I am doing, and I am not neglecting my household responsibility, they accepted it. Now I do not have any problems from them anymore. Instead, I get support from them. My business changed their and the community's negative view of women doing business. [BWE1]

DISCUSSION

The study findings suggest that entrepreneurship helps women in Bangladesh to build agency through a gradual and evolutionary context-driven process, which conditions and shapes BWEs' unique experiences of Bangladesh's cultural and institutional constraints. Navigating their way through the four-stage process, BWEs incur considerable suppression due to the deeply rooted patriarchal norms of the country. Numerous BWEs go through the process at the expense of their psychological and physical wellbeing. This highlights the dark side of the entrepreneurship experience, which contrasts sharply with the idealized and romanticized notion of entrepreneurship as the "Holy Grail of elevation and emancipation" (Verduijn and Essers, 2013, p. 100). Indeed, the costs involved in the process of procuring agency through entrepreneurship may be far higher than one commonly assumes, especially when countenanced in the context of patriarchal societies such as Bangladesh.

Mainstream entrepreneurship focuses heavily on the success side, depicting entrepreneurs as heroes unencumbered by sociocultural context factors (Khan et al., 2007; Weik, 2011). This study identifies the risks and costs to the individual women during their struggles in the entrepreneurial venture. It shows that they succeed by procuring or creating self-agency while interacting with their unique contexts and sociocultural situations. Our findings show that not only do BWEs borrow agency, but they also use it to develop self-agency through entrepreneurship. In this respect, our study finds that the benefits of entrepreneurship transcend financial independence and wealth accumulation, since entrepreneurial activity allows them to release their "strengths and powers" (Alkhaled and Berglund, 2018, p. 878) and helps BWEs to liberate themselves from the shackles embedded deep within Bangladesh's patriarchal society. As they navigate their way through their entrepreneurial journey, many BWEs begin to attain autonomy, dignity and social status, and through this they develop the psychological strength to be able to develop and exert self-agency.

Our study also finds that BWEs from lower social class backgrounds face multiple disadvantages due to a complex interweaving of gender, religion and social class within Bangladesh. Agency requires the freedom and ability to exercise choice (Ali et al., 2017; Altan-Olcay, 2016). For BWEs, especially at the beginning stage of entrepreneurship, the level and ability to exercise agency are limited due to their lack of and access to resources. Engaging in entrepreneurship within their societal context, Bangladeshi women are handicapped by a lack of equal access to economic opportunities, education and other resources. Faced with weak access to resources and significant hindrances, BWEs adopt a range of active and passive coping mechanisms, ranging from passive endurance and silent withdrawal to active confrontation of inequities and injustices.

As wealth and financial independence increase through entrepreneurship, they also serve to alter household power relations and they enable BWEs to participate more openly in the public domain. This appears to be the starting point of a chain of events, leading to what numerous researchers identify as the link between women's entrepreneurship and gender equality (Al-Dajani and Marlow, 2013; Alkhaled and Berglund, 2018; Altan-Olcay, 2016; Berglund and Johansson, 2007). Our findings concur with the view that entrepreneurs who can free themselves from the constraints of their environments are more likely to be satisfied with other aspects of their lives (Jennings et al., 2016). The trigger point to freeing themselves from the many shackles and constraints of the external environment appears to be the change in power and status within BWEs' homes.

The final stage of the agency process is when BWEs begin to build and exert collective agency. At this stage, the literature and experience suggest that true and lasting opportunities for women in entrepreneurship "emerge from social structural reforms to eliminate discrimination" (Calás et al., 2009, p. 556). Simply encouraging and having more women enter into entrepreneurship without fundamentally addressing the patriarchal social norms that are deeply embedded in the institutional structure will do little to enact social change, other than force more women to navigate the vicious circular wall of oppressive social norms.

The results of this study point to the shortcoming of enacting policies and initiatives within developing-country contexts that push for women entrepreneurship without simultaneously addressing the constraints arising from the patriarchal nature of the country's society. Instead, policymakers should work toward creating an inclusive environment in which women and men can participate in public and private life together. Such change needs to take place at the point of inception, namely in the family and schools, where the coming generations' psychosocial development occurs (Calás et al., 2009). In other words, both girls and boys have to learn appropriate gender behaviors from the very beginning of their lives.

Gender equitable norms need cultivation at the individual, family and societal levels simultaneously. As Bullough et al. (2017) suggested, societal-level acceptance of women participating in the economy may take a generation or two to become embedded at the family level. Furthermore, as BWEs exert their agency and become role models to other women, they simultaneously start to engage in cultivating and exercising collective agency, and intentionally or unknowingly begin the process of promoting gender equity whose goal is not only improving the wellbeing of women and girls, but also promoting respectful and caring behavior between men and women (Sayem and Nury, 2013). This means that programs to stimulate women's business development and having successful women entrepreneurs as role models and mentors for aspiring women entrepreneurs are very important. This supports Byrne et al.'s (2019) call for integrating role models into entrepreneurship initiatives to combat stereotypes and trigger change.

Our identification of the four-stage process illustrates that while women in Bangladesh navigate their individual agency-building through entrepreneurship, they can influence and bring about social change through the force of collective agency. In this respect, our study echoes and supports the critical perspective of women's entrepreneurship as a vehicle beyond wealth creation to one as an engine of social change (Datta and Gailey, 2012).

CONCLUSION

Our study broadens the understanding of women's entrepreneurship by exploring women's agency and entrepreneurship in Bangladesh, a developing country in South Asia, which is characterized by patriarchal sociocultural norms. Although the qualitative nature of the study and the small sample size hinders generalization, the study contributes to the entrepreneurship literature. First, our study identifies a four-stage process through which Bangladeshi women entrepreneurs acquire and exercise agency. Within this, we also note the heterogeneity of experiences by women entrepreneurs arising from the intersection of gender, religion and social class in Bangladesh.

Next, the study shows how, as the agency process unfolds, women entrepreneurs nurture and begin to exercise a collective agency that moves them beyond themselves. Gradually, individual agency seeps into a collective form and starts to challenge the constraining patriarchal attitudes and norms of Bangladeshi society. Consequently, the struggles of these women are not purely economic in nature, but perhaps, more importantly, they are social struggles for equity and just standing in society. Our study underscores the importance of taking account of the cultural and institutional setting, since the context heavily shapes the experiences of people within them. In our study, we find that BWEs are not the conventional heroic entrepreneurs found in Western, developed-country settings; instead, they are knowingly or unknowingly agents of social change.

REFERENCES

Al-Dajani, H. and Marlow, S. (2010). Impact of women's home-based enterprise on family dynamics: Evidence from Jordan. *International Small Business Journal*, **28** (5), 470–86.

Al-Dajani, H. and Marlow, S. (2013). Empowerment and entrepreneurship: A theoretical framework. *International Journal of Entrepreneurial Behavior & Research*, **19** (5), 503–24.

Ali, F. (2013). A multi-level perspective on equal employment opportunity for women in Pakistan. *Equality, Diversity and Inclusion: An International Journal*, **32** (3), 289–309.

Ali, F., Malik, A., Pereira, V. and Ariss, A.A. (2017). A relational understanding of work–life balance of Muslim migrant women in the west: Future research agenda. *International Journal of Human Resource Management*, **28** (8), 1163–81.

Alkhaled, S. and Berglund, K. (2018). "And now I'm free": Women's empowerment and emancipation through entrepreneurship in Saudi Arabia and Sweden. *Entrepreneurship & Regional Development*, **30** (7–8), 877–900.

Alliance for Financial Inclusion (2017). Expanding women's financial inclusion in Bangladesh: Through MSME financial policies. Case Study No. 5. Accessed at https://www.afi-global.org/sites/default/files/publications/2017-02/AFI_bangladesh_case%20study_AW_digital.pdf.

Altan-Olcay, Ö. (2016). The entrepreneurial woman in development programs: Thinking through class differences. *Social Politics: International Studies in Gender, State & Society*, **23** (3), 389–414.

Bandura, A. (2001). Social cognitive theory: An agentic perspective. *Annual Review of Psychology*, **52** (1), 1–26.

Bandura, A. (2006). Toward a psychology of human agency. *Perspectives on Psychological Science*, **1** (2), 164–80.

Barragan, S., Erogul, M.S. and Essers, C. (2018). "Strategic (dis)obedience": Female entrepreneurs reflecting on and acting upon patriarchal practices. *Gender, Work & Organization*, **25** (5), 575–92.

Baughn, C.C., Chua, B.-L. and Neupert, K.E. (2006). The normative context for women's participation in entrepreneurship: A multi-country study. *Entrepreneurship: Theory and Practice*, **30** (5), 687–708.

Berglund, K. and Johansson, A.W. (2007). Entrepreneurship, discourses and conscientization in processes of regional development. *Entrepreneurship & Regional Development*, **19** (6), 499–525.

Bullough, A., Renko, M. and Abdelzaher, D. (2017). Women's business ownership: Operating within the context of institutional and in-group collectivism. *Journal of Management*, **43** (7), 2037–64.

Byrne, J., Fattoum, S. and Garcia, M.C.D. (2019). Role models and women entrepreneurs: Entrepreneurial superwoman has her say. *Journal of Small Business Management*, **57** (1), 154–84.

Calás, M.B., Smircich, L. and Bourne, K.A. (2009). Extending the boundaries: Reframing "entrepreneurship as social change" through feminist perspectives. *Academy of Management Review*, **34** (3), 552–69.

Colaizzi, P.F. (1978). Psychological research as the phenomenologist views it. In R.S. Valle and M. King (eds), *Existential Phenomenological Alternatives for Psychology* (pp. 48–71). Oxford: Oxford University Press.

Cope, J. (2005). Researching entrepreneurship through phenomenological inquiry: Philosophical and methodological issues. *International Small Business Journal*, **23** (2), 163–89.

Creswell, J.W. (2007). *Qualitative Inquiry and Research Design: Choosing Among Five Approaches* (2nd edn). Thousand Oaks, CA: Sage.

Daily Star (2017). Women-led SMEs need easy loans. 29 September. Accessed at https://www.thedailystar.net/business/women-led-smes-need-easy-loans-experts-1469167.

Datta, P.B. and Gailey, R. (2012). Empowering women through social entrepreneurship: Case study of a women's cooperative in India. *Entrepreneurship Theory and Practice*, **36** (3), 569–87.

Dy, A.M., Marlow, S. and Martin, L. (2017). A web of opportunity or the same old story? Women digital entrepreneurs and intersectionality theory. *Human Relations*, **70** (3), 286–311.

Garud, R., Hardy, C. and Maguire, S. (2007). Institutional entrepreneurship as embedded agency: An introduction to the special issue. *Organization Studies*, **28** (7), 957–69.

Hattab, H. (2012). Towards understanding female entrepreneurship in Middle Eastern and North African countries: A cross-country comparison of female entrepreneurship. *Education, Business and Society: Contemporary Middle Eastern Issues*, **5** (3), 171–86.

Itani, H., Sidani, Y.M. and Baalbaki, I. (2011). United Arab Emirates female entrepreneurs: Motivations and frustrations. *Equality, Diversity and Inclusion: An International Journal*, **30** (5), 409–24.

Jansen, G.G. and Pippard, J.L. (1998). The Grameen Bank in Bangladesh: Helping poor women with credit for self-employment. *Journal of Community Practice*, **5** (1–2), 103–23.

Jennings, J.E., Jennings, P.D. and Sharifian, M. (2016). Living the dream? Assessing the "entrepreneurship as emancipation" perspective in a developed region. *Entrepreneurship Theory and Practice*, **40** (1), 81–110.

Kantor, P. (2002). Gender, microenterprise success and cultural context: The case of South Asia. *Entrepreneurship Theory and Practice*, **26** (4), 131–43.

Kazemi, F. (2000). Gender, Islam, and politics. *Social Research*, **67** (2), 453–74.

Khan, F.R., Munir, K.A. and Willmott, H. (2007). A dark side of institutional entrepreneurship: Soccer balls, child labour and postcolonial impoverishment. *Organization Studies*, **28** (7), 1055–77.

Klyver, K., Nielsen, S.L. and Evald, M.R. (2013). Women's self-employment: An act of institutional (dis)integration? A multilevel, cross-country study. *Journal of Business Venturing*, **28** (4), 474–88.

Lincoln, Y.S. and Guba, E.G. (1985). *Naturalistic Inquiry*. Thousand Oaks, CA: Sage.

Minniti, M. and Naudé, W. (2010). What do we know about the patterns and determinants of female entrepreneurship across countries? *European Journal of Development Research*, **22** (3), 277–93.

Misangyi, V.F., Weaver, G.R. and Elms, H. (2008). Ending corruption: The interplay among institutional logics, resources, and institutional entrepreneurs. *Academy of Management Review*, **33** (3), 750–70.

Naguib, R. and Jamali, D. (2015). Female entrepreneurship in the UAE: A multi-level integrative lens. *Gender in Management: An International Journal*, **30** (2), 135–61.

Naved, R.T. and Persson, L.A. (2010). Dowry and spousal physical violence against women in Bangladesh. *Journal of Family Issues*, **31** (6), 830–56.

Sayem, A.M. and Nury, A.T.M.S. (2013). An assessment of attitude towards equitable gender norms among Muslim women in Bangladesh. *Women's Studies International Forum*, **40**, 102–10.

Schuler, S.R., Hashemi, S.M., Riley, A.P. and Akhter, S. (1996). Credit programs, patriarchy and men's violence against women in rural Bangladesh. *Social Science & Medicine*, **43** (12), 1729–42.

Sen, A. (1999). *Development as Freedom*. Oxford: Oxford University Press.

Steyaert, C. and Hjorth, D. (2008). *Entrepreneurship as Social Change: A Third New Movements in Entrepreneurship Book* (Vol. 3). Cheltenham, UK and Northampton, MA, USA: Edward Elgar Publishing.

Steyaert, C. and Katz, J. (2004). Reclaiming the space of entrepreneurship in society: Geographical, discursive and social dimensions. *Entrepreneurship & Regional Development*, **16** (3), 179–96.

Tlaiss, H.A. (2014). Women's entrepreneurship, barriers and culture: Insights from the United Arab Emirates. *Journal of Entrepreneurship*, **23** (2), 289–320.

Tlaiss, H.A. (2015). How Islamic business ethics impact women entrepreneurs: Insights from four Arab Middle Eastern countries. *Journal of Business Ethics*, **129** (4), 859–77.

Verduijn, K. and Essers, C. (2013). Questioning dominant entrepreneurship assumptions: The case of female ethnic minority entrepreneurs. *Entrepreneurship & Regional Development*, **25** (7–8), 612–30.

Warnecke, T. (2013). Entrepreneurship and gender: An institutional perspective. *Journal of Economic Issues*, **47** (2), 455–63.

Weik, E. (2011). Institutional entrepreneurship and agency. *Journal for the Theory of Social Behaviour*, **41** (4), 466–81.

Welter, F. and Smallbone, D. (2008). Women's entrepreneurship from an institutional perspective: The case of Uzbekistan. *International Entrepreneurship and Management Journal*, **4** (4), 505–20.

Zaman, H. (1999). Violence against women in Bangladesh: Issues and responses. *Women's Studies International Forum*, **22** (1), 37–48.

4. The influence of institutional and in-group collectivism on women's entrepreneurship

Pedro Torres and Mário Augusto

INTRODUCTION

Women are increasingly involved in entrepreneurship, and the trends of women's entrepreneurship reveal positive change, but it is recognized that women's business ownership still lags behind that of men (Pandey and Amezcua, 2018). Thus, women's entrepreneurship is a topic of crescent interest. Conceptually, it is acknowledged that there is no ideal context for entrepreneurship (Welter et al., 2017); that is, several combinations of antecedent conditions can lead to this outcome. The same can happen in women's entrepreneurship. Thus, it is important to understand which combination of conditions (i.e., configurations) favour women's self-employment to inform future policies aiming to promote women's entrepreneurship. This research focuses on institutional collectivism and in-group collectivism and considers the role of self-protective leadership ideals. The study employs a configurational approach to address the literature gaps identified below. Besides identifying the configurations that lead to high levels of women's self-employment, it contributes to understanding the importance of institutional and in-group collectivism, which are unclear.

Self-employment involves the start-up of new business organizations with their own legal identity, which is considered a definition of entrepreneurship (Woodside et al., 2016). In fact, the rates of self-employment are often used as a measure of entrepreneurship (Lin et al., 2000; Bullough and Luque, 2015; Bullough et al., 2017b). Governmental policies can either promote or hinder entrepreneurial activity (Acs et al., 2016). It is suggested that policy-makers should shift their focus from incentives to societal culture (Dennis Jr, 2011; Pandey and Amezcua, 2018). It is also noted that cultural factors can provide a fertile area of inquiry regarding self-employment (Minniti and Naudé, 2010). However, findings regarding associations between cultural and entrepreneurial outcomes are remarkably inconsistent (Hayton and Cacciotti, 2013) and the interplay and nuances of women's entrepreneurship and culture remain under-studied (De Bruin et al., 2006; Bullough et al., 2017a). Uncertainty avoidance and individualism–collectivism are considered to be most important cultural dimensions affecting entrepreneurship (Hayton et al., 2002). The role of collectivism is considered particularly important for women's self-employment. Collectivism refers to the belief that people are part of close and interconnected groups that protect and provide security throughout life, in which group loyalty is valued rather than individual achievements (Gelfand et al., 2004). The literature has long ago recognised the potential importance of collectivism for understanding entrepreneurship (e.g., Morris et al., 1994; Tiessen, 1997), but only recently has this stream of research been included in women's entrepreneurship research. Past research noted that the implications of collectivism to women business owners justify the dichotomization of this construct (e.g., Bullough et al., 2017b) into institutional collectivism and in-group collectivism. Institutional collectivism practices tend to underscore collective interests, while in-group collectivism reflects how much individuals depend on their families or organizations (House and Javidan, 2004). Bullough et al. (2017b) claimed that the freedom to pursue individuals' goals, combined with support from the in-group, provides the most favourable context for women entrepreneurship, thereby suggesting that in-group collectivism is more important than institutional collectivism for women's entrepreneurship. However, many questions remain open and more research is needed.

Women's self-employment can be seen as an act of institutional disintegration (Klyver et al., 2013), which implies leadership. The entrepreneur is often viewed as a leader (Vecchio, 2003) and the culture influences what is expected of leaders (Stelter, 2002). The integration of leadership theory into entrepreneurship research has been advocated (Cogliser and Brigham, 2004). However, few studies addressed this issue and only recently has it been discussed in the literature. Stephan and Pathak (2016) suggest that two culturally-endorsed implicit leadership theories have the most impact on entrepreneurship: charismatic/value-based leadership and self-protective leadership. While charismatic/value-based leadership is often seen as effective and desirable (Den Hartog et al., 1999), self-protective leadership is considered to be negative (Bullough and Luque, 2015). Nevertheless, there is some controversy regarding the impact of self-protective leadership. It is hypothesized that environments that endorse self-protective leadership can discourage women from participating in entrepreneurial leadership (e.g., Bullough and Luque, 2015). But, Torres and Augusto (2019a) found that the presence of self-protective leadership ideals can contribute to achieve high levels of women's self-employment. To shed light on the role of self-protective leadership ideals, this research considers this construct as a possible antecedent condition of women's self-employment.

The idea that the relationship between collectivism and women's self-employment is non-linear is being increasingly proposed in the literature (e.g., Autio et al., 2013; Bullough et al., 2017b). In the same vein, this research takes a configurational approach and employs qualitative comparative analysis (QCA), in particular fuzzy-set qualitative comparative analysis (fs/QCA). QCA uses Boolean algebraic techniques to analyse pair-wise combinations of antecedents and outcome conditions to identify those leading to an outcome. This method is recognised as a well-structured method to identify configurations (i.e., combinations of conditions) associated with an outcome of interest (Wagemann et al., 2016). As noted by Schneider et al. (2010), fs/QCA presents several advantages, such as: asymmetrical causality is allowed; combinations of antecedent conditions, rather than single conditions, are considered to be linked to the outcome; the idea of *equifinality* is captured (i.e., multiple causal paths lead to the same outcome) and links between the various combinations of causal conditions and the outcome are expressed as necessary and sufficient conditions. Thus, this method embraces the notion that there is no ideal context for entrepreneurship (Welter et al., 2017). Moreover, with this method it is acknowledged that the relationship between collectivism and women's self-employment is non-linear (Autio et al., 2013; Bullough et al., 2017b).

This study makes two important contributions to women's entrepreneurship literature. First, it is shown that different configurations can lead to high levels of women's self-employment. Second, the obtained configurations contribute to clarify the role of collectivism. While low institutional collectivism should be combined with high in-group collectivism when uncertainty avoidance practices are absent, high institutional collectivism requires the absence of in-group collectivism and the presence of self-protective leadership ideals to achieve high levels of women's self-employment. These findings have implications for both researchers and policy-makers, which are highlighted at the end of the chapter.

THEORETICAL BACKGROUND

Women's Entrepreneurship and Culture Practices

Past research highlighted the importance of cultural factors as an area of inquiry regarding self-employment (e.g., Minniti and Naudé, 2010). In fact, the call for more research into the way in which societal culture can encourage women's entrepreneurship is increasingly emphasized. There is a trend towards giving more attention to cultural practices than to cultural values (e.g., Thai and Turkina, 2014). Cultural practices are likely to have a more direct influence on entrepreneurship behaviour (Stephan and Pathak, 2016). They reflect descriptive norms of typical behaviour in a culture (Stephan and Uhlaner, 2010). Individuals can easily apply what they perceived to be usual societal behaviours (Nolan et al., 2008). Thus, cultural practices are more closely linked to behaviour and societal outcomes (Javidan et al., 2006).

The Global Leadership and Organizational Behavior Effectiveness (GLOBE) study includes cultural practices and has identified nine dimensions (House et al., 2004): (1) performance orientation; (2) assertiveness; (3) future orientation; (4) humane orientation; (5) institutional collectivism; (6) group collectivism; (7) gender egalitarianism; (8) power distance; and (9) uncertainty avoidance. Among these dimensions, uncertainty avoidance and collectivism are considered to be the most important affecting entrepreneurship (Hayton et al., 2002). Uncertainty avoidance refers to the extent to which a society relies on social norms, rules and procedures to minimize unpredictability of future events. This dimension reflects the extent to which individuals tend to be anxious regarding the unpredictability of the future (Shane, 1995). As mentioned above, collectivism refers to the belief that people are part of close and interconnected groups that protect and provide security throughout life, in which group loyalty is valued rather than individual achievements (Gelfand et al., 2004). Cultures with low collectivism tend to be more focused on the individual rather than the group (Dorfman et al., 2004). An individualist societal culture values individual achievements and relies on the belief that people can be independent and self-reliant. Thus, individualistic cultures are likely to favour proactivity and independent actions (Baughn and Neupert, 2003). In general, cultures that embrace uncertainty and promote the pursuit of individual interests are perceived to be more favourable to the development of entrepreneurial behaviour (e.g., Frese and Gielnik, 2014). However, it is suggested that the entrepreneurial activity is positively related to individualism in highly developed countries and negatively related to individualism in coun-tries in other stages of development (Pinillos and Reyes, 2011). Tiessen (1997) suggests that individualism and collectivism together influence entrepreneurial behaviour, advocating a balance (i.e., not very high and not very low collectiv-ism would be desirable).

The GLOBE study considers two types of collectivism: institutional col-lectivism and in-group collectivism. While institutional collectivism tends to encourage collective action, in-group collectivism refers to the extent to which individuals express pride, loyalty and cohesiveness in their families (or organ-izations). According to Bullough et al. (2017b), when institutional collectivism is high the society tends to reward women staying close to home. In this case, the society only supports women entrepreneurship that will benefit the collective. However, these authors also suggested that women could benefit from being part of a loyal collective, which can provide resource support. At the in-group level, they noted that collectivism could either hinder or help women's entrepreneurship. Low in-group collectivism can encourage women to pursue individual businesses. However, women may lack emotional, financial and/or resource support from their in-group. Bullough et al. (2017b) claim that the freedom to pursue individual goals, combined with support from the in-group, might provide the most favourable context for women's entrepreneurship. Thus, it is suggested that in-group collectivism is more important than institutional collectivism for women's entrepreneurship.

Women's Self-employment and Culturally-endorsed Leadership Ideals

Women are less likely than men to choose self-employment (Klyver et al., 2013). Vejsiu (2011) suggests that men tend to be more 'loyal' to self-employment than women. Past research suggests that women may have less entrepreneurial self-efficacy and thus often do not consider business ownership (e.g., Wilson et al., 2007; Forlani, 2013). Women's self-employment can be seen as an act of institutional disintegration (Klyver et al., 2013), which implies leadership.

Entrepreneurs are often viewed as leaders (Vecchio, 2003). Likewise, women who embrace self-employment can be viewed as leaders because self-employment implies the start-up of new business organizations. Leaders are likely to behave in line with what is commonly expected and accepted by followers (Collinson, 2006). Leadership implies an individual's ability to influence, motivate and enable others to contribute to the success of their organizations (House et al., 2004). Individuals who perceived their profiles to be aligned with culturally-endorsed leadership ideals tend to have higher propensity to engage in entrepreneurial activity (Gupta et al., 2008). The context influences what is expected of leaders (Stelter, 2002).

The GLOBE study presents six culturally-endorsed leadership ideals: (1) charismatic/value-based leadership; (2) team-oriented leadership; (3) participative leadership; (4) humane-oriented leadership; (5) autonomous leadership; and (6) self-protective leadership. Charismatic/value-based leadership and self-protective leadership ideals have been more associated with entrepreneurship (Stephan and Pathak, 2016). Charismatic/value-based leadership is performance-oriented and inspirational. Moreover, it is grounded on values of integrity, self-sacrifice and vision. Self-protective leadership is characterized as being self-focused and competitive, and it is associated with behaviours that are status conscious, conflict causing, face saving and procedural.

It is suggested that charismatic/value-based leadership could be positively linked to women's participation in leadership (Bullough and Luque, 2015), which is consistent with the idea that women would be more likely to excel in contexts that encourage empathy, cooperation and sensitivity (Groves,

2005). Furthermore, women tend to be authentic (Eagly, 2005), conflict solving (Westermann et al., 2005), gentle (Rudman and Glick, 1999) and sensitive to the needs of followers (Groves, 2005). This leads to the notion that culturally-endorsed self-protective leadership ideals would discourage women's entrepreneurship (Bullough and Luque, 2015). However, the results obtained by Bullough and Luque (2015) did not support this claim. In contrast, recent research suggests that culturally-endorsed self-protective leadership can favour both entrepreneurship and early-stage entrepreneurial activity (Torres and Augusto, 2019b). Furthermore, there is evidence that its presence could be part of the solution to increase the level of women's self-employment (Torres and Augusto, 2019a).

According to Stephan and Pathak (2016), to be successful, entrepreneurs may have to focus on self-interests and exhibit competitive behaviour. Women tend to face a constant struggle in perceiving themselves as entrepreneurs (Verheul et al., 2005). Women are often led to develop careers which are seen by the society as being more appropriate for them (Carter et al., 2003). Furthermore, in general, entrepreneurship can be associated with a deviation from the norms (Garud and Karnøe, 2001). Thus, in contrast with previous formulations, it can be hypothesized that women are more likely to choose self-employment options in cultures that endorse self-protective leadership ideals.

The Interplay Between Culture Practices and Leaderships Ideals

It is recognized that women face, at the societal cultural level, institutional limitations and strong role expectations, which can influence their engagement in entrepreneurship activities (Minniti and Nardone, 2007). Societal cultures that embrace uncertainty can provide a more favourable environment for developing risk-taking and innovative actions (Clercq et al., 2010). Hence, the absence of uncertainty avoidance practices could be linked with high levels of women's self-employment. However, according to Bullough and Luque (2015), women tend to have more affinity with future planning. Therefore, women could prefer contexts that minimize the unpredictability of future events. Thus, because self-protective leadership tends to be more predictable, it could be associated to women's self-employment. Self-protective leadership is likely to be more acceptable in societal cultures characterized by low levels of collectivism since they are more focused on the individual (Dorfman et al., 2004). Nevertheless, it is acknowledged that self-protective leadership includes attributes such as face saving (which relates to the desire to express pride), which can be associated with in-group collectivism (Stephan and Pathak, 2016).

Bullough et al. (2017b) suggested that women's business ownership is associated with both forms of collectivism (institutional and in-group collectivism), but they also conceptualize that the two types of collectivism do not operate in isolation from each other. Furthermore, although several combinations of cultural practices and culturally-endorsed implicit leadership ideals can benefit entrepreneurial behaviour, none of the simple antecedent conditions is necessary individually (Torres and Augusto, 2019b). In the same vein, the present study hypothesizes that the presence or absence of a simple antecedent condition is neither necessary nor sufficient to achieve high levels of women's entrepreneurship. It is proposed that there are combinations of simple antecedent conditions that are sufficient to identify countries with high levels of women's self-employment.

DATA AND METHOD

Data

Following previous studies on women's entrepreneurship (e.g., Lin et al., 2000; Bullough and Luque, 2015; Bullough et al., 2017b), the rate of self-employed females was used as a measure of women's entrepreneurship (WSE), which captures the share of working women who are business owners. The data was obtained from the World Bank database. Regarding the antecedent conditions of women's entrepreneurship, data from the GLOBE study (House et al., 2004) was used. The GLOBE project is a multi-method programme and involved over 160 researchers from 62 countries, and surveyed 17 370 middle managers and 951 local companies and three industry sectors. The GLOBE study used rigorous statistical procedures and constructed validity was assessed. The data collected from the World Bank was extracted for years that are temporally close to the GLOBE data, respecting temporal ordering. Following Bullough et al. (2017b), the mean score for each country was computed covering the years 2004 to 2008. Matching the data from the two data sources (GLOBE and World Bank databases), a sample of 20 countries was obtained (see Table 4.1).

The GLOBE study is used in previous research (Autio et al., 2013; Bullough et al., 2017b) because it employs rigorous statistical procedures. Uncertainty avoidance practices (UAP) were measured using the following item: 'most people lead (should lead) highly structured lives with few unexpected events'. Regarding leadership ideals, the GLOBE study included 121 leader attribute and behaviour items, considering a wide array of traits, skills, behaviours and abilities potentially relevant to leadership emergence and effectiveness (the complete procedure can be seen in House et al., 2004, chapters 6 to 11). Leader attributes were rated on a 7-point Likert type scale (from 1 = 'this behaviour or characteristic greatly inhibits a person from being an outstanding leader' to 7 = 'this behaviour or characteristic contributes greatly to a person being an outstanding leader'). The items were grouped into 21 primary dimensions

Table 4.1   *Countries included in the analysis and respective scores*

Country	Code	WSE %	UAP	IC	IGC	SPL
Argentina	ARG	19.27	3.65	3.66	5.51	3.45
Australia	AUS	13.74	4.39	4.29	4.17	3.05
Austria	AUT	10.67	5.16	4.3	4.85	3.07
Czech Republic	CZE	10.70	4.44	3.6	3.18	3.13
Denmark	DNK	5.33	5.22	4.8	3.53	2.81
Finland	FIN	8.41	5.02	4.63	4.07	2.55
France	FRA	7.54	4.43	3.93	4.37	2.81
Greece	GRC	31.28	3.39	3.25	5.27	3.49
Hungary	HUN	9.40	3.12	3.53	5.25	3.24
Ireland	IRL	7.28	4.3	4.63	5.14	3.00
Italy	ITA	20.50	3.79	3.68	4.94	3.25
Japan	JPN	13.88	4.07	5.19	4.63	3.60
Netherlands	NLD	9.87	4.7	4.46	3.7	2.87
New Zealand	NZL	12.96	4.75	4.81	3.67	3.19
Poland	POL	21.99	3.62	4.53	5.52	3.52
Portugal	PRT	23.34	3.91	3.92	5.51	3.10
Slovenia	SVN	12.71	3.78	4.13	5.43	3.61
Spain	ESP	13.68	3.97	3.85	5.45	3.38
Sweden	SWE	5.77	5.32	5.22	3.66	2.81
United States	USA	5.88	4.15	4.2	4.25	3.15

Note: WSE = Women's self-employment; UAP = Uncertainty avoidance societal practices; IC = Institutional collectivism; IGC = In-group collectivism; SPL = Self-protective leadership.

of leadership and reduced to six global leadership dimensions using factor analysis. One of these factors is self-protective leadership (SPL), which includes five primary dimensions: self-centred, status-conscious, conflict inducer (internally competitive), face saver and procedural (bureaucratic). Regarding collectivism, the GLOBE study used four questions to measure institutional collectivism practices (IC), using a Likert-type scale ranging from one to seven. For example, respondents should answer the following question: 'In this society, leaders encourage group loyalty even if individual goals suffer'. To measure in-group collectivism (IGC), four items were also used, including items such as the following: 'In this society, aging parents generally live at home with their children'.

Method

To identify combinations of cultural practices and culturally-endorsed lead-ership ideals leading to high levels of women's self-employment, fuzzy-set qualitative comparative analysis (fs/QCA) was adopted as a research approach (Ragin, 2008). Different from regression-based methods, which rely on covar-iation to identify the average net effects of single variables, QCA identifies configurations of conditions that are jointly associated with an outcome (Fiss, 2007). The focus on configurational models rather than additive and linear ones justifies the choice of the method (Schneider and Eggert, 2014). Methods that are based on symmetric relations between the predictors and the outcomes may show some difficulty in capturing non-linear relations (see, for example, Woodside, 2017). Fs/QCA captures non-linearity. Thus, since the relation between collectivism and women's self-employment is likely to be non-linear (Autio et al., 2013; Bullough et al., 2017b) fs/QCA is a suitable method. Fs/QCA allows the identification of the combinations of conditions that lead to a given outcome, taking into account possible asymmetric effects of the condi-tions (in some configurations, the presence of a given condition may contribute to reaching the outcome and, in other contexts, it may be its absence that leads to the outcome) (Torres et al., 2017). The method implies the examination of relationships between the outcome of interest and all possible combinations of binary states (i.e., presence or absence) of antecedent conditions. It allows the identification of configurations that indicate necessary and sufficient con-ditions for an outcome of interest (Ordanini et al., 2014). Because it has been asserted that there is no ideal context for entrepreneurship to thrive (Welter et al., 2017), fs/QCA is an adequate method to identify different combinations of conditions (i.e., configurations) that consistently lead to high rates of women's self-employment. Moreover, fs/QCA is suitable for the analysis of a small number of cases, that is, between 15 and 60 cases (Fiss, 2011). Hence, fs/QCA was considered especially suitable for the research at hand, which considers 20 cases.

Fs/QCA starts with the transformation of raw data into fuzzy scores (which are defined in the [0,1] interval), a process termed calibration (Ragin, 2008), which requires setting three anchor points that define full set membership of a case in a set, full non-membership, as well as a cross-over point of maximum ambiguity. Each of these thresholds translates into a specific fuzzy value and it is standard to use the following fuzzy values of 0.95, 0.05 and 0.50, respectively (see Ragin, 2008). Given the lack of any external substantive criteria for setting the qualitative anchors, the thresholds for full membership, non-membership and for the cross-over point in this study were defined using the 90th, 10th and 50th percentiles of the original values of each condition.

This procedure is in line with much previous research using this method (e.g., Torres and Augusto, 2019b).

The second step involves the testing of whether individual conditions are logically necessary for the outcome. This analysis is required to avoid later steps that wrongly assume relationships of logical necessity (Schneider and Wagemann, 2012). Ragin (2008) suggested two criteria for this analysis: consistency and trivialness of necessity. The consistency threshold used to assess necessary conditions should be larger than the one used for sufficient conditions. Following Schneider et al. (2010), the threshold of 0.90 in terms of consistency was considered to be adequate for the analysis of necessary conditions. Furthermore, to be considered necessary, individual conditions should present a non-negligible coverage, thereby indicating that they are not trivial.

Finally, regarding the configurational analysis, several authors recommend avoiding values less than 0.75 for the consistency threshold, and suggest that using values of 0.80 or higher will be preferable (e.g., Ragin, 2009). Thus, only configurations with consistency values above the 0.80 threshold will be considered acceptable in this study. Additionally, 'core' and 'peripheral' conditions should be identified to assess the relative importance of each condition. To make this distinction both the parsimonious and the intermediate solutions presented in the configurational analysis needed to be considered. According to Fiss (2011, p. 403): 'core conditions are those that are part of both parsimonious and intermediate solutions, and peripheral conditions are those that are eliminated in the parsimonious solution and thus only appear in the intermediate solution'.

RESULTS

Analysis of Necessary Conditions

The results show that none of the simple antecedent conditions is necessary to achieve a high level of women's self-employment. All consistency values are below the 0.90 threshold, as can be seen in Table 4.2.

High consistency values were obtained for the following conditions: the presence of self-protective leadership (0.828), the presence of in-group collectivism (0.783), the absence of uncertainty avoidance practices (0.837) and the absence of institutional collectivism (0.786). In addition, all these conditions have high coverage, indicating that they are not trivial. Hence, the results suggest that these are important conditions to achieve the outcome of interest.

Table 4.2   Analysis of necessary conditions

WSE	Consistency	Coverage
UAP	0.444	0.430
~UAP	0.837	0.781
IC	0.489	0.497
~IC	0.786	0.701
IGC	0.783	0.731
~IGC	0.435	0.421
SPL	0.828	0.794
~SPL	0.447	0.421

Notes: WSE = Women's self-employment; UAP = Uncertainty avoidance societal practices; IC = Institutional collectivism; IGC = In-group collectivism; SPL = Self-protective leadership. The tilde '~' represents negation.

Analysis of Sufficient Conditions

The configurational analysis suggests that there are several combinations of conditions that can be associated with high levels of women's self-employment. Five configurations were obtained (WSE1a; WSE1b; WSE2a; WSE2b; WSE3), which are presented in Figure 4.1. Following Fiss's (2011) notation, black circles indicate the presence of a condition, circles with a cross indicate its absence, blank spaces indicate a situation in which the causal condition may be either present or absent, large circles indicate core conditions and small circles indicate peripheral conditions.

The results present a high overall consistency (0.873) and coverage (0.823). Hence, the obtained configurations can be associated with women's self-employment, and account for about 82 per cent of membership in this outcome. All configurations present acceptable consistency (≥ 0.819) and coverage (≥ 0.277). While both WSE1a and WSE1b configurations combine the absence of uncertainty avoidance practices (~UAP) and the presence of self-protective leadership (SPL), in WSE1a the former condition is core and the latter is peripheral, and in WSE1b the importance of the conditions changes, SPL is core and ~UAP is peripheral. This combination of antecedent conditions has highest coverage (0.745) and unique coverage (0.104), which indicates that this is the most frequent configuration associated with high levels of women's entrepreneurship. As shown in Figure 4.1, Argentina is a good example of a country that presents this configuration; it has low UAP and high SPL scores and exhibits a high percentage of women's self-employment.

The five configurations include ~UAP and/or SPL, which confirms the importance of these conditions for women's self-employment. In the WSE2a configuration, the ~UAP is core and it is combined with the absence of insti-

Configuration	WSE 1a	WSE 1b	WSE 2a	WSE 2b	WSE 3
UAP	⊗	⊗	⊗	⊗	
IC			⊗	⊗	●
IGC			●	●	⊗
SPL	●	●			●
Example	Argentina		Portugal		Japan
Consistency	0.836	0.836	0.819	0.819	0.846
Raw coverage	0.745	0.745	0.608	0.608	0.277
Unique coverage	0.104	0.104	0.052	0.052	0.076
Overall consistency	0.873				
Overall raw coverage	0.823				

⊗ = absence of a condition
● = presence of a condition

Note: WSE = Women's self-employment; UAP = Uncertainty avoidance societal practices; IC = Institutional collectivism; IGC = In-group collectivism; SPL = Self-protective leadership. Blank spaces indicate 'don't care'. Large circles indicate core conditions and small ones indicate peripheral conditions.

Figure 4.1   Analysis of sufficient conditions

tutional collectivism (~IC) and with the presence of in-group collectivism (IGC). In WSE2b, the combination is similar to WSE2a (~UAP*~IC*IGC), but ~UAP is a peripheral condition and ~IC and IGC are core conditions. This configuration presents the second highest coverage (0.608), but the least unique coverage (0.052) (i.e. this configuration presents the lowest proportion of cases that can be explained exclusively by this configuration). The country with high women's self-employment rates that is exclusively explained by this configuration is Portugal. The WSE3 configuration combines IC, ~IGC and SPL, and the latter is a core condition. This configuration has a low raw coverage 0.277; only two countries can be associated with this configuration: Japan and New Zealand. It is interesting to note that when IGC is present, IC is absent, and vice versa. The configurations show that ~UAP requires SPL or the joint combination of ~IC and IGC, while SPL requires ~UAP or the joint combination of IC and ~IGC. These findings can shed new light on the role of collectivism and are discussed in the next section.

Among the nine countries that fit the ~UAP*SPL configuration (WSE1a and WSE1b), only two countries have women's self-employment scores below 0.50, meaning that this combination of conditions correctly predicts seven (Argentina, Greece, Italy, Japan, Poland, Slovenia and Spain) out of nine cases. The outliers are Hungary and the United States (these two countries have a score of ~UAP and SPL above 0.50, but have low levels of women's self-employment). Regarding configuration ~UAP*~IC*IGC (WSE2a and WSE2b), six (Argentina, Greece, Italy, Portugal, Slovenia and Spain) out of seven countries are correctly predicted. Only Hungary is not correctly predicted. Finally, only two countries, New Zealand and Japan, fit the configuration IC*~IGC*SPL (WSE3), and they both have scores above 0.50 on women's self-employment. The obtained configurations show that several combinations are sufficient to yield the desired outcome, but none of them can be considered to be necessary. The findings presented herein can guide policy-makers aiming to design policies that encourage women entrepreneurship.

DISCUSSION

The results show that societal cultures that endorse self-protective leadership can be favourable to women's entrepreneurship if the society embraces uncertainty (configurations WSE1a and WSE1b) or presents simultaneously high levels of institutional collectivism and low levels of in-group collectivism (configuration WSE3). These results contrast with previous propositions, which suggested that culturally-endorsed self-protective leadership ideals could discourage women's participation in entrepreneurship (Bullough and Luque, 2015). But they are in line with more recent research (Torres and Augusto, 2019a). A possible interpretation is that women should be self-protective and competitive to engage in entrepreneurial activities. It is easier to do so if the society culturally endorses a more self-focused and competitive leadership style. Furthermore, because women tend to have more affinity with future planning, they could prefer contexts that minimize the unpredictability of future events (Bullough and Luque, 2015) and self-protective leadership tends to be more predictable. Thus, if the society endorses leadership that is self-centred, status-conscious, internally competitive, face saving and procedural it may favour the emergence of women's entrepreneurship. Entrepreneurship can be associated with a deviation from the norms (Garud and Karnøe, 2001) and women's self-employment can be seen as an act of institutional disintegration (Klyver et al., 2013). If the society endorses self-protective leadership, it would be easier for women to break predefined gender role prescriptions.

However, the presence of culturally-endorsed self-protective leadership is not necessary. Configurations WSE2a and WSE2b (~UAP*~IC*IGC) do not include this condition. These solutions are associated with cultures that embrace uncertainty, as well as low institutional collectivism and high in-group collectivism. This result suggests that women's entrepreneurship can be higher in cultures that embrace uncertainty and promote the pursuit of individual interests, which is in line with previous literature. For example, Bullough et al. (2017b) recognized that this context may favour risk-taking and independent thinking, which might drive entrepreneurial behaviours. However, the presence of in-group collectivism in this configuration suggests that women may need the support of their families, close friends and colleagues to start their own businesses. Women may need cultural practices that promote loyalty and cohesiveness (i.e., in-group collectivism), which are usually linked with the social and emotional skills at which women excel (Groves, 2005). This result is consistent with the notion that women's entrepreneurship requires freedom to pursue individual goals combined with support from the in-group (Bullough et al., 2017b).

Nevertheless, the configuration WSE3 (SPL*IC*~IGC) includes low in-group collectivism and high institutional collectivism. As mentioned above, the presence of SPL in this configuration shows that women's business ownership and entrepreneurship can also be nurtured in societies that culturally endorse self-focused leadership. But the presence of collectivism at the societal level is surprising. Societies that value individual achievements are perceived more favourable to entrepreneurial activity (Frese and Gielnik, 2014). In contrast, societies with high institutional collectivism tend to reward women staying close to home (Bullough et al., 2017b). However, only two countries fit into this configuration: Japan and New Zealand. Hence, this should be interpreted with caution, because they have particular characteristics that might justify this combination. Moreover, either the presence of institutional collectivism or the absence of in-group collectivism are peripheral conditions.

These findings suggest that the importance of collectivism should be relativized. The most frequent configuration (~UAP*SPL) does not include the presence of collectivism or its absence. Furthermore, when collectivism at the societal level is present, collectivism at the in-group level should be absent, and vice versa (~UAP*~IC*IGC or SPL*IC*~IGC). They do not operate in isolation from each other. However, the level of institutional and in-group that favours women's participation in entrepreneurship depends on other cultural factors, namely, the absence of uncertainty avoidance practices and the presence of self-protective leadership ideals. Thus, linking collectivism, leadership and women's entrepreneurship yields new insights. In addition, this research further highlights the notion that the relationship between collectivism and women's self-employment is non-linear.

Two main contributions to the literature can be highlighted. First, it is shown that different configurations can be associated to high levels of women's entrepreneurship. Second, the obtained configurations clarify the role of institutional collectivism and in-group collectivism. Furthermore, since governments are shifting their efforts from incentives to societal culture, the findings presented herein contribute to better understanding the influence of cultural practices and culturally-endorsed leadership ideals on women's entrepreneurship. Cultural practices are difficult to change, but not as difficult as cultural values. It takes time to change culture, but knowing the combinations of conditions that lead to high rates of women's entrepreneurship can be helpful to guide this effort. Considering the cultural conditions that characterize their country, policy-makers can choose the path that best suits their society.

As with any research, this study is not without limitations, which could be addressed in future research. Using the rate of women's self-employment to measure women's entrepreneurship is in line with the literature, but it may not capture innovative Schumpeterian entrepreneurship. Although cultural practices take time to change, it is recognized that data from the GLOBE study were not completely up to date. Using data from GEM that respects temporal ordering minimizes the effect of this situation. Future research could replicate this study with new data. In addition, opportunity-based and necessity-based self-employment is not distinguished, which can limit the insights on women's self-employment as a choice. Future research could explore these issues. Finally, there are countries that do not fit into the obtained configurations, which calls for further research.

CONCLUSION

This research contributes to better understanding the interplay of women's entrepreneurship, collectivism and self-protective leadership ideals. Using an application of QCA, several combinations of antecedent conditions that lead to high levels of women's entrepreneurship were identified. The analysis shows that individually none of them can be considered necessary for achieving the desired outcome. The findings show that cultural endorsement of self-protective leadership ideals can be positively associated with women's entrepreneurship. Regarding collectivism, it is shown that low institutional collectivism should be combined with high in-group collectivism when societal culture embraces uncertainty, while self-protective leadership ideals should be combined with high institutional collectivism and low in-group collectivism to achieve high levels of women's self-employment. Therefore, the dichotomization of collectivism should be taken into account in future research, and complex and non-linear relationships between this construct and women's self-employment should be considered. The findings provide a framework (at least a first draft) to policy-makers aiming to promote women's entrepreneurship by changing societal culture. Cultural practices are difficult to change, but governments should make an effort to reduce uncertainty avoidance. Policy-makers should also promote the society's endorsement of self-protective leadership because it can be associated with high levels of women's entrepreneurship. Policy-makers should be aware of the combination of conditions that facilitates the emergence of women's entrepreneurship. Considering the cultural characteristics of their own countries, governments can promote the changes that are needed. Furthermore, policy-makers can develop new training programmes for women focusing on coping with cultural obstacles to women's entrepreneurship. Knowledge about what is expected from leaders in a given society, in particular women leaders, might be a first step to prepare women to face cultural barriers and engage in women's entrepreneurship.

ACKNOWLEDGEMENT

This work has been funded by national funds through FCT – Fundação para a Ciência e a Tecnologia, I.P., Project UIDB/05037/2020.

REFERENCES

Acs, Z., T. Åstebro, D. Audretsch and D.T. Robinson (2016), 'Public policy to promote entrepreneurship: A call to arms', *Small Business Economics*, **47** (1), 35–51.

Autio, E., S. Pathak and K. Wennberg (2013), 'Consequences of cultural practices for entrepreneurial behaviors', *Journal of International Business Studies*, **44** (4), 334–62.

Baughn, C.C. and K.E. Neupert (2003), 'Culture and national conditions facilitating entrepreneurial start-ups', *Journal of International Entrepreneurship*, **1** (3), 313–30.

Bullough, A. and M.S.D. Luque (2015), 'Women's participation in entrepreneurial and political leadership: The importance of culturally endorsed implicit leadership theories', *Leadership*, **11** (1), 36–56.

Bullough, A., F. Moore and T. Kalafatoglu (2017a), 'Research on women in international business and management: Then, now, and next', *Cross Cultural and Strategic Management*, **24** (2), 211–30.

Bullough, A., M. Renko and D. Abdelzaher (2017b), 'Women's business ownership: Operating within the context of institutional and in-group collectivism', *Journal of Management*, **43** (7), 2037–64.

Carter, N.M., W.B. Gartner, K.G. Shaver and E.J. Gatewood (2003), 'The career reasons of nascent entrepreneurs', *Journal of Business Venturing*, **18** (1), 31–9.

Clercq, D.D., W.M. Danis and M. Dakhli (2010), 'The moderating effect of institutional context on the relationship between associational activity and new business activity in emerging economies', *International Business Review*, **19** (1), 85–101.

Cogliser, C.C. and K.H. Brigham (2004), 'The intersection of leadership and entrepreneurship: Mutual lessons to be learned', *The Leadership Quarterly*, **15** (6), 771–99.

Collinson, D. (2006), 'Rethinking followership: A post-structuralist analysis of follower identities', *The Leadership Quarterly*, **17** (2), 179–89.

De Bruin, A., C.G. Brush and F. Welter (2006), 'Introduction to the special issue: Towards building cumulative knowledge on women's entrepreneurship', *Entrepreneurship Theory and Practice*, **30** (5), 585–93.

Den Hartog, D.N., R.J. House, P.J. Hanges, S.A. Ruiz-Quintanilla and P.W. Dorfman (1999), 'Culture specific and cross-culturally generazible implicit leadership theories: Are attributes of charismatic/transformational leadership universally endorsed?', *The Leadership Quarterly*, **10** (2), 219–56.

Dennis Jr, W.J. (2011), 'Entrepreneurship, small business and public policy levers', *Journal of Small Business Management*, **49** (1), 92–106.

Dorfman, P., P.J. Hanges and F.C. Brodbeck (2004), 'Leadership and cultural variation', in R.J. House, P.J. Hanges, M. Javidan, P.W. Dorfman and V. Gupta (eds), *Culture, Leadership and Organizations: The GLOBE Study of 62 Societies*, Thousand Oaks, CA: Sage, pp. 669–719.

Eagly, A.H. (2005), 'Achieving relational authenticity in leadership: Does gender matter?', *The Leadership Quarterly*, **16** (3), 459–74.

Fiss, P.C. (2007), 'A set-theoretic approach to organizational configurations', *Academy of Management Review*, **32** (4), 1180–98.

Fiss, P.C. (2011), 'Building better causal theories: A fuzzy set approach to typologies in organization research', *Academy of Management Journal*, **54** (2), 393–420.

Forlani, D. (2013), 'How task structure and outcome comparisons influence women's and men's risk-taking self-efficacies: A multi-study exploration', *Psychology & Marketing*, **30** (12), 1088–107.

Frese, M. and M.M. Gielnik (2014), 'The psychology of entrepreneurship', *Annual Review of Organizational Psychology and Organizational Behavior*, **1**, 413–38.

Garud, R. and P. Karnøe (2001), 'Path creation as a process of mindful deviation', in R. Garud and P. Karnøe (eds), *Path Dependence and Creation*, Mahwah, NJ: Lawrence Erlbaum Associates, pp. 1–38.

Gelfand, M.J., D.P.S. Bhawuk, L.H. Nishi and D.J. Bechtold (2004), 'Individualism and collectivism', in R.J. House, P.J. Hanges, M. Javidan, P.W. Dorfman and V. Gupta (eds), *Culture, Leadership and Organizations: The GLOBE Study of 62 Societies*, Thousand Oaks, CA: Sage, pp. 437–512.

Groves, K.S. (2005), 'Gender differences in social and emotional skills and charismatic leadership', *Journal of Leadership & Organizational Studies*, **11** (3), 30–46.

Gupta, V.K., D.B. Turban and N.M. Bhawe (2008), 'The effect of gender stereotype activation on entrepreneurial intentions', *Journal of Applied Psychology*, **93** (5), 1053–61.

Hayton, J.C. and G. Cacciotti (2013), 'Is there an entrepreneurial culture? A review of empirical research', *Entrepreneurship and Regional Development: An International Journal*, **25** (9/10), 708–31.

Hayton, J.C., G. George and S.A. Zahra (2002), 'National culture and entrepreneurship: A review of behavioral research', *Entrepreneurship Theory and Practice*, **26** (4), 33–52.

House, R.J. and M. Javidan (2004), 'Overview of GLOBE', in R.J. House, P.J. Hanges, M. Javidan, P.W. Dorfman and V. Gupta (eds), *Culture, Leadership and Organizations: The GLOBE Study of 62 Societies*, Thousand Oaks, CA: Sage, pp. 9–28.

House, R.J., P.J. Hanges, M. Javidan, P. Dorfman and V. Gupta (2004), *Culture, Leadership, and Organizations: The GLOBE Study of 62 Societies*, Thousand Oaks, CA: Sage.

Javidan, M., R.J. House, P.W. Dorfman, P.J. Hanges and M.S.D. Luque (2006), 'Conceptualizing and measuring cultures and their consequences: A comparative review of GLOBE's and Hofstede's approaches', *Journal of International Business Studies*, **37** (6), 897–914.

Klyver, K., S.L. Nielsen and M.R. Evald (2013), 'Women's self employment: An act of institutional (dis)integration? A multilevel, cross-country study', *Journal of Business Venturing*, **28** (4), 474–88.

Lin, Z., G. Picot and J. Compton (2000), 'The entry and exit dynamics of self-employment in Canada', *Small Business Economics*, **15** (2), 105–25.

Minniti, M. and C. Nardone (2007), 'Being in someone else's shoes: The role of gender in nascent entrepreneurship', *Small Business Economics*, **28** (2/3), 223–38.

Minniti, M. and W. Naudé (2010), 'What do we know about patterns and determinants of female entrepreneurship across countries?', *European Journal of Development Research*, **22** (3), 277–93.

Morris, M.H., D.L. Davis and J.W. Allen (1994), 'Fostering corporate entrepreneurship: Cross-cultural comparisons of the importance of individualism versus collectivism', *Journal of International Business Studies*, **25** (1), 65–89.

Nolan, J.M., P.W. Schultz, R.B. Cialdini, N.J. Goldstein and V. Griskevicius (2008), 'Normative social influence is underdetected', *Personality and Social Psychology Bulletin*, **34** (7), 913–23.

Ordanini, A., A. Parasuraman and G. Rubera (2014), 'When the recipe is more important than the ingredients: A Qualitative Comparative Analysis (QCA) of service innovation configurations', *Journal of Service Research*, **17** (2), 134–49.

Pandey, S. and A.S. Amezcua (2018), 'Women's business ownership and women's entrepreneurship through the lens of U.S. federal policies', *Small Business Economics* (in press).

Pinillos, M.-J. and L. Reyes (2011), 'Relationship between individualist–collectivist culture and entrepreneurial activity: Evidence from Global Entrepreneurship Monitor data', *Small Business Economics*, **37** (1), 23–37.

Ragin, C.C. (2008), *Redesigning Social Inquiry: Fuzzy Sets and Beyond*, Chicago, IL: University of Chicago Press.

Ragin, C.C. (2009), 'Qualitative Comparative Analysis using fuzzy sets (fsQCA)', in C.C. Ragin and B. Rihoux (eds), *Configurational Comparative Methods: Qualitative Comparative Analysis (QCA) and Related Techniques*, Los Angeles, CA: Sage, pp. 87–122.

Rudman, L. and P. Glick (1999), 'Feminized management and backlash toward agentic women: The hidden cost to women of a kinder, gentler image of middle managers', *Journal of Personality and Social Psychology*, **77** (5), 1004–10.

Schneider, C.Q. and C. Wagemann (2012), *Set-theoretic Methods for the Social Sciences: A Guide to Qualitative Comparative Analysis*, Cambridge: Cambridge University Press.

Schneider, M.R. and A. Eggert (2014), 'Embracing complex causality with the QCA method: An invitation', *Journal of Business Market Management*, **7** (1), 312–28.

Schneider, M.R., C. Schulze-Bentrop and M. Paunescu (2010), 'Mapping the institutional capital of high-tech firms: A fuzzy-set analysis of capitalist variety and export performance', *Journal of International Business Studies*, **41** (2), 246–66.

Shane, S. (1995), 'Uncertainty avoidance and the preference for innovation championing roles', *Journal of International Business Studies*, **26** (1), 47–68.

Stelter, N.Z. (2002), 'Gender differences in leadership: Current social issues and future organizational implications', *Journal of Leadership & Organizational Studies*, **8** (4), 88–99.

Stephan, U. and S. Pathak (2016), 'Beyond cultural values? Cultural leadership ideals and entrepreneurship', *Journal of Business Venturing*, **31** (5), 505–23.

Stephan, U. and L.M. Uhlaner (2010), 'Performance-based vs socially supportive culture: A cross national study of descriptive norms and entrepreneurship', *Journal of International Business Studies*, **41** (8), 1347–64.

Thai, M.T.T. and E. Turkina (2014), 'Macro-level determinants of formal entrepreneurship versus informal entrepreneurship', *Journal of Business Venturing*, **29** (4), 490–510.

Tiessen, J. (1997), 'Individualism, collectivism, and entrepreneurship: A framework for international comparative research', *Journal of Business Venturing*, **12** (5), 367–84.

Torres, P. and M. Augusto (2019a), 'Cultural leadership ideals and cultural practices leading to women's participation in transformational entrepreneurial leadership', in V. Ratten and P. Jones (eds), *Transformational Entrepreneurship*, London, UK and New York, USA: Routledge, Taylor & Francis Group, pp. 136–57.

Torres, P. and M. Augusto (2019b), 'Cultural configurations and entrepreneurial realisation', *International Journal of Entrepreneurial Behavior & Research*, **25** (1), 112–28.

Torres, P., M. Augusto and P. Godinho (2017), 'Predicting high consumer-brand identification and high repurchase: Necessary and sufficient conditions', *Journal of Business Research*, **79**, 52–65.

Vecchio, R.P. (2003), 'Entrepreneurship and leadership: Common trends and common threads', *Human Resource Management Review*, **13** (2), 303–27.

Vejsiu, A. (2011), 'Incentives to the self-employment decision in Sweden', *International Review of Applied Economics*, **25** (4), 379–403.

Verheul, I., L. Uhlaner and R. Thurik (2005), 'Business accomplishment, gender and entrepreneurial self-image', *Journal of Business Venturing*, **20** (4), 483–518.

Wagemann, C., J. Buche and M.B. Siewer (2016), 'QCA and business research: Work in progress or a consolidated agenda?', *Journal of Business Research*, **69** (7), 2531–40.

Welter, F., T. Baker, D.B. Audretsch and W.B. Gartner (2017), 'Everyday entrepreneurship – A call for entrepreneurship research to embrace entrepreneurial diversity', *Entrepreneurship Theory and Practice*, **41** (3), 311–21.

Westermann, O., J. Ashby and J. Pretty (2005), 'Gender and social capital: The importance of gender differences for the maturity and effectiveness of natural resource management groups', *World Development*, **33** (11), 1783–99.

Wilson, F., J. Kickul and D. Marlino (2007), 'Gender, entrepreneurial self-efficacy, and entrepreneurial career intentions: Implications for entrepreneurship education', *Entrepreneurship Theory and Practice*, **31** (3), 387–406.

Woodside, A.G. (2017), 'Preface', in A.G. Woodside (eds), *The Complexity Turn: Cultural, Management, and Marketing Applications*, Cham: Springer, pp. v–xviii.

Woodside, A.G., P.M. Bernal and A. Coduras (2016), 'The general theory of culture, entrepreneurship, innovation, and quality of life: Comparing nurturing versus thwarting enterprise start-ups in BRIC, Denmark, Germany, and the United States', *Industrial Marketing Management*, **53**, 136–59.

PART II

Women's emancipation from traditional family roles

5. You are well-educated, so why do you want to start a venture? Cultural norms of women's entrepreneurship in Ethiopia

Magdalena Markowska and Tigist Tesfaye Abebe

INTRODUCTION

Women's entrepreneurship is increasing (Brush et al., 2017); in 2011, 39 per cent of entrepreneurs across the world were women (Kelley et al., 2012). The percentage of women entrepreneurs in sub-Saharan Africa is even higher, although most are informal entrepreneurs; for example, in Ethiopia women account for 73 per cent of informal entrepreneurship (CSA, 2010). Given that entrepreneurship has been proposed as the panacea to most problems (Baker and Welter, 2015) and 'a tool or mechanism for overcoming the sorts of constraints that are faced by people in disadvantaged circumstances' (Baker and Powell, 2016, p. 44), many believe that women entrepreneurs could help to fight poverty and increase women's economic empowerment in developing and emerging economies (De Vita et al., 2014; Ngino and Maina, 2014; UNESCAP, 2017; Wasihun and Paul, 2010).

Women's participation in the economy and, more specifically, in entrepreneurship is important. However, the culture that prevails in developing and emerging economies often constrains women's activities (Brush et al., 2018; Mabsout and Van Staveren, 2010; Roomi et al., 2009). Many limitations on women are grounded in gender-based social norms and values. Women are considered to be subordinate to men, which can reduce their right to education, their autonomy and their access to other institutional and financial support mechanisms (Zehra and Achtenhagen, 2018). In other words, in contexts dominated by male norms, the types of activities open to women are often restricted – for the most part by the need for women to comply with traditional cultural values and norms.

How can women be empowered in patriarchal cultures? How can the legitimacy constraints on women's entrepreneurship be reduced? How can women's access to education and other resources be increased in such cultures? How can we change society's perception of educated women who aspire to entrepreneurship as a valuable and desired career? The existing research investigates these issues focusing on individual women (Berglund et al., 2018), which, although helpful, overlooks the importance of the social and institutional context. In this chapter, we adopt a more contextualized lens to highlight the need to understand entrepreneurial activity *in a particular context* (Brush et al., 2009; 2017; Welter, 2011) and to ensure that context is part of the story (Zahra et al., 2014). For example, in developing countries and emerging economies, women's entrepreneurship tends to be part of the informal economy (ILO, 2009). Also, businesses owned by women are often smaller, grow more slowly and are less profitable (Bardasi et al., 2011; Hallward-Driemeier, 2013). Because the gender norms and values of the social context determine what women can or cannot do, this social context shapes women's entrepreneurship (Jamali, 2009). In other words, the way that context and entrepreneurship are intertwined has the potential to either enable or constrain particular behaviours and influence the dynamics of entrepreneurial endeavours (Markowska and Lopez-Vega, 2018).

To examine our research question of *what cultural constraints limit attractiveness of entrepreneurship as a career for educated women in Ethiopia*, we employ a multiple case study strategy to explore how five Ethiopian women educated to at least bachelor's degree level, have overcome the cultural challenges and legitimized their entrepreneurial endeavours. Our choice to study educated women in Ethiopia was based on the fact that, despite government efforts to change the institutional framework and encourage women's engagement in entrepreneurship, in Ethiopia gender inequality and female subordination are very present (Amine and Staub, 2009; Kalantaridis and Fletcher, 2012). For instance, the 2015 Global Gender Gap Report ranks Ethiopia 124th out of 145 countries for magnitude and scope of gender disparities. Also, it appears that educated women in Ethiopia face other, often social challenges related to their labour market decisions (Richardson et al., 2004).

Our contextualized analysis demonstrates that, although Ethiopia's institutional context is moving in the right direction and is providing facilities for women entrepreneurs (e.g., women-focused policy programmes to encourage women's entrepreneurship, entrepreneurship development programmes), changing the cultural context and society's perceptions is more difficult. Our study shows, also, that education and family support are important for legitimizing the woman's decision to become an entrepreneur and to start a venture.

This chapter contributes to research that proposes a contextualized view of entrepreneurship and suggests that when evaluating entrepreneurial activity in developing-country and emerging-economy contexts, we need to understand the social, cultural and/or gender norms and values. We contribute by identifying three cultural aspects that limit the attractiveness of entrepreneurship as a career for educated women: (1) being ostracized by family and society for choosing entrepreneurship over regular employment; (2) dislike of the type of business; and (3) censure for prioritizing business over the role of mother. We show, also, that appropriateness and perception of the opportunities and challenges involved in female entrepreneurship is contextually bound and that educated women entrepreneurs are prepared to face the cultural obstacles. They strive to create both value and jobs, particularly for other women, and see the need for business networks to allow them to nurture and advance their ventures and to thrive in the long term. We argue that increasing gender equality is likely to increase the legitimacy of female entrepreneurship. We suggest the need for systemic change in order for female entrepreneurship to be accepted and to flourish in Ethiopia. This change must include greater gender equality and a change to cultural beliefs about what is appropriate for Ethiopian women, and promotion of female entrepreneurship.

WOMEN AND ENTREPRENEURSHIP

Women's entrepreneurship is driven by both individual and contextual factors (Brush et al., 2017) and women are both pulled and pushed into entrepreneurship. However, support programmes tend to target the individual woman and focus on improving women's entrepreneurial skills and attitudes (Berglund et al., 2018). Research shows that women have less access than men to education and entrepreneurial experience (ILO, 2014), which has led to the assumption that the smaller number of women entrepreneurs is due to lack of appropriate skills and experience. The so-called 'under-performance hypothesis' (Du Rietz and Henrekson, 2000) suggests that women can be 'fixed' to allow them to become successful entrepreneurs (Ahl, 2006; Marlow, 2009; 2013). Directly or indirectly, women are accused of deviating in their business management from the way men run businesses, and are expected to get on 'the right track' by changing or adjusting their behaviours to an aspiration to run high-growth firms, to network differently, to participate in further education and to identify as entrepreneurs (García and Welter, 2013; Wu et al., 2019).

   However, this hypothesis has been rejected on the basis of clear evidence that performance differences between men and women are sector dependent rather than being related to individual characteristics (Du Rietz and Henrekson, 2000; Robb and Watson, 2012; Watson, 2002). Nevertheless, policy, research and general discourse tend to focus on the need to 'improve' women rather than the need to change existing norms, values and structures. This applies, particularly, to patriarchal cultures in developing countries and emerging economies where women suffer discrimination (Zehra and Achtenhagen, 2018).

CONTEXTUALIZING WOMEN ENTREPRENEURSHIP

Identifying an entrepreneurial opportunity depends heavily on human capital and the contextual variables (Brush et al., 2017), particularly informal institutions (Welter and Smallbone, 2008) in the form of codes of conduct, values and norms (Welter and Smallbone, 2011). In the context of entrepreneurship, the social and institutional environment dictates what forms of work are allowed or not for women and whether entrepreneurship is perceived as reserved for males or open, also, to women. In many societies, the woman's role is predominantly that of carer (Achtenhagen and Welter, 2003) and women experience huge difficulties when trying to combine labour market activity with family and household responsibilities (Gimenez-Nadal et al., 2012).

An understanding of the local culture is crucial for understanding entrepreneurship. The culture, which includes the codes of conduct, values, norms and non-codified attitudes embedded in society (Welter and Smallbone, 2011), shapes individual perceptions about what society desires and expects. The culture can be viewed as the 'rich complex of meanings, beliefs, practices, symbols, norms, and values prevalent among people in a society' and as the 'underlying system of values peculiar to a specific group or society' (Schwartz, 2006, p. 138). More specifically, cultural values and norms influence what is considered desirable and legitimate. Cultural norms are important for prescribing behaviour in general and career choices in particular. Norms refer to notions about how individuals should 'be' and should act, and socialization into specific behavioural norms shapes men's and women's repertoires of acceptable choices and trajectories (Welter and Smallbone, 2011). Therefore, individual behaviour is shaped by the local culture and cultural values and the social and gender norms internalized from childhood, which can establish a life cycle of social and gender socialization and stereotyping (Ahl, 2007).

Because entrepreneurship is viewed by many as a masculine endeavour (Ahl, 2004), women entrepreneurs are considered not the norm, but as 'the other' and as less successful (García and Welter, 2013). Women are socialized to believe that they are not particularly suited to entrepreneurship. For example, Wilson et al. (2007) show that, among women and men in possession of the same knowledge, men's self-efficacy is much higher. Therefore, to fully comprehend women's entrepreneurship, it is important to understand the social and institutional conditions.

WOMEN ENTREPRENEURSHIP IN ETHIOPIA

Entrepreneurship in Ethiopia is dominated, overall, by women (Gelan and Wedajo, 2013), although this trend changes with increasing venture size. More specifically, according to the 2010 Central Statistical Agency of Ethiopia (CSA) survey (Kipnis, 2013), while 73.5 per cent of urban micro-enterprises are run by women, women's respective ownership of small and medium sized ventures is 13.7 per cent and 30 per cent. The majority of Ethiopian women entrepreneurs are informal entrepreneurs who engage in entrepreneurship at the subsistence level mostly in petty trade, food processing, retailing and hairdressing (De Vita et al., 2014). However, there is a growing number of educated women entrepreneurs in the formal sector (Solomon, 2010).

Ethiopia is a traditional, patriarchal, landlocked country, located in the horn of Africa. It is the second most populous country in Africa, with near to 110 million inhabitants in 2019, and is a cultural, ethnic and religious melting pot (Addis Getahun and Tafete Kassu, 2014). It includes over 80 different ethnic groups and languages, multiple religions and strong family norms. Some 70 per cent of the population are young and unemployed. There is still relatively high illiteracy, particularly in rural regions and among women. Ethiopia is one of the poorest countries in the world, with annual per capita income of USD 772 (World Bank, 2018). The Ethiopian government sees the solution to this problem as encouragement of entrepreneurship – especially involving women – to create employment, and has put in place a number of policies to support that aim (FDRE, 2016). Ethiopia has some good policies, laws and guidelines, but lacks institutional capacity for their implementation (Woldegies, 2016). Encouragement of entrepreneurship is related to the recent transformation of the Ethiopian economy into a free market economy where capitalism is practised and privatization is allowed (FDRE, 2016).

Despite the high percentage of women entrepreneurs, women's ventures lack legitimacy. Ethiopian women entrepreneurs are disadvantaged both economically and societally (Abagissa, 2013; Zewde & Associates, 2002). The obstacles they face include: low levels of human and financial capital; high levels of domestic responsibility; low levels of education; and lack of female role models. Several studies show that, for many marginalized women, establishing their own enterprise is their only employment means (Abagissa, 2013; Kelley et al., 2014; Kew et al., 2015). Women are not generally allowed to own property and, consequently, do not have the collateral required for bank loans (Belwal et al., 2012). Research shows that, compared to men, women face greater difficulty in growing their businesses, participate in fewer business-oriented networks, lack capital and assets, suffer lower status in society and tend to be less assertive and confident in their ability to succeed in business (Abagissa, 2013; Kelley et al., 2014).

Since male dominance is ingrained in Ethiopia's culture and, as in many other parts of the country, women are still considered subordinate to men (Cherinet and Mulugeta, 2003; Fox, 2019), patriarchy and gender inequality prevail. Many of Ethiopia's traditional sayings present women in a very negative light (Allo, 2018). 'A woman's country is her husband and her livelihood is her character' and 'as a soul is in its creator, a woman is in her master' (Fox, 2019) are examples of popular aphorisms portraying women as inferior to men, which reflects Ethiopia's patriarchal structure and societal values that subordinate women to men, 'while relentlessly upholding male privilege' (Allo, 2018). As a result, women and their contributions and achievements are marginalized, while men are presented as capable, competent, credible, authoritative and knowledgeable. Similarly, there are many barriers to girls' education and development of self-worth (Adego, 2014). In many rural regions, in particular, there is a belief that girls do not belong in school and that educated women will never succeed (Singh and Belwal, 2008). Also, in the Ethiopian context, entrepreneurs are assumed to be male with wives who support their activities. In addition, Woldegies (2016) notes that the Amhara (the largest ethnic group in Ethiopia) silence women and hinder their freedom of speech and human capacity through male domination.

Although Ethiopia has implemented several reforms aimed at increasing gender equality, families with scarce resources invest more in their sons' rather than their daughters' education (Richardson et al., 2004). Many girls drop out of school at around the age of 15 for gender and cultural reasons (e.g., early marriage, avoidance of sexual assaults, domestic work, subsistence activities, etc.). From a young age, girls learn that they should not have career ambitions and that their families are unlikely to support their education (Singh and Belwal, 2008) or encourage them to follow a career. However, Woldegies (2016) suggests that women's engagement in income-generating activities allows them to participate in household decisions.

Finally, in the Ethiopian context, public discourse about gender equality is non-existent or marginal (Allo, 2018). Although the institutional context is changing – Ethiopia has introduced progressive gender equality laws, which are enshrined in its constitution (Federal Democratic Republic of Ethiopia, 1995) – these have yet to be implemented in daily practice. Ellen Alem, a UNICEF Ethiopia gender and development specialist, notes that 'the problem is in translating those [equality laws] to reality' (*Independent*, 2019).

Table 5.1   *Descriptive data about the five participating entrepreneurs*

Case	Age	Marital status	Children	Education	Experience as entrepreneur	Sector
Amarech	31	Married	2	Master's in Paediatrics	4 years	Childcare
Bethelhem	36	Divorced	3	Bachelor's in Business Management	6 years	Food
Chaltu	31	Single	no	Bachelor's in Electrical engineering	7 years	Fashion
Desta	42	Married	5	Bachelor's in nursing	8 years	Healthcare
Zeritu	35	Married	3	Master's in child nutrition	3 years (closed business in early 2020)	Counselling & training

METHOD

To investigate what cultural constraints hinder attractiveness of entrepreneurship as a career for educated women in Ethiopia, we chose a multiple case study strategy to explore women's entrepreneurship in a particular context. We used convenience sampling to select five cases of educated Ethiopian women entrepreneurs, to highlight the opportunities and difficulties they experienced in pursuing entrepreneurship. All five cases were active women entrepreneurs in Addis Ababa, Ethiopia, in 2019, when we conducted our first interviews. One of our entrepreneurs closed her business for financial reasons in April 2020, but her story remains relevant for our study. Table 5.1 provides descriptive data on the five entrepreneurs. We collected our data through semi-structured interviews, which were conducted in Amharic and, later, translated into English. They focused on the women's life stories and the motivations for the entrepreneur journey, the challenges and opportunities they experienced and their hopes for the future. Each of our entrepreneurs was interviewed twice, first in early 2019 and then in early 2020. All the interviews were recorded and transcribed verbatim before being translated. We analysed the data using Gioia's (Gioia et al., 2013) first- and second-order coding and conducted comparative analysis across cases. Specifically, we analysed the stories of our individual entrepreneurs, looked for similarities and differences among entrepreneurs, and identified patterns and themes in the data.

THE CASES

Amarech

Amarech, a 31-year-old mother of two, had opened her day nursery four years earlier. Although she wanted to serve her community and generate employment for others, especially women, she had a practical reason for her entrepreneurial endeavour. She originally had worked at the university and, after a period of maternity leave, wanted to return to work, but had no one to care for her baby. Two years prior to her maternity, she had proposed the notion of a day nursery for the children of university employees, but, what was perceived as a novel idea, lacked support from the university's management. Following a second period of maternity leave, her day nursery proposal was successful and the first university nursery was established as a non-profit business, with Amarech as its manager. After less than a year, during which she helped more than 50 mothers, Amarech decided it was time to strike out on her own. Initially, she faced several problems, including access to funding and negative perceptions of her day nursery, but she was determined. Amarech told us that the support of her mother, the wider family and, especially, her husband were crucial. She was proud of her achievement: 'I have reached this point where people recognize me for my abilities and skills, especially my mother because she feels proud of me'. Amarech believes that her education was important, but that her entrepreneurial endeavour would have failed without emotional and financial support from her husband to set up the centre and the contribution made by her mother by providing the physical space she needed for her project.

Bethlehem

At the age of 36, Bethlehem divorced and became an entrepreneur to provide for herself and her three children. Although her family supported her financially, they were not sympathetic to her business, which was an injera bakery (injera is the traditional Ethiopian bread). Although the memory of her family's and friends' disapproval of a university educated woman engaging in a baking business remained raw, she never doubted that she had made the right choice. Despite several difficulties, including obtaining a government licence to trade, she became independent and achieved a good standard of living for her family. Bethlehem was employing four women and two men and felt she was a good employer. However, her venture had involved her having to balance work and family obligations, particularly difficult since she was a single parent. She was clear that: 'It is the time for women to move forward and prove their identity in society'.

Chaltu

Chaltu was aged 31 at the time of the first interview. She studied electrical engineering at university, but, for as long as she could remember, she had wanted to be a fashion designer. Seven years earlier, after finishing her bachelor's degree and experiencing difficulty finding employment she liked, she decided to start a business to produce traditional dresses. Her family was opposed to the idea. Her father said: 'No need to think about it, you are educated enough, so why do you want to start a venture – focus on getting a job'. Therefore, she embarked on her entrepreneurial journey initially without any family support. After numerous problems and, eventually, with help from her family, she established a venture which, at the time, was employing around 20 other women. She is recognized in society and is actively engaged in helping other women start their own ventures. She offers advice on market strategies and available government schemes. She believes strongly that women are the pillars of the family, society and the nation.

Desta

Eight years before the first interview, Desta had established a healthcare centre with her husband, a medical doctor. She was aged 42 at the time, and was mother to five children, the oldest just under 15 years old. She originated from a rural part of Ethiopia, but after their marriage, she and her husband moved to Addis Ababa where he practised medicine. She quickly realized that life in the city differed hugely from life in rural Ethiopia. Initially, she wanted to work as a hospital nurse, but it was difficult to find a job which offered or accommodated childcare. Eventually, she concluded that she must start her own business. Her husband was very supportive and they decided to open a healthcare centre, which she would manage and he would work in as a doctor. Her hope was both to help the patients who attended the centre and to provide employment for others, particularly women. She had to overcome numerous problems, including financial problems, competition with established hospitals, access to resources and negative perceptions about what she, a woman and a mother, was doing. However, her business grew. She believes that education is important for building women's self-confidence and competences.

Zeritu

Zeritu, who was 35, lived with her husband and three small children. For three years prior to our first interview, she had been running a counselling and training service, but had given it up to study for another degree. Her decision to become an entrepreneur was based on a gap she identified in the market. She realized that many Ethiopian mothers knew little about how and when to wean their babies. She had completed a master's degree in complementary child nutrition and the lifelong impact on the development of introducing solids into an infant's diet. She decided to establish a business to allow her to share her knowledge. She needed financial support from her husband. Although she enjoyed her work as a counsellor, her husband made her close it down when the business began to lose money. Zeritu believes that he was right to do this and that women should respect God, marry and become mothers and, only then, devote their energies to developing their talents and enjoying life. She believes that if a woman entrepreneur does not have time for the family or if the business affects her or the family's health, her first duty must be to the family. She believes that an Ethiopian woman who is a mother and wife is respected, but that this respect is lost if she prioritizes business over family.

FINDINGS

Our data show that culture in Ethiopia is not conducive to women's choice of entrepreneurship as a career and that one of the main consequences of Ethiopia's cultural norms and rules is lack of legitimacy for women's entrepreneurial activities. Our interviews highlighted several important points: (1) two of the women had been rejected by their families and ostracized by society for their decisions to become entrepreneurs rather than find jobs (Amarech and Chaltu), while (2) one was judged for the type of business she decided to open (Bethelhem) and (3) two interviewees experienced negative judgements for prioritizing their business over their roles as mothers (Desta and Zeritu). In what follows, we discuss these three aspects in more detail.

Entrepreneurship: a Legitimate Career?

Although government and the broader institutional context advocate entrepreneurship as the solution to unemployment, Ethiopian society is not abreast of these developments. Our entrepreneurs referred to the problems related to convincing family and friends that entrepreneurship was a legitimate career path for a woman, particularly an educated woman. While the necessity for informal entrepreneurship among poor and less well-educated women is being recognized, entrepreneurship by educated women continues to be disapproved of. For example, Bethelhem reflected that 'having a first degree in business management, put me under pressure from friends to look for employment rather than establish my own business'. Similarly, Chaltu's father was unsympathetic to Chaltu starting her own business and expressed concern about her and her future. He questioned why she or any other educated woman would want to become an entrepreneur if they could find a good job. His comments reflect the common perception that entrepreneurship is not a valued or legitimate activity for women and that employment, especially in the public sector, is considered more socially appropriate.

Even if the family supported the decision to become an entrepreneur, the type of business was not always acceptable, as in the case of Bethelhem. Her family was not against her becoming an entrepreneur, but they thought that owning and running a traditional injera bakery was not appropriate for an educated woman. However, Bethelhem considered it as legitimate as any other business. Eventually, she was able to convince her family to support her and she created employment for six more people.

Clashing Ideals: Motherhood Versus Entrepreneurship

Another problem experienced by our entrepreneurs was combining motherhood with entrepreneurship. First, given the patriarchal culture and traditional family model, women in Ethiopia generally have sole responsibility for the household and childcare; men contribute very little or not at all to these chores. Hence, for women who work, combining being primary carer with work responsibilities can be difficult. All five interviewees had found the family–work balance difficult and almost impossible without the help of partners or family.

Second, being a wife and mother are paramount for women. Women's careers are not encouraged by society because they (are likely to) affect the family negatively. Career-oriented women need to deal with being stigmatized as favouring career achievements ahead of their families. Zeritu exemplified this view: 'Moms can be entrepreneurs, but that shouldn't come before their children and I feel sorry for moms who have to travel, say to Dubai, for a one month stay which means leaving their baby to the care of an untrained Nanny'. Zeritu believed that women entrepreneurs should exploit their talents for the good of society, but should not focus on profit. She argued that:

> Specially for a married woman, her husband has to provide for the woman not because she is less [than he is] but because she is noble and deserves to be provided for. A mother who is pregnant or breast feeding or taking care of a young child until the age of four should not worry about providing for her family; she is doing big things already by giving birth and taking care of babies – any additional burden will be too much for her.

On the one hand, this extract highlights the special job that women are 'destined' to perform, but, on the other hand, it highlights gender inequality. Achieving independence and equality was considered by Zeritu as disrespectful to her husband and would result in her being ostracized by her family. She said: 'what good will be the money or the land she has got to show her equality with a husband if she loses her family? What is the use of money if this becomes more valuable than her family? What use will it be if she is on her own?'

To sum up, it would seem that increasing women's entrepreneurship in Ethiopia will require a change in the perceptions of both men and women about what is appropriate for women to engage in and how motherhood can be combined with entrepreneurship. To change cultural values and norms, and ideas about gender equality, will require implementation of structural changes and the introduction of new norms.

Creating Opportunities for Women's Entrepreneurship

The entrepreneurs we studied had experienced numerous difficulties, but had managed to overcome them. They emphasized the importance of education and networking and the emotional, moral and financial support of family and exposure to role models.

Education and networking
Bethelhem believed that education was the primary prerequisite for the realiza-tion of potential and acquisition of entrepreneurial tools and skills. Education and networking provided an awareness of development programmes and gov-ernment policies, and opportunities for access to micro loans to enable women to become entrepreneurs. She believed that access to bank loans and other forms of financing was one of the most important enablers of women-owned businesses and that her awareness of the available schemes allowed her to exploit them. However, many women did not know what was available and believed that government should focus on awareness campaigns. Amarech emphasized the importance of education and its effect on confidence. She explained:

> It is challenging especially socializing with the important people and getting the help you need from others is tough for women and the time it demands still puts the women in a dilemma. But when you realize it, it is a very exciting and rewarding experience. I feel that I can make something happen from nothing. I feel like I don't need to hope things will happen, instead I can make them happen if I want them enough.

Although these entrepreneurs had overcome these obstacles and negative per-ceptions, they stressed the need for overarching changes to societal norms and values. They were very aware of the difficulties related to being a woman and being a woman entrepreneur in Ethiopia. Although there can be no expectation of overnight changes, this does not mean that efforts should not be made to improve the status of women entrepreneurs. Chaltu wanted: 'women to be given equal opportunity as well as being subjected to an equal burden as men. Every child should be given the same opportunity to succeed in their education and at the same time, they should share household burdens equally'.

Family as the gatekeeper

Research shows the importance of family to the entrepreneurial endeavour (Bird and Wennberg, 2016; Edelman et al., 2016; Kirkwood, 2012). Family can be the source of support and material resources to facilitate the entrepreneurial activity (De Bruin et al., 2007). In developing countries and emerging economies, in particular, many entrepreneurial firms are family businesses with several members of the same family participating. Families are rich repositories of both tangible and intangible resources (Alsos et al., 2014). In Ethiopia, family is more than the nuclear family (parents and children) and includes grandparents, aunts and uncles, and cousins and their respective families, all of whom need to support the woman entrepreneur.

Family is crucial for the formation of cultural and social expectations. For example, the family defines what is or is not appropriate for the woman to engage in (Hashim et al., forthcoming). Chaltu told us that her family, particularly her father, was opposed to her decision to start her own business. They argued that, because she was educated, if she wanted to work, she should find employment rather than engage in entrepreneurship, which in her father's eyes was a subsistence activity not worthy of a well-educated person. Family structure – being a wife and mother – complicates the decision to start a business (Gudeta and van Engen, 2018; Solomon, 2010). For example, Desta emphasized that it was more difficult for married women to start a venture if the husband did not support them. Also, being a mother was an additional strain. Women who are involved in business have to take responsibility, also, for the household and childcare.

Amarech felt lucky that her mother and her husband had supported her. She was proud to be an entrepreneur: 'Thanks to family support, I have reached a point where people recognize me for my abilities and skills. Especially my mother, because she feels proud of me'. Also, Desta emphasized the support she received from her husband: 'My husband is a medical doctor and when I was deciding to launch the business of health care centre, he was my supporter not only emotionally, but by his professional contribution to the business'. Hence, family can be a source of support or a barrier (De Bruin et al., 2007).

The role of female role models

Given the institutional and social context in Ethiopia, women need to be convinced about their value, potential and abilities. They need successful female role models to increase their self-efficacy (Bandura, 1997). Female role models attract the participation of young women and convince them that entrepreneurship is a viable choice and that they have the necessary skills and abilities to pursue such a career. For example, Chaltu said, 'I was highly inspired by those women who run their enterprises successfully and decided that I also wanted to establish a venture on my own'. She believes that role models allow women to overcome the negative perceptions of family. At the same time, support programmes for women are needed to provide training and skills needed for entrepreneurial endeavours.

DISCUSSION

Although women's entrepreneurship is growing worldwide, we need a contextualized understanding of the phenomenon. Extant research stresses the importance of context (Welter, 2011), yet it usually emphasizes the role of institutional environment (Brush et al., 2017). The institutional context refers to the constitutional, legal and organizational forces, including family law and property rights, allowing/restricting women's ownership of land (Welter and Smallbone, 2011). Institutional context has a tremendous impact on both male and female entrepreneurship and exerts pressure for conformance to behaviours considered legitimate for those groups (Welter and Smallbone, 2011). Institutional context tends to limit women's behaviours more than men's behaviours and to privilege men at the expense of women (Mabsout and Van Staveren, 2010). Our study highlights the need to see context as more nuanced and the importance of culture and cultural values in prescribing desired behaviours. More specifically, we show the contextual complexity of an environment where formal institutional context undergoes changes to encourage, while the gender and cultural norms and traditions continue to ostracize women, particularly educated ones, for choosing entrepreneurship as a career. We argue that systemic changes to the social context are needed to utilize women's potential and empower them to become entrepreneurs. While some studies focus on how to incentivize individual women to engage in entrepreneurial careers, we argue that this approach is not sufficient to empower women. The findings from our study show that cultural norms and tradition play a role in legitimizing entrepreneurship as a viable career path for women. We argue that perceptions of women's entrepreneurship need to be changed and that women's entrepreneurship needs to be 're-valued'.

Cultural Constraints

Our findings confirm the existence of gender-based constraints on women entrepreneurship in Ethiopia but stress the role of education for overcoming them. Extant research shows that women in developing countries and patriarchal societies tend to be raised to be unambitious, to be perfect and to be less worthy than men (Mekonnen and Cestino, 2017; Zehra and Achtenhagen, 2018). We found that educated women in Ethiopia are ambitious and self-confident and see themselves as valuable members of society, ready to prove their potential. This suggests that education is crucial for enabling the socialized gender norms to be overridden. However, it appears that education also acts as a double-sided sword in this context. While it liberates women, building both their confidence and competence (Kelley et al., 2015), it also subjects them to more social pressure regarding their career choices. More specifically, we found that with an increasing level of women's education, social ostracism increases and reduces the perceived appropriateness of entrepreneurship as a career for educated women. This is why we subscribe to the arguments in Wasihun and Paul (2010, p. 234) that 'the challenge is less about trying to increase the number of women entrepreneurs and more about how to legitimize and strengthen the base of their activity'.

Further, in contrast to extant literature which shows that mothers' entrepreneurial activity is encouraged (Richomme-Huet et al., 2013; Naldi et al., 2019), our data show that women are ostracized for engaging in business activity at the expense of their family. Additionally, although extant literature suggests that women entrepreneurs are widely supported by their families and friends (De Bruin et al., 2007; Edelman et al., 2016), it appears that in Ethiopia family provides a gatekeeping function restricting women's entry into entrepreneurship, particularly that of educated women. Thus, the goal should be to change society's systemic values, which see entrepreneurship as less attractive and legitimate than paid employment and as less legitimate and appropriate for women compared to men.

We argue that to change the status quo it is not enough to change the formal institutional context through the imposition of new family laws, for example; it needs huge effort to be put into changing societal perceptions of gender equality and women's entrepreneurship (Mekonnen and Cestino, 2017). This presupposes a more holistic approach to gender equality and an assumption that entrepreneurship policies should not include the traditional role-stereotyping which confines women largely to their traditional gender roles (Zehra and Achtenhagen, 2018). At the same time, women must have greater self-awareness. They must recognize that the aspiration to become an entrepreneur will require them to fight against longstanding cultural values and attitudes (Kelley et al., 2013). Finally, although government has taken many positive steps, there is a need for bottom-up advocacy to showcase the true value and potential of women entrepreneurs. More female role models are needed and, especially, Ethiopian women entrepreneurs who have developed ventures, based on their own choices, and are part of the formal sector of the economy (Hailemariam et al., 2017).

In summary, to encourage women's entrepreneurship will require two simultaneous developments. First, a change to Ethiopia's cultural and gender values, so that women are considered equal to men and have similar rights to men (such as allowed by the property law), and men's participation in household chores and childcare is seen as the norm. Second, there need to be more entrepreneurship development programmes aimed at educating and supporting women. Education builds both confidence and competence and can change society's perception of women (Kelley et al., 2015). Woldegies (2016) argues that economically empowered women develop self-confidence and claim power with respect to issues that affect them negatively. We found that education has a similar effect on women and their confidence.

CONCLUSIONS

This chapter has argued that it is not enough to focus on developing the skills and aptitudes of individual women and that what is needed is a change to social and cultural perceptions, norms and values, to improve gender equality and increase and legitimize women's entrepreneurship. In addressing our research question, we found that social and cultural norms and traditions play an important role in educated women's decisions to engage in entrepreneurship as a career; in particular we identified (1) ostracism by family and society for becoming an entrepreneur rather than finding a job; (2) objection to the type of business; and (3) censure for prioritizing business over the role of mother as key cultural constraints. Our findings suggest that educated women feel able to explore an entrepreneurial career, but need the support of their family to avoid social censure.

We suggest policy makers should launch campaigns to promote entre-preneurship as a legitimate and desirable career for women and showcase successful women entrepreneurs, both with and without family responsibili-ties. Further, the study contributes to debate on the importance of contextual conditions on (the dynamics of) entrepreneurship (Acs et al., 2008; Welter, 2011). Without a good understanding of the cultural norms and the woman's role in Ethiopian culture, the existing development programmes will be only moderately successful. What is needed is an education policy governing both boys' and girls' early education, which teaches them about entrepreneurship and gender equality, so that both women and men are exposed and sensitized to the benefits of entrepreneurship and equality values.

Limitations and Avenues for Future Research

Our study has some limitations. First, we study only women entrepreneurs; exploring how the social network including family members, particularly husbands and the women's parents, view women's entrepreneurship would shed more light on the perceptions towards entrepreneurship as a career for educated women. Second, we present only the view of women who had successfully embarked on an entrepreneurship career. We believe that including the views of women who failed to overcome the constraints would enrich our findings.

We believe that research exploring different dimensions of culture and different cultural norms and their impact on changing beliefs about equality and women's engagement in entrepreneurship, could contribute to a better understanding of entrepreneurship as a legitimate career for women. Also, an exploration of the interplay between institutional and cultural norms would advance our knowledge about how to effectively legitimize women's entrepreneurship and improve gender equality.

REFERENCES

Abagissa, J. 2013. Challenges confronting women in micro and small enterprises in Addis Ababa, Ethiopia. *Ethiopian Journal of Business and Economics*, 3(1): 95–139.

Achtenhagen, L. and Welter, F. 2003. Female entrepreneurship in Germany: Context, development and its reflection in German media. In J.E. Butler (ed.), *New Perspectives on Women Entrepreneurs* (pp. 71–100). Greenwich: Information Age Publishing.

Acs, Z., Desai, S. and Hessels, J. 2008. Entrepreneurship, economic development and institutions. *Small Business Economics*, 31: 219–34.

Addis Getahun, S. and Tefate Kassu, W. 2014. *Culture & Customs of Ethiopia*. Westport, CT: Greenwood Press.

Adego, T. 2014. Challenges and prospects of women operated micro and small enterprises: A case of Aksum City administration, Ethiopia. *European Journal of Business and Management*, 6(28): 143–55.

Ahl, H. 2004. *The Scientific Reproduction of Gender Inequality: A Discourse Analysis of Research Texts on Women's Entrepreneurship*. Malmö: Liber AB.

Ahl, H. 2006. Why research on women entrepreneurs needs new directions. *Entrepreneurship Theory and Practice*, 30(5): 595–621.

Ahl, H. 2007. Gender stereotypes. In S. Clegg and J. Bailey (eds), *International Encyclopedia of Organization Studies* (pp. 544–7). London: Sage.

Allo, A. 2018. The power of Ethiopia's gender-balanced cabinet. Aljazeera. Accessed 14 May 2020 at https://www.aljazeera.com/indepth/opinion/power-ethiopia-gender -balanced-cabinet-181019110930577.html.

Alsos, G., Carter, S. and Ljunggren, E. 2014. Kinship and business: How entrepreneurial households facilitate business growth. *Entrepreneurship & Regional Development*, 26(1–2): 97–122.

Amine, L.S. and Staub, K.M. 2009. Women entrepreneurs in sub-Saharan Africa: An institutional theory analysis from a social marketing point of view. *Entrepreneurship & Regional Development*, 21(2): 183–211.

Baker, T. and Powell, E. 2016. Let them eat bricolage? Toward a contextualized notion of inequality of entrepreneurial opportunity. In F. Welter and W.B. Gartner (eds),

A Research Agenda for Entrepreneurship and Context (pp. 41–53). Cheltenham, UK and Northampton, MA, USA: Edward Elgar Publishing.

Baker, T. and Welter, F. 2015. Bridges to the future. In T. Baker and F. Welter (eds), *The Routledge Companion to Entrepreneurship* (pp. 3–17). London: Routledge.

Bandura, A. 1997. *Self-efficacy: The Exercise of Control*. New York: Freeman.

Bardasi, E., Sabarwal, S. and Terrell, K. 2011. How do female entrepreneurs perform? Evidence from three developing regions. *Small Business Economics*, 37(4): 417.

Belwal, R., Tamiru, M. and Singh, G. 2012. Microfinance and sustained economic improvement: Women small-scale entrepreneurs in Ethiopia. *Journal of International Development*, 24: S84–S99.

Berglund, K., Ahl, H., Pettersson, K. and Tillmar, M. 2018. Women's entrepreneurship, neoliberalism and economic justice in the postfeminist era: A discourse analysis of policy change in Sweden. *Gender, Work & Organization*, 25(5): 531–56.

Bird, M. and Wennberg, K. 2016. Why family matters: The impact of family resources on immigrant entrepreneurs' exit from entrepreneurship. *Journal of Business Venturing*, 31(6): 687–704.

Brush, C., de Bruin, A. and Welter, F. 2009. A gender-aware framework for women's entrepreneurship. *International Journal of Gender and Entrepreneurship*, 1(1): 8–24.

Brush, C., Ali, A., Kelley, D. and Greene, P. 2017. The influence of human capital factors and context on women's entrepreneurship: Which matters more? *Journal of Business Venturing Insights*, 8: 105–13.

Brush, C., Edelman, L., Manolova, T. and Welter, F. 2018. A gendered look at entrepreneurship ecosystems. *Small Business Economics*, 53(2): 393–408.

Cherinet, H. and Mulugeta, E. 2003. Towards gender equality in Ethiopia: A profile of gender relations. Stockholm: Swedish International Development Cooperation Agency (SIDA).

CSA 2010. The 2007 Population and Housing Census of Ethiopia: Statistical report at country level. Statistical report Central Statistical Agency, Addis Ababa.

De Bruin, A., Brush, C. and Welter, F. 2007. Advancing a framework for coherent research on women's entrepreneurship. *Entrepreneurship Theory and Practice*, 31(3): 323–39.

De Vita, L., Mari, M. and Poggesi, S. 2014. Women entrepreneurs in and from developing countries: Evidences from the literature. *European Management Journal*, 32(3): 451–60.

Du Rietz, A. and Henrekson, M. 2000. Testing the female underperformance hypothesis. *Small Business Economics*, 14(1): 1–10.

Edelman, L., Manolova, T., Shirokova, G. and Tsukanova, T. 2016. The impact of family suport on young entrepreneurs' start-up activities. *Journal of Business Venturing*, 31(4): 428–48.

Federal Democratic Republic of Ethiopia (FDRE). 1995. The constitution of the Federal Democratic Republic of Ethiopia. Available at http://www.ethiopia.gov.et/constitution.

Federal Democratic Republic of Ethiopia (FDRE). 2011/2016. *Micro and Small Enterprise Development Policy & Strategy*. Addis Ababa.

Fox, J. 2019. Ethiopia's fight for gender equality, *RTE*. Accessed at https://www.rte.ie/news/world/2019/0425/1045550-ethiopia-women/.

García, M.-C.D. and Welter, F. 2013. Gender identities and practices: Interpreting women entrepreneurs' narratives. *International Small Business Journal*, 31(4): 384–404.

Gelan, D. and Wedajo, G. (2013). Factors affecting entrepreneurial orientation level of business women: The case of Gambela region of Ethiopia. Accessed at SSRN 2261488.

Gimenez-Nadal, J.I., Molina, J.A. and Ortega, R. 2012. Self-employed mothers and the work–family conflict. *Applied Economics*, 44(17): 2133–47.

Gioia, D.A., Corley, K.G. and Hamilton, A.L. 2013. Seeking qualitative rigor in inductive research: Notes on the Gioia methodology. *Organizational Research Methods*, 16(1): 15–31.

Gudeta, K.H. and van Engen, M. 2018. Work–life boundary management styles of women entrepreneurs in Ethiopia: 'Choice' or imposition? *Journal of Small Business and Enterprise Development*, 25(3): 368–86.

Hailemariam, A., Kroon, B. and van Veldhoven, M. 2017. Understanding motivation of women entrepreneurs in Ethiopia. In Tatiana S. Manolova, Candida G. Brush, Linda F. Edelman, Alicia Robb and Friederike Welter (eds), *Entrepreneurial Ecosystems and Growth of Women's Entrepreneurship: A Comparative Analysis*. Cheltenham, UK and Northampton, MA, USA: Edward Elgar Publishing.

Hallward-Driemeier, M. 2013. *Enterprising Women: Expanding Economic Opportunities in Africa*. Washington, DC: World Bank Publications.

Hashim, S., Naldi, L. and Markowska, M. (forthcoming). 'The Royal Award goes to…' Legitimacy processes for female-led family ventures. *Journal of Family Business Strategy*.

ILO. 2009. The informal economy in Africa: Promoting transition to formality: Challenges & Strategies. Geneva: International Labour Organization.

ILO. 2014. Effectiveness of entrepreneurship development interventions for women entrepreneurs. Geneva: International Labour Organization.

Independent. 2019. Ethiopia has made positive changes for women's equality, but will it tackle sexism and harassment head on?. *Independent*. 4 January.

Jamali, D. 2009. Constraints and opportunities facing women entrepreneurs in developing countries. *Gender in Management: An International Journal*, 24(4): 232–51.

Kalantaridis, C. and Fletcher, D. 2012. Entrepreneurship and institutional change: A research agenda. *Entrepreneurship & Regional Development*, 24(3–4): 199–214.

Kelley, D., Brush, C., Greene, P. and Litovsky, Y. 2013. Global Entrepreneurship Monitor 2012 Women's Report, 2016. Accessed at www.gemconsortium.org.

Kelley, D., Brush, C., Greene, P., Herrington, M., Ali, A. and Kew, P. 2014. Women's Entrepreneurship. Special report. Global Entrepreneurship Monitor (GEM).

Kelley, D., Brush, C., Greene, P., Herrington, M., Ali, A. and Kew, P. 2015. GEM special report: Women's entrepreneurship. Accessed at www. gemconsortium.org.

Kelley, D., Singer, S. and Herrington, M. 2012. Global Entrepreneurship Monitor 2011: Global report. London: Global Entrepreneurship Research Association. Accessed at www. gemconsortium.org.

Kew, J., Namatovu, R., Aderinto, R. and Chigunta, F. 2015. *Africa's Young Entrepreneurs: Unlocking the Potential for a Brighter Future*. GEM Special Report.

Kipnis, H. 2013. *Financing Women-Owned SMEs: A Case Study in Ethiopia*. Accessed at https://2012-2017.usaid.gov/sites/default/files/documents/1860/Financing%20Women-Owned%20SMEs.pdf.

Kirkwood, J. 2012. Family matters: Exploring the role of family in the new venture creation decision. *Journal of Small Business and Entrepreneurship*, 25(2): 141–54.

Mabsout, R. and Van Staveren, I. 2010. Disentangling bargaining power from individual and household level to institutions: Evidence on women's position in Ethiopia. *World Development*, 38(5): 783–96.

Markowska, M. and Lopez-Vega, H. 2018. Entrepreneurial storying: Winepreneurs as crafters of regional identity stories. *The International Journal of Entrepreneurship and Innovation*, 19(4): 282–97.

Marlow, S. 2009. The myth of the underperforming female entrepreneur. Paper presented at the *Institute for Small Business and Entrepreneurship* (ISBE) *Enterprising Matters*: Institute for Small Business and Entrepreneurship.

Marlow, S. 2013. Why can't a woman be more like a man? Critically evaluating contemporary analyses of the association between gender and entrepreneurship. *Regions Magazine*, 292(1): 10–11.

Mekonnen, H.D. and Cestino, J. 2017. The impact of the institutional context on women's entrepreneurship in Ethiopia: Breaking the cycle of poverty? In M. Ramirez Pasillas, E. Brundin and M. Markowska (eds), *Contextualizing Entrepreneurship in Emerging Economies and Developing Countries*. Cheltenham, UK and Northampton, MA, USA: Edward Elgar Publishing.

Naldi, L., Baù, M., Ahl, H. and Markowska, M. 2019. Gender (in)equality within the household and business start-up among mothers. *Small Business Economics*. doi:10 .1007/s11187-019-00275-1.

Ngino, T. and Maina, L. 2014. Challenges facing women entrepreneurs in Africa: The case of Kenyan women entrepreneurs. *International Journal of Advances in Management, Economics & Entrepreneurship*, 1(2): 1–8.

Richardson, P., Howarth, R. and Finnegan, G. 2004. *The Challenges of Growing Small Businesses: Insights from Women Entrepreneurs in Africa*. Geneva: International Labour Office.

Richomme-Huet, K., Vial, V. and d'Andria, A. 2013. Mumpreneurship: A new concept for an old phenomenon? *International Journal of Entrepreneurship and Small Business*, 19(2), 251–75.

Robb, A.M. and Watson, J. 2012. Gender differences in firm performance: Evidence from new ventures in the United States. *Journal of Business Venturing*, 27(5): 544–58.

Roomi, M., Harrison, P. and Beaumont-Kerridge, J. 2009. Women-owned small and medium enterprises in England: Analysis of factors influencing the growth process. *Journal of Small Business and Enterprise Development*, 16(2): 270–88.

Schwartz, S.H. 2006. A theory of cultural value orientations: Explication and applications. *Comparative Sociology*, 5(2), 137–82.

Singh, G. and Belwal, R. 2008. Entrepreneurship and SMEs in Ethiopia: Evaluating the role, prospects and problems faced by women in this emergent sector. *Gender in Management: An International Journal*, 23(2): 120–36.

Solomon, D. 2010. *Desk Review of Studies Conducted on Women Entrepreneurs of Ethiopia*. Private Sector Development Hub/ Addis Ababa Chamber of Commerce and Sectoral Associations.

UNESCAP 2017. *Fostering Women's Entrepreneurship in ASEAN: Transforming Prospects, Transforming Societies*. Accessed at https://www.unescap.org/sites/ default/files/ESCAP-FWE-ASEAN-full_0.pdf.

Wasihun, R. and Paul, I. 2010. Growth determinants of women-operated micro and small enterprises in Addis Ababa. *Journal of Sustainable Development in Africa*, 12(6): 233–46.

Watson, J. 2002. Comparing the performance of male- and female-controlled businesses: Relating outputs to inputs. *Entrepreneurship Theory and Practice*, 26(3): 91–100.

Welter, F. 2011. Contextualising entrepreneurship: Conceptual challenges and ways forward. *Entrepreneurship Theory and Practice*, 35(1): 165–84.

Welter, F. and Smallbone, D. 2008. Women's entrepreneurship from an institutional perspective: The case of Uzbekistan. *International Entrepreneurship and Management Journal*, 4(4), 505–20.

Welter, F. and Smallbone, D. 2011. Institutional perspectives on entrepreneurial behavior in challenging environment. *Journal of Small Business Management*, 49(1): 107–25.

Wilson, F., Kickul, J. and Marlino, D. 2007. Gender, entrepreneurial self-efficacy, and entrepreneurial career intentions: Implications for entrepreneurship education. *Entrepreneurship Theory and Practice*, 31(3): 387–406.

Woldegies, B.D. 2016. Research highlighting options for gender empowerment in Amhara Regional State, Ethiopia. *South African Review of Sociology*, 47(1): 58–80.

World Bank. 2018. *Country – Ethiopia. Overview.* Accessed at https://data.worldbank .org.

Wu, J., Li, Y. and Zhang, D. 2019. Identifying women's entrepreneurial barriers and empowering female entrepreneurship worldwide: A fuzzy-set QCA approach. *International Entrepreneurship and Management Journal*, 15(3): 905–28.

Zahra, S.A., Wright, M. and Abdelgawad, S.G. 2014. Contextualization and the advancement of entrepreneurship research. *International Small Business Journal*, 32(5): 479–500.

Zehra, K. and Achtenhagen, L. 2018. If policy (half-heartedly) says 'yes', but patriarchy says 'no': How the gendered institutional context in Pakistan restricts women entrepreneurship. In S.Y. Yousafzi, A. Lindgreen, S. Saeed, C. Henry and A. Fayolle (eds), *Contextual Embeddedness of Women's Entrepreneurship: Going Beyond a Gender Neutral Approach* (pp. 18–32). London: Routledge.

Zewde & Associates. 2002. *Jobs, Gender and Small Enterprises in Africa: Women Entrepreneurs in Ethiopia. A Preliminary Report.* Geneva: ILO, IFP/SEED-WEDGE, October.

6. From empowerment to emancipation: women's entrepreneurship cooking up a stir in South Africa

Bridget N. Irene, William K. Murithi, Regina Frank and Bernadette Mandawa-Bray

INTRODUCTION

While wealth creation has been considered to be the primary objective of most entrepreneurial activities, there is evidence to suggest that women's reasons for engaging in entrepreneurship go further (Zahra and Wright, 2011; Ali and Mohamud, 2013). Academic scholars have pointed out that adopting a gender-neutral approach in entrepreneurship research and policy may contribute to the failure to untangle the complex web of interwoven socio-economic and politically constructed realities created by gendered institutions, thereby failing to adequately understand and promote women's entrepreneurship (Lansky, 2000; Ahl and Marlow, 2012; Marlow and Swail, 2014).

More recently, a growing body of literature has explored women's entrepreneurship and its contextual embeddedness (Liu et al., 2019; Roos, 2019; Xheneti et al., 2019; Yousafzai et al., 2019). This follows an extensive critique of prior women's entrepreneurship literature. For instance, Fayolle et al. (2015) posit that research on women's entrepreneurship focuses more on the causal relationships between direct conditions and arrangements in the business environment (for both genders) and women's entrepreneurial activities rather than pursuing a more 'reflexive, theoretically informed' understanding of the embedded contexts. They argue that this 'universal one fit for all' approach (Aldrich, 2009) and 'extreme decontextualization' (Welter et al., 2014) does not respond to the call for the nuanced and fluid conceptualisation of gender that is deeply rooted in historical and traditional contexts (Marlow and Martinez Dy, 2018). Accordingly, we introduce key characteristics of the context of our study – South Africa – which, despite its collection of cultures and sub-cultures, can be characterised as a predominantly patriarchal society (see Coetzee, 2001). Overall, this particular context informs and sustains the normative, hierarchical subjugation that shapes women's lives and influences their opportunities (Marlow and McAdam, 2013).

In this chapter, we reinforce the importance of continued research on the bilateral relationship between gender equality and economic empowerment (World Bank, 2012). Previous empirical studies covering half a century and a variety of contexts confirm that gender equality has a positive effect on female education, employment and ultimately economic development (Hossain, 2012; Kabeer and Natali, 2013). These macro-level findings, complemented by a wealth of micro-level data, indicate that women's access to economic opportunities not only reduces the probability of household poverty but yields a variety of positive outcomes on household ability and human capital (Kabeer, 2012; World Bank, 2012). As women make up 50 per cent of the world's population, these findings provide a clear rationale for including women in economic growth processes in the pursuit of equality, inclusiveness and success of development agendas. Conversely, there is evidence to suggest that economic growth alone is often insufficient in the promotion of gender equality, as growth outcomes appear to be far more positive when juxtaposed with other factors such as access to resources and education for women (Kabeer, 2012). At the same time, recent findings (e.g. Irene et al., 2019) suggest that entrepreneurship has a positive impact on women that transcends economic growth and provides a basis and a point of departure for this chapter.

Against this backdrop, the chapter seeks to achieve the following aims. First, the chapter examines how women's entrepreneurship has been conceptualised and considers the specific socio-cultural context and perhaps traditional views of women and their roles in South African society. Second, the chapter explores the notion of emancipation as both provocative and timely in the current debates on women's entrepreneurship and empowerment. The chapter draws on conceptualisations of emancipation by Laclau (1996), Rindova et al. (2009) and Verduijn et al. (2014) as a basis to explore and interpret South African women entrepreneurs' narratives. By analysing women's entrepreneurship through the dual lens of empowerment and emancipation, this chapter offers an alternative and complementary understanding to the widely accepted, narrow view of entrepreneurship as a means for economic wealth creation. By exploring the correlation between entrepreneurship, culture and emancipation, this chapter primarily aims to answer the following research question:

RQ: To what extent does entrepreneurship contribute to the emancipation of women entrepreneurs in patriarchal societies such as South Africa?

This chapter makes a worthwhile contribution to the literature on women's entrepreneurship, empowerment, emancipation, and African entrepreneurship. Perhaps the most striking is the story of social and systemic exclusion the women tell, and the resilience demonstrated by women entrepreneurs in particular, for whom entrepreneurship not only presents a way out of poverty but also a way out of a life of total dependence and obscurity. Drawing on the narratives of these women, we paint a tapestry analogous to culture, in their life stories on the 'road to freedom' where entrepreneurship becomes the enabler to 'break free' from gendered structures and barriers.

WOMEN'S ENTREPRENEURSHIP AND EMANCIPATION IN SOUTH AFRICA

Culture and Women's Entrepreneurship

This chapter begins by discussing the concept of culture to provide context to our study on women entrepreneurs in South Africa and the importance of entrepreneurship for their empowerment and emancipation. Culture represents the fabric of every society. Although there is no universal definition of the concept due to its complex and multifaceted nature, there are various definitions of culture. For this chapter, we adopt the definition that culture refers to those customary beliefs and values that ethnic, religious and social groups transmit fairly unchanged from generation to generation (Guiso et al., 2006).

Within the area of entrepreneurship, culture has been linked to the distribution of entrepreneurial efforts in an economy (Acs and Lappi, 2019). It plays a significant role in terms of influencing entrepreneurial behaviour, with some (e.g. Anisya and Mueller, 2000) arguing that entrepreneurs tend to reflect those values that dominate their national culture. While several approaches have over time been adopted to understand cultural influences on entrepreneurship, Hofstede's conceptualisation of national culture as a six-dimensional construct (i.e. power distance, individualism, masculinity, uncertainty avoidance, long-term orientation, and indulgence) continues to dominate entrepreneurship literature (Hofstede, 1980; Hayton et al., 2002; Hofstede et al., 2010; Siu and Lo, 2013; Autio et al., 2013). Despite its wide use, Hofstede's conceptualisation has been criticised for assuming that cultures are homogeneous within nations and that all individuals belonging to a particular culture endorse the same cultural roles and meanings (Valliere, 2019). Moreover, Hofstede's theory of national culture cannot be used effectively to explain gender inequality as it masks the underlying enablers of patriarchy and diverts attention from meaningful non-violent strategies that women have adopted to deal with this real hindrance in their path to emancipation (Nagra, 2018). The above weaknesses are addressed in socio-cultural studies of entrepreneurship, often drawing on institutional theory to explore contexts (Boettke and Coyne, 2009; Welter, 2011) and analysing the link between human behaviour and institutions (see North, 1990; Hall and Jones, 1999; Acemoglu and Robinson, 2012).

While both formal and informal institutions make up the 'rules of the game' in a society (Acs and Lappi, 2019), culture represents the informal institutions.

In the context of sub-Saharan Africa, one important cultural norm that is deeply ingrained in most societies and affects women entrepreneurs is patriarchy (Titi Amayah and Haque, 2017). Patriarchal power structures in sub-Saharan Africa are particularly pervasive, also when compared to other regions of the world, resulting in high levels of gender inequality across various domains (World Economic Forum, 2017). Patriarchal societal norms and institutions are reflected in socially defined gender roles, with women and men being unequally positioned in society, both in spatial and economic terms (Bugra, 2014). A key feature of such societies is male domination and female subordination, which is evidenced in various forms and dimensions ranging for example from household to workplace suppression of women (Cinar, 2019). In response to gender discrimination in the labour market (Marlow, 1997; Buttner and Moore, 1997; Aidis et al., 2004; Smith-Hunter and Boyd, 2004; Carrasco Miro, 2016), many women tend to engage in entrepreneurial activities. Yet as women are expected to conform to stringent socio-cultural traditions, women entrepreneurs predominantly engage in business activities that are in line with their traditional reproductive roles and that are culturally acceptable (Langowitz and Minniti, 2007; Nchimbi and Chijoriga, 2009). Correspondingly, their practical needs tend to include such considerations as proximity of child-care services to the business location and focusing on business activities typically considered to be suitable for women, such as services and catering.

In their recent paper, Brush et al. (2017) bridge the gap between micro- and macro-level women's entrepreneurship studies by studying the influence of context and human capital factors (education, perceived capabilities) on business start-ups by gender and regions of varying developmental levels. Results of their multi-level study show that equality in entrepreneurship-specific capability self-perceptions plays a more important role than education levels in closing the gender gap across start-up phases and types of business processes. Nevertheless, they call for more research needed on the consideration of individual-level factors (e.g. start-up finance) and cultural factors (e.g. family role expectations).

Also, Torres and Augusto (2019) explore the link between culture and entrepreneurship by studying entrepreneurial intentions and early-stage entrepreneurial activity separately while examining different configurations of culturally endorsed implicit leadership theories and cultural practices that lead to entrepreneurial behaviour. Their findings suggest that there is no single path to stimulate entrepreneurship that works for all countries, yet also suggest the need for further fine-grained studies on cultural practices.

In summary, culture has a notable influence on women's entrepreneurship, such as women's participation in the business, business entry motives, nature of business chosen and financing of new start-ups (Basu and Altinay, 2002). It is worth noting that although the context of this study, South Africa, has unique characteristics compared to other countries in the sub-Saharan African region, the literature suggests that it is a predominantly patriarchal society (see Coetzee, 2001).

Women's Entrepreneurship and Empowerment

The need to promote women's economic independence is not new. Indeed, in 1995 the Beijing Declaration and Platform for Action declared to '[p]romote women's economic independence, including employment' (United Nations, 1995, p. 10), '[e]nsure women's equal access to economic resources, including land, credit, science and technology, vocational training, information, communication and markets, as a means to further the advancement and empowerment of women' (United Nations, 1995, pp. 11–12).

Entrepreneurship empowers women to emancipate themselves from subordination, patriarchy and labour market discrimination (Alkhaled and Berglund, 2018). The link between emancipation and empowerment has been identified as an important one in the literature, with these two divergent concepts often used interchangeably (Alkhaled and Berglund, 2018). Alkhaled and Berglund note that the conceptual pairing has emerged as an important concept in the study of women's entrepreneurship. It follows that a better understanding of the relationship between women's entrepreneurship and emancipation can be achieved by exploring the role of empowerment.

Empowerment enables people to develop capacities through which they can act successfully within the existing system and structures of power (Inglis, 1997). Accordingly, Al-Dajani and Marlow (2013) define empowerment as a continuous cycle where one's abilities to control choices, decisions and actions to act with others to effect social change are enhanced. They argue that the process of empowerment results in both economic and social independence for women entrepreneurs. While the importance of non-economic dimensions of empowerment has also been highlighted in the literature (Al-Dajani, 2007), the economic dimension has dominated the discourse on international policy in recent years (Kabeer, 2012).

The conceptualisation of women's empowerment shows clear overlaps between different definitions, with common themes that are market-related yet also with significant differences. The main difference is the extent to which economic empowerment is seen mainly as an end in itself or a means to other development goals. The second difference is that 'empowerment' is defined in some instances in purely economic terms (i.e. World Bank and

ICRW) while in other instances there is room for a spill-over into other areas of women's lives. Finally, differences exist in terms of the perception of the impact of market-related forces in women's economic empowerment. The higher the level of inequalities in the distribution of land or capital resources and education, the less likely there would be economic empowerment or poverty alleviation (Kabeer, 2012; Baker and Welter, 2018; Liu et al., 2019). In line with Al-Dajani and Marlow (2013), we argue that empowerment is a process and not a goal, the application of which is directly relevant to people who lack power by way of marginalisation, social exclusion, discrimination and social equality. Inequalities, particularly in asset distribution, influence growth outcomes.

Emancipatory Entrepreneurship

Empowerment and emancipation are often used interchangeably even though they are two divergent concepts (Alkhaled and Berglund, 2018). In line with the central tenets of this chapter, empowerment is conceptualised as a process involving an individual's development of the capacities to decide and act successfully (e.g. Inglis, 1997; Al-Dajani and Marlow, 2013). Emancipation, on the other hand, refers to the process of critically analysing, and bringing about resistance to challenge and subvert power.

For this chapter, entrepreneurship is defined as the efforts of an individual or group to create new economic, social, institutional and cultural environments (Rindova et al., 2009). This definition covers an array of change-oriented activities and projects. Entrepreneuring diverges from the broader set of change initiatives to the extent that its focus is to create something new, for example a new product or service, a new market or, more generally, a new set of possibilities for the individual or group and/or for other stakeholders. This definition is consistent with previous studies that defined entrepreneurship in terms of the creation of newness (Lumpkin and Dess, 1996; Ireland et al., 2003).

This study builds on Rindova's framework of emancipatory entrepreneuring, which may involve 'breaking free' from authority and 'breaking down' perceived limitations or obstacles. For men and women alike, engaging in entrepreneurship, therefore, is not only about exploiting existing opportunities, but also to overcome or eliminate perceived barriers in their environments (Ahl, 2006; Hu et al., 2020). Notably, these barriers may be intellectual, psychological, economic, social, institutional or cultural and are reproduced in many ways, beyond strictly economic, legal or political means (Irene, 2018). Similarly, this study explores the perceived significance of 'authoring' and 'making decisions' for women entrepreneurs when coordinating resource exchanges and managing stakeholder interpretations (Rindova et al., 2009).

As indicated above, the desire for autonomy is one of the principal factors that motivate individuals to venture into entrepreneurship (Sethi and Saxena, 2013). It has also been identified as a major motivational factor for women entrepreneurs in African contexts, given the societal view of women and the penchant for stereotyping. The drive towards autonomy refers to the desire for independence which, in effect, becomes a desire to do work of one's choice and at one's pace, defining one's own rules of the game, taking initiative, making independent and innovative choices and being responsible and accountable to oneself rather than some external authority for performance (Irene et al., 2019).

The letter 'e' in emancipation represents an abbreviation of 'ex' and denotes two distinctive but related activities: (a) breaking free (as in 'excommunicate') and (b) breaking up (as in 'my ex-husband'), hence indicating two forms of increased autonomy. While 'breaking free' indicates the desire to be free to follow one's chosen paths, 'breaking up' points towards the ambition to 'imagine and create a better world' (Sarasvathy et al., 2003, p. 155). The implications of both these derivations are embodied in theorising and conceptualising entrepreneurial activities. For instance, Baker and Nelson (2005) demonstrate in their seminal study how entrepreneurs without formal and professional education sought to break free from extreme resource constrictions by using wide-ranging sets of:

'amateurish' and 'rudimentary' skills with little regard to craft or professional boundaries' to engage in 'activities that other firms ... would reject as impermissible.' ... In so doing, they developed a deep knowledge of what they could get away with and which apparent constraints they ... [could] ignore and even disdain. (2005, p. 345)

This implies that female entrepreneurs can 'break free' by evading existing tough-pressing obstacles. The concept of 'breaking up' also resonates with the Schumpeterian view of entrepreneurship as 'creative destruction'; nonetheless, the emancipatory view transcends the Schumpeterian view by incorporating both the 'breaking free' and 'breaking up' variables. Thus, the difference between both schools of thought arises from the impact of different conceptualisations of autonomy on entrepreneurial activities (Block et al., 2017). It reiterates the fact that entrepreneurship encompasses the creation and amplification of cracks in otherwise stable (and potentially rigidified) socio-economic relationships that enforce barriers on certain types of entrepreneurial activities that the women may consider valuable (Henderson and Weiler, 2010; Block et al., 2013).

In analysing the exact nature of the need and desire for autonomy, new directions are opened for entrepreneurship research. The recognition that escaping from or removing constraints as a vital objective of women's entrepreneurship advocates for more rigorous and systematic cogitation of the interplay between the real experience of constraints and the extent to which women entrepreneurs pursue change with their entrepreneuring. Finally, the emancipatory perspective suggests extending the understanding of entrepreneurship as a driver for economic wealth creation by considering entrepreneurship as an agent for social change to understand its emancipatory potential, particularly patriarchal contexts (Simmons et al., 2014).

Such an approach will also eliminate the institutionalised distinction between regular and social entrepreneurship. It would suggest that such a distinction is unnecessary and potentially invalid, given that women entrepreneurs not only seek to improve their economic situations, but they achieve this through the impact of broader social change (Weber et al., 2008).

Emancipation and Oppression: Two Sides of the Same Coin?

Adopting a critical approach to emancipation often entails having a positive outlook as it is inclined towards liberating 'human beings from the circumstances that enslave them' (Horkheimer, 1982, p. 244). As a result, most studies seek to advance the premise of boosting all forms of freedom. Accordingly, Rindova et al. (2009) focus their research on seeking 'to broaden the focus of entrepreneurship research by drawing attention to the emancipatory aspects of entrepreneuring' (p. 478). Rather than envisioning 'entrepreneuring' simply as engaging in economic activities with profitable outcomes, they define it as 'efforts to bring about new economic, social, institutional, and cultural environments through the actions of an individual or group of individuals' (p. 477). By doing so, Rindova et al. (2009) provide a premise for the conceptualisation of entrepreneurship as an intrinsically emancipatory activity, while extending valuable insights regarding the emancipatory agendas embedded in many entrepreneurial endeavours. In opposition to this view, Verduijn and Essers (2013) question the idealisation of entrepreneurship as a 'Holy Grail' of elevation and emancipation (Verduijn et al., 2014, p. 100). This thus leaves the lingering question on the divergence between Rindova et al. (2009) and Verduijn and Essers (2013) on whether or not entrepreneurship is emancipatory.

Instead of engaging with the above contested 'either–or' debate, we assume an 'as-well-as' stance which argues that emancipation and oppression are dual forces which are in constant tension with each other, and both intrinsic potentials of entrepreneurship, in line with the arguments of Laclau (1996) and Verduijn et al. (2014) on emancipation. Laclau's starting point is 'there is no emancipation without oppression, and there is no oppression without the presence of something which is impeded in its free development by oppressive forces' (Laclau, 1996, p. 1). Accordingly, entrepreneurship could be viewed as a two-sided phenomenon, comprising emancipation and oppression in a continuously tense relationship (see Figure 6.1). Women's entrepreneurship can thus be visualised as continually leaning either towards emancipation, autonomy and freedom or towards oppression.

Verduijn and Essers (2013) apply Laclau's views on emancipation to entrepreneurship and propose distinguishing four views of the phenomenon: two macro-accounts (utopian and dystopian interpretations of entrepreneurship) and two micro-accounts (heterotopian vs paratopian views of entrepreneurship). When juxtaposed, they help understand the tension between emancipation and oppression at the macro- and micro-levels of entrepreneurship in any given context. According to Verduijn and Essers (2013), Laclau's knowledge of emancipation derives from a utopian vision of a better world, viewing emancipation as portraying a superior future reality when compared to the current reality (i.e. more just, equitable, safe, etc.). A utopian view leans towards a more macro-oriented kind of emancipation that 'tends to draw our attention to those acts that seek to fundamentally challenge broader social structural modes of domination' (Huault et al., 2014, p. 42). The utopians define emancipation as the act of liberating 'human beings from the circumstances that enslave them' (Horkheimer, 1982, p. 244). Their view of entrepreneurship focuses on how it can be used to address the larger social-structural challenges (Huault et al., 2014). Examples of this view include reports specifying entrepreneurship as a societal agent for poverty alleviation, wealth creation and well-being (Sarasvathy and Venkataraman, 2011). The utopian view is hinged on the notion that it would be possible, though not easy, to create conducive environments for people to live freely, uninterrupted by oppressive relations of power.

To develop a nuanced understanding of women's entrepreneurship in South Africa, we study women's reflections on their entrepreneurial journeys as part of their lived experiences, including their goals, ambitions and constraints. Accordingly, for this study, a heterotopian view of entrepreneurship is adopted; here the focus is on micro-manifestations of emancipation as typified by the localised engagement in everyday practices through which entrepreneurs create local environments of empowerment, struggles towards freedom and liberation, and alternative identity politics (i.e. 'hetero-topia').

In summary, drawing on Laclau's (1996) theory of emancipation, the framework of emancipatory entrepreneuring by Rindova et al. (2009) and extending the work of Verduijn et al. (2014), we propose the following theoretical framework to conceptualise the tensions of women's entrepreneurship in South Africa (Figure 6.1):

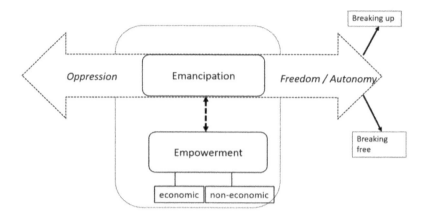

Figure 6.1   *Theoretical framework for women's entrepreneurship in South Africa*

The Context: Women's Entrepreneurship in South Africa

This chapter presents an analysis of women's entrepreneurship in South Africa, thereby responding to the call for further research in underexplored contexts, particularly in the Global South. This study draws on empirical data collected from urban women entrepreneurs in South Africa based on our belief that even this particular, delimited geographic context can offer rich research opportunities to further the understanding the of socio-cultural influences on women's entrepreneurship. This focus also allows us to present, discuss and illustrate our findings in a more meaningful way, as well as raise questions for directions for future research.

   South Africa is a multicultural, multiracial and deeply segregated country in terms of the rural and urban divide. While its economic advancement compared to other countries in the sub-Saharan Africa region is notable, South Africa remains characterised by high levels of unemployment, poverty, crime and inequality (Ncanywa, 2019). Statistics show that between 2000 and 2018, the unemployment rate in South Africa averaged 26 per cent, with around 38 per cent being concentrated in the age group 15–34 (StatsSA, 2018). The South African government implemented several interventions to address these challenges, including strategies and goals summarised in the country's National Development Plan Vision 2030 (Ncanywa, 2019). Notwithstanding that this saw a notable reduction in poverty levels since the birth of democracy in 1994, high levels of poverty, inequality and unemployment lingered (Davis and Thurlow, 2010). This persistence has defined the role of entrepreneurship as a means of unlocking the potential of the South African economy for employment creation and ultimately poverty and inequality reduction.

Government efforts have therefore been focused on developing entrepreneurship (especially SMEs), an area where women generally form the majority of the informal and less active sectors (Okeke-Uzodike, 2019). Women account for 51 per cent of South Africa's population, and about 35.4 per cent of its economically active population (StatsSA, 2018). In post-apartheid South Africa, unemployment rates for males from poorer households have led to increased participation of women in entrepreneurial activities (Casale and Posel, 2005). It follows that women entrepreneurs play an important role in South Africa's economy. Consequently, the South African government has implemented deliberate public policies and strategies aimed at promoting women's empowerment and gender equality in business, including considerable financial packages in the form of grants, training and consultative services and other funding to women-owned MSMEs (Okeke-Uzodike, 2019). Unfortunately, these efforts have not resulted in a corresponding increase in the inclusion of women in the main formal sectors, with some (e.g. Okeke-Uzodike, 2019) observing that South African women experience notable gender-based income gaps compared to men. A study on women entrepreneurs in Kwazulu Natal notes that women across South Africa are generally marginalised, with economic activities across most sectors still dominated by men (Okeke-Uzodike et al., 2018). This was attributed to historical cultural practices that saw women restricted to roles associated with domestic responsibilities. In South Africa, historical policies and laws also deliberately favoured men, predominantly white men (Mathur-Helm, 2004). Evidently, despite consistent calls for the need to eliminate gender inequality and empower and emancipate women, traditional institutions and practices that hail males as the dominant gender still hold ground in most societies (Hartmann, 2010), including South Africa.

To further understand women's entrepreneurship in the tension between oppression, emancipation and empowerment, we therefore draw on the experiences of women entrepreneurs in South Africa to gain an insight into how women turn to entrepreneurship as a means of emancipation from perceived gender barriers imposed by patriarchal societal norms and values.

METHODOLOGY

Interpretive Phenomenological Approach (IPA)

While prior studies have investigated entrepreneurship as a source of emancipation (e.g. Rindova et al., 2009; Jennings et al., 2016) there is a dearth of empirical research on emancipatory women's entrepreneurship specifically in Africa. This establishes a need to investigate the overarching motivation for African women engagement in entrepreneurship and to explore its role for women to achieve economic freedom and (further) emancipation (Irene, 2018).

In this study, an interpretive phenomenological approach (IPA) was adopted. IPA is a qualitative approach that is used to study participants' lived experiences to understand what's hidden in them (Smith and Osborn, 2015). IPA allows the generation of an in-depth understanding of the potential of entrepreneurial behaviours of women as a tool to overcome cultural and contextual environment using data collected in the Republic of South Africa, hence responding to the call by Cálas et al. (2009) to reframe entrepreneurship from 'an economic activity with possible social change outcomes' to 'entrepreneurship as a social change activity with a variety of possible outcomes.'

IPA has become a dominant qualitative research method in social sciences because it 'recognizes that humans are sense-making organisms' (Smith and Osborn, 2015, p. 41). This methodological approach enables an in-depth understanding of women's perceptions of entrepreneurship and the correlation between entrepreneurship and culture (Goulding, 2005).

Exploring the correlation between entrepreneurship and forms of emancipation (Rindova et al., 2009), the IPA methodology helps interpret the narratives and understand the lived experiences of the African women entrepreneurs and the complexities they face. Using data from interview narratives, insight is gained into cultural and socioeconomic aspects of women's entrepreneurship.

Sampling Process and Data Collection

The sample for this research was drawn from a population of South African women entrepreneurs using purposive and snowballing sampling techniques. Adopting IPA, we sought to establish a purposeful sample of respondents based in South Africa (Patton and Cochran, 2002) with the experience and characteristics to provide us with 'rich, fine-grained and insightful data'.

Data were collected by face-to-face interviews involving 60 women entrepreneurs and 10 focus group discussions involving 8–10 participants per session. The total sample size is 152 (combined). The criteria for inclusion included: (a) women who founded their own business; (b) businesses two years old or more; (c) women with family responsibilities. The data were collected through various networks including the Businesswomen's Association of South Africa (BWA), Fine Women, Leading Women of Africa (LWA) and the Department of Trade and Industry (DTI).

The first phase of the data collection involved face-to-face semi-structured interviews that lasted on average one and a half hours, each providing 'rich, fine-grained and insightful data' (Al-Dajani et al., 2015). The interviews were tape-recorded and transcribed by a professional with a good understanding of the local accent. To ensure the validity of the data, upon completion of the transcribing process, the transcripts were sent to the participants to ensure that their thoughts, feelings and perceptions were adequately captured. The second phase of data collection involved focus group interviews with a selected group of women entrepreneurs. Focus groups are considered useful for eliciting feedback on sensitive issues (Madriz, 2003). Thus, the focus groups provided an opportunity for interaction between the interviewer and participants, which is appropriate as a pre-test and for exploration (Cyr, 2016). Through the focus groups, researchers were able to observe how the participants expressed disapproval or objections as well as their sensitivity on some of the traditional-cultural practices (Cyr, 2016). This allowed the triangulation of the individual views and experiences of the women entrepreneurs (Kitzinger, 1994). Using these two data collection methods the study was able to capture some of the cultural and contextual challenges that the women entrepreneurs encountered in South Africa, the factors that influenced their decisions to start businesses, and evidence relating to emancipation. Therefore, careful consideration was made to capture the meanings of the respondents' experiences adequately, thus allowing and establishing relationships that may ordinarily go unnoticed to come to the fore (Irene, 2016).

Data Analysis

Laclau's (1996) and Rindova et al.'s (2009) conceptualisations of emancipation form the basis for the data analysis. The data are analysed according to the interpretative phenomenological approach (IPA) proposed by Smith (2004). This involves examining each participant's response in detail as to how their personal experience addresses the research questions. The main research question that guided this study was 'to what extent does entrepreneurship contribute to the emancipation of women entrepreneurs in patriarchal societies such as South Africa?' Speaking with our respondents, this 'translated' into open-ended questions on why they decided to start their businesses; how they perceived entrepreneurship, in particular in the context of their society-prescribed roles as home-makers and caregivers in South Africa; and what were the unique influences of entrepreneurship on 'breaking free' from their gendered socio-cultural standing.

Once transcribed, the data were transferred to N'Vivo, and a search conducted for themes and patterns (Alkhaled and Berglund, 2018). The first stage was to establish codes within the N'Vivo (see Table 6.1), based on key drivers of women's entrepreneurship and constructs of emancipation. The second stage involved revisiting the data to identify patterns. During the two stages of analysis, the co-authors had regular interaction sessions in order to ensure that the analysis process was able to identify and preserve the cultural integrity

Table 6.1   Reference points by age groups (interviews)

All Variables	Age Group 20–30	Age Group 31–40	Age Group 41–50	Age Group 51–60	Reference points (**)
Socio-cultural Freedom	5	19	35	12	71
Financial or Economic Freedom	5	10	10	2	27
Breaking Up	3	12	18	12	45
Breaking Free	3	8	15	8	34
Gender Roles	2	7	13	15	37
Traditional Views	1	5	13	11	30
Gender Stereotyping	2	4	8	6	20
Patriarchy	2	3	11	0	16
Training and Seminars	3	8	16	9	36
Policies	6	12	11	6	35
Access to Resources	3	11	8	5	27
Education (formal and informal)	4	14	7	2	27
Mentoring	1	5	9	1	16
Networking	1	3	4	0	8
Number of respondents	**13**	**54**	**64**	**21**	**152**
% of total respondents	8%	36%	42%	14%	100%

Notes: ** indicates the number of related quotes found in the data. Participants may have made more than one statement that could be associated with the nodes.

of the empirical context while understanding and reflecting on the limitations of the socially constructed situation (Alkhaled and Berglund, 2018). This also allowed the researchers to exercise reflexivity throughout the process, highlighting any potential deviations from the objectives of the study and inevitable limitations that could have affected the process of analysis (Essers, 2009).

FINDINGS AND DISCUSSION

This study aimed to gain deeper insights into the role of entrepreneurship as an emancipatory agent for women in traditional African contexts. It explored women's perceptions of patriarchal dominance resulting from the accumulation of economic, social and cultural capital. Findings disclose the power relations within the realities in which women entrepreneurs operate. Additionally, this study contributes to a more nuanced understanding of emancipation, namely in respect of areas where women wish to seek autonomy or freedom from, breaking free and breaking up (see Figure 6.1).

The Link between Empowerment and Emancipation

The terms 'empowerment' and 'emancipation' are often used interchangeably even though they are two divergent concepts (Alkhaled and Berglund, 2018). In line with the central tenets of this chapter, empowerment is conceptualised as a process involving an individual's development of the capacities to decide and act successfully (e.g. Inglis, 1997; Al-Dajani and Marlow, 2013). In the fields of development economics, empowerment is often equated with economic empowerment only. Emancipation, on the other hand, refers to the process of critically analysing, and bringing about resistance to challenge and subvert power. This distinction allows researchers to query what the 'social turn' might mean for women entrepreneurs and see what potential shortcomings there may be in this turn.

There is a renewed and growing call for a shift in the focus of women's entrepreneurship as a 'desirable' economic activity with predominantly positive outcomes to a focus on the dark side of entrepreneurship. In analysing the two-headed phenomenon of empowerment and emancipation while also considering non-economic benefits and context, we find that both concepts are inseparable. Empowerment is embedded in emancipation, and emancipation is triggered when individuals develop the capabilities to 'successfully act within existing systems and structures of power'. Using the interpretive phenomenological approach (IPA), we apply these concepts to the narratives of 152 women entrepreneurs to explore their perceptions on their empowerment as well as their views on how the government or other stakeholders could empower them further.

The findings revealed six main areas of capacity building consistent with the literature that women's entrepreneurial motivations transcend economic benefits and emphasised the importance of formal contexts such as policies as well as informal institutional contexts such as traditions and norms (Al-Dajani and Marlow, 2013; Al-Dajani et al., 2015). The data analysis showed that women considered entrepreneurship as a place where they experienced 'freedom' en route to emancipation. Responses helped us to establish which capabilities (these) women require to successfully build resistance through which they could subvert existing powers as a means to emancipate themselves.

Women considered the following as empowering: (a) access to resources; (b) education (formal and informal); (c) mentorship; (d) networking; (e) government policies; and (f) training and seminars. The data showed that education (formal and informal) as well as training and seminars, were dominant themes (23 per cent and 38 per cent). This indicates that women entrepreneurs consider the acquisition of knowledge more empowering than financial assistance, as illustrated by the following quotes:

> Women should go for training. We need training more than we need money. (Retailer)

> For some reason, the government thinks that they can just keep throwing money at women and that will settle everything. What is the difference, if we are not collecting from the government, we will collect from the men? At the end of the day, we still don't have our own. I believe in the Chinese saying: Don't give me fish, teach me how to fish. If I know how to get the money for myself, then I don't need to wait for the government or for a man to give me. (Contractor)

Essentially, they considered their subservient roles to be synonymous with spousal over-dependence which is born out of their inability to fend for themselves.

These sentiments were also echoed by most of the respondents as they advocated for education and training (Table 6.2). It must also be noted that while there are no official restrictions to the education of the girl child, in most cases the cost of training of more than one child is often too much for parents who are left with no choice but to educate only some of their children. Typically, this leads parents to choose their sons to be educated rather than their daughters (Irene and Hussain, 2020).

Government policies featured high in interview responses, with women indicating that current policies were neither inadequate nor did they effectively empower businesswomen:

> Government need to come back to us with skills and how to go further with upgrading and improving our business because we are less skilled. (Hairdresser)

> There is a lot of bureaucracy, there's a lot of corruption and there's also a lot of frustration with our BEE codes. (Retailer)

> I think the legislation in our country is disabling for businesses. (Lawyer)

> Government should help women to feel confident in themselves by making resources available to them. (Retailer)

The inability to access resources was also mentioned as a factor that further hinders women's empowerment. This is consistent with the literature on women entrepreneurs that highlights access to finance as a major challenge facing women (Irene et al., 2019).

Table 6.2   *Reference points for empowerment*

Empowerment Nodes	Source Number*	Reference Point**	Direct Quotes
Access to Resources	25	25	'There is [*sic*] very little opportunities for women post-apartheid especially as most of us don't have any degrees. We don't have money, no property that can be used to borrow money for business. We have no choice but to depend on men for money and some women remain in abusive relationships because they cannot stand on their own feet, they need the men.' 'I had to keep on fighting for the business to be sustained and the banks and creditors to believe in my business, especially because I am a woman. If I were a man, it would have been different. That is why it was very important for me to be successful in the business so that I can raise my head high and say, I am a woman and I did it.' (Contractor)
Education (formal and informal)	21	27	'I think you need to have your basic education and also to know what's going on in the world so that you know how to run a business.' 'Yes, they need to empower women, to give them tools to run a business. They need to give them education.' (Restaurant owner) 'Obviously if you have a limiting culture then that could play a role but if you are educated then you should be able to do whatever you want to do.' (Retailer)
Mentorship	13	16	'I would be lying if I say I don't have a mentor. It is important that you sometimes have a sounding board. As an entrepreneur, you find that sometimes when there are challenges, you need to just bounce them off someone, because it gives you a bit of perspective and I mean when you are running as an entrepreneur, it gives you a mental challenge; if you don't have a sounding board especially as a woman, it is going to be really challenging.' (Wholesaler)
Networking	6	8	'Networking is absolutely crucial. We wouldn't be where we are today without that. I mean our website is not great, it doesn't do half the work that it needs to do, and we don't do any advertising or cold calling but I'm busy all the time because of my networks.' (PR consultant)

Empowerment			Direct Quotes
Nodes	Source Number*	Reference Point**	
Government Policies	32	35	'The Govt keep making promises they never keep. Every year they tell us all the good things they plan for businesswomen but year in year out, we wait and nothing. Then come up with new things that we must comply with to qualify for the help. The banks don't borrow [*sic*] us money because we don't have property. How can we get property without money to pay for the property? The govt should help us even if it is to train us and let us take care of our families.' (Preschool owner)
Training and Seminars	34	35	'We're not like men, it is a vicious world for women, that is why I think women should be trained.' (Interior decorator) 'And my weaknesses are my lack of formal business training.' (Wholesaler) 'Us women, we mostly start our businesses without any training or skills to run a business. Women are opening a lot of businesses and employing a lot of people, but they are also struggling due to lack of knowledge. The government should step in and provide the opportunity for us to develop our skills and compete with men on the same level.' (Restaurateur)
Total	131	146	

Notes: * indicates the responses; ** indicates the number of related quotes found in the data. Participants may have made more than one statement that could be associated with the nodes.

Emancipation of South African Women Entrepreneurs

Women are faced with formal and informal institutional constraints at both macro and micro levels which lead to a sense of agency in their engagement in entrepreneurial activities (Brush et al., 2017). In exploring emancipation empirically, this study focuses on two elements: (a) 'breaking free' by evading existing tough-pressing obstacles; and (b) 'breaking up' by striving to imagine and create a better world (Rindova et al., 2009).

We interviewed women from different age and cultural groups as well as different socio-economic groups. Our findings reveal that narratives of women between the ages of 30 and 50 included sentiments that can be associated with the concepts of breaking up and breaking free, while younger women (under the age of 20) and older women (over 50) did not comment on respective issues. One explanation could be that younger women are still under or just coming out of the protective care of their parents and have not fully grasped or experienced some of the challenges mentioned in this study. As for older women, we argue that there is a sense of acceptance and feeling that there is nothing that can be done to change the social structures and their reality.

> I think that was in the day; because you see now that the women are more successful, more independent, I think women are definitely taking over. I think it is a lot of both because before now there was [*sic*] all these laws about women can't do this or can't do that? But I also think it has a bit of negative influence with women sitting down and not wanting to do anything. (Over 50 years old)

> So there was that and I also worked in engineering and architecture for some years and that's a very male-dominated world. And I don't know how, I think it's just my personality, but I didn't come out of that world thinking that I was just a pretty young thing, I could hold my own against anybody who was thinking I am just a young girlie in business. And I did have quite a lot of supporters who were men who could see me for my ability to do stuff, like one of my mentors, he was a businessman and he was very supportive of me when I wanted to go into business. I think in Southern Africa and mostly in Africa in general, women have a much more subservient role in the society and I don't make it a big thing but I'm not afraid to stand up to people if I feel that they are not giving me the credit that I deserve even though I'm a woman. (30–40 years old)

The reference points for the nodes coding and some sample quotes are displayed in Table 6.3.

The above confirms that women's perception of freedom aligns with the notion of entrepreneuring-as-emancipatory, namely 'pursuit of freedom and autonomy relative to an existing status quo ... [seeking] to disrupt the status quo and change her position in the social order ... and ... the social order itself' (Rindova et al., 2009, p. 478).

Table 6.3   *Reference points for emancipation*

Emancipation			Direct Quotes
Nodes	Source Number*	Reference Point**	
Breaking Free	32	34	'This is what my life was like, and my mother's experience too, until I decided I had had enough. I don't want my daughter to experience this too, so the cycle has to be broken.' (Contractor)
			'I need to have financial independence and freedom do things my way and to be a role model for my daughters and their friends.' (Consultant)
			'I'm very passionate about our entrepreneurship because I think our country relies on it. The big corporations (such as the one I worked for) do not understand how to support small business especially those in the informal economy. And that is where women businesses are in this country.' (Incubator owner)
			'That means women will not get the support to help them break free from all these limiting forces in our culture.' (Contractor)
Breaking Up	40	45	'Most people think that empowerment is money alone. No, giving people the platform to make decisions concerning their lives, their health, their careers, actually, about everything. That is empowerment. That is what women need.' (Optometrist)
			'Have you ever wondered why there is even a glass ceiling? It is because they want to maintain the status quo at home, and they believe empowering women will shift that balance. It is just men looking out for men. That is why we need to break this system and end the discrimination against women.' (Incubator owner)
			'Most of us are not educated, that is why the men treat us the way they want. We need the education so we can be on an equal level with the men and also be able to make better decisions.' (Contractor)
Total	72	79	

Notes: * indicates the responses; ** indicates the number of related quotes found in the data.
Participants may have made more than one statement that could be associated with the nodes.

The narratives of our participants show how they have taken their engagement in entrepreneurship into context and crafted a complex process on the road to emancipation. In line with Rindova et al. (2009), these narratives reveal that most women's journey to emancipation began with a shift in the 'status quo' in their experience of different forms of patriarchy (explicit or implied) in the legal systems, in the workplace, in society or at home.

The desire for autonomy is a principal factor in women's motivation to engage in entrepreneurial activities and it refers to the desire for independence which, in effect, becomes a desire to do work of one's choice and at one's pace, defining one's own rules of the game, taking initiative, making independent and innovative choices and being responsible and accountable to oneself rather than some external authority for performance (Irene et al., 2019). Our data also indicate that the processes of 'breaking up' and 'breaking free' are actualised through both self-empowerment and the empowerment of others; namely, women entrepreneurs contribute to their personal development and the development of others, thereby creating and indeed accelerating social change. Women entrepreneurs in South Africa believe in 'giving back' and 'freeing others' to change potential perspectives, to develop opportunities for other women, and create potential work. Our findings showed that women were more inclined to employ women when setting up their businesses.

The findings also reveal that more women (66 per cent) indicated they were motivated by socio-cultural factors. This is also an indication of women breaking free from the age-old saying that a woman's place is in the kitchen. Women no longer desire to be considered as homemakers whose reward is their children and a lifetime of provision; they want to be acknowledged for their attributes and achievements just as much as men. According to some respondents:

> My father made a lot of money, so I was well off, suddenly my mother found herself in a place where she has kids to look after and she has no skills and no personal income because it all belonged to my father and he took it all away. I think seeing my mother coming from this gorgeous woman where she had everything to this woman that was broken and had no skills, I mean she didn't even know how to cook properly, suddenly she was thrown into this place where she had no money, and she couldn't get a job, and I just said to myself 'I would never be that woman'. That I will be so reliant on a man that if something goes wrong, I just can't do anything. That experience is not responsible for my achievements, but it did lighten me up to the fact that I am never, ever going to be like that. I will never be that dependent on any man. (Incubator owner)

> Success means freedom for me to express who I am and also for me to uplift and support others. I've done a lot of work in social development, a lot of work with the poorest of the poor to help them identify opportunities; unfortunately, I became poor through that. It's really about expressing who I am, seeing opportunities, exploring those opportunities but bringing others with me. I pride myself when people who

had no idea about energy, who had no idea about the environment could suddenly learn about it and then become converts. If I can put it that way. (Preschool owner)

Now, I make more money than working for someone else and I have the flexibility I need to care for my kids. I have also earned the respect of a lot of people who never thought anything of me when I was just a struggling mother of three. Now they refer to me as a businesswoman and treat me as such. (Boutique owner)

For us to understand the notion of 'breaking up' and 'breaking free' in the context of African women entrepreneurs, the role of patriarchy (a cultural norm) had to be explored. In particular, South African women's desire for emancipation can best be understood in the context of the prevailing patriarchal culture in South Africa. Interestingly, 'patriarchy' as such was rarely mentioned by women. This may be a reflection of the infancy of gender equality in general in South Africa, with a lack of informed and critical public debate on patriarchy and emancipation in mainstream media.

It also confirms the relevance and appropriateness of IPA as a research method when collecting and analysing data in contexts where respondents are unfamiliar with certain terminology. Our findings confirm existing discussions about patriarchy that explain women's need to break free from institutional barriers and portray emancipation and empowerment as processes comprising everyday practices of power and dominance within formal and informal institutional structures in which women entrepreneurs operate.

In the existing entrepreneurship literature, patriarchal socio-cultural values and associated gender ideologies tend to be associated negatively with women's entrepreneurship (Al-Dajani and Marlow, 2010; Tlaiss, 2015). This is in line with our findings which confirm prior research on African women entrepreneurs that mostly portray gender ideologies and socio-cultural values as factors that inhibit women and limit their choices (Tlaiss, 2015; Irene, 2018). Our participants' narratives indicate a positive correlation between gender roles, gender stereotyping and (the lack of) socio-cultural freedom. Accordingly, patriarchy can also be considered as an enabler for gender roles and traditional views of women, and unequal access to resources and education.

According to some participants:

And the women are very conservative, and they are expected to stay home and just bring up the children, and they are not encouraged to have careers. They are not encouraged to become entrepreneurs; they are actually encouraged to be housewives. (Hairdresser)

There is a notion that every money [*sic*] a woman has is from a man and if she does not submit to the authority of men, she cannot have any money. I watched my mother as I was growing up. She never had anything except the ones [*sic*] my father gave her, and she could not even afford to buy [a] present for us without asking money from him. (Lawyer)

In my culture, the greatest achievement you can have as a woman is to be married to someone 'important' while the men are recognised and praised for their achievements. Even when you have money as a woman, it is deemed to have come from the men. (Wholesaler)

In SA women have subjective freedom where you are given consideration but only to a certain extent. We are continuously living in the shadow of the men. (Contractor)

How can you say there is gender equality when girls are disadvantaged from birth? In my culture, when a man says I have 2 and a half children, he means he has 2 sons and a daughter. The daughter is half a child. The only value she brings is the dowry he will collect when he marries her off and the money he will continue to get from his in-laws for as long as she remains married. (Retailer)

The reference points for the nodes coding and some sample quotes are displayed in Table 6.4.

Notably, older respondents tended to express their desire for 'freedom' and 'autonomy', their need to 'break free' from existing structures more poignantly than younger respondents. Such thoughts are voiced together with their preference for access to further training than finance, to further their businesses. This can be interpreted in two ways: (a) older women are survivors of the Apartheid regime of enslavement and inaccessibility of education for the black and minority communities, thus, they continue to fight to 'break free' post-Apartheid; (b) younger women have access to education and have not experienced inequality to the extent that the older women have. While this mirrors prior studies (e.g. Kabeer, 2013), more work needs to be done to understand fully the correlation and interdependencies between these influencing factors. Similarly, it would be worthwhile investigating if and how the South African culture has changed post-Apartheid, and the influences of such socio-historical factors on women's entrepreneurship throughout the country.

IMPLICATIONS AND CONCLUSIONS

This chapter contributes to the discourse on the emancipatory potential of entrepreneurship for women, with a particular focus on women's entrepreneurship in patriarchal societies such as South Africa. By considering the socio-cultural context of women entrepreneurs and analysing their stories and perspectives, our study shows how women's motivations and decisions to engage in entrepreneurial activities go beyond their need of economic subsistence, namely embracing their much broader need for socio-cultural freedom and autonomy. Findings indicate the potential of entrepreneurship to eliminate

Table 6.4   *Reference points for freedom or autonomy*

Nodes	Freedom		Direct Quotes
	Source Number*	Reference Point**	
Socio-cultural	72	119	'Having my own business gives me freedom and confidence as I see the way people have treated me differently since I started my own business. Even my husband's attitude is now more supportive compared to when I was doing the 9–5 job.' (Building contractor)
			'In my culture, the greatest achievement you can have as a woman is to be married to someone "important" while the men are recognised and praised for their achievements. Even when you have money as a woman, it is deemed to have come from the men. I started my business so I can be independent and gain social recognition or status if you wish.' (Restaurateur)
			'One of my aunts is very well respected and highly successful. I see the way she is respected by so many people in our society to the exclusion of all other women. It made me realise that while they always say a woman's place is in the kitchen, a successful woman will command the respect of men just like my aunt. She is a major source of inspiration and I aspire to be like her rather than just be an invisible Influencer.' (Beautician)
Financial and Economic	21	25	'I wanted to work for myself as I was not earning enough from my previous job. I could never do enough with the money, yet it was demanding and not giving me enough time to fulfil my role at home.' (Hairdresser)
			'For me, success means being financially and emotionally independent.' (Contractor)
Total	93	144	

Notes: * indicates the responses; ** indicates the number of related quotes found in the data.
Participants may have made more than one statement that could be associated with the nodes.

a myriad of perceived barriers to women participating fully in economic and social activities. Accordingly, this study extends the debate beyond the economic empowerment of women entrepreneurs and uncovers the intangible dimensions of empowerment and emancipation that entrepreneurship offers to South African women.

This study contributes to the analytical scholarship on women's engagement with entrepreneurship by clearly distinguishing between empowerment as a process for achieving individual autonomy within structures, and emancipation as an act of dismantling social restrictions so that this freedom can be extended to others within the society. Findings of this study support previous studies that entrepreneurship is undeniably an agent of change for empowerment and emancipation of women in general, in emerging economies.

Whilst shining light on women's entrepreneurship in South Africa, this study is not without its limitations. These can, however, be addressed through further research. First, the chapter presents the perceptions of only 152 women entrepreneurs, with a large number of these reached through business networks such as the Businesswomen's Association of South Africa (BWA), Leading Women of Africa (LWA) and the Department of Trade and Industry (DTI). Accordingly, there may be a bias towards 'better-connected' urban women entrepreneurs. Future studies may explore a greater number of entrepreneurs in more diverse settings, namely in rural and different built environments.

Second, for this study, we didn't capture the ethnicity, religion and several other socio-demographic factors of our respondents, therefore potential questions on how these factors could shape women's entrepreneurship have not been addressed. However, South Africa is a very diverse country, with a mixed population of different ethnicities and heritages. Future research could investigate, in greater depth, if and how ethnicity, religion and changing socio-demographic and socio-cultural factors influence women's entrepreneurship across South Africa. Similarly, an extensive multi-level study building on Laclau's four views of emancipation could produce a comprehensive understanding of systemic and individual factors explaining levels of entrepreneurship in South Africa.

Third, comparative studies exploring women's entrepreneurship in different African countries could further contribute to a more general appreciation of influences on and of women's entrepreneurship across the continent.

Finally, detailed studies of women's entrepreneurship across different patriarchal (and/or matriarchal) societies could contribute towards more generalisable yet situated gendered entrepreneurship theory-building.

The findings will allow the development of a more nuanced understanding of women's entrepreneurship worldwide, advancing the entrepreneurship research and gender studies, and supporting respective policy development.

REFERENCES

Acemoglu, D. and J.A. Robinson (2012), *Why Nations Fail: The Origins of Power, Prosperity and Poverty* (1st edn), New York: Crown.

Acs, Z. and E. Lappi (2019), 'Entrepreneurship, culture and the epigenetic revolution: A research note', *Small Business Economics*, accessed at https://doi.org/10.1007/s11187-019-00230-0.

Ahl, H. (2006), 'Why research on women entrepreneurs needs new directions', *Entrepreneurship Theory & Practice*, **30** (5), 595–621.

Ahl, H. and S. Marlow (2012), 'Exploring the dynamics of gender, feminism and entrepreneurship: Advancing debate to escape a dead-end?', *Organization*, **19** (5), 543–62.

Aidis, R., K. Bishop, S. Ederveen, J. Fidrmuc, J.P. Fidrmuc, J. Köllö, T. Mickiewicz et al. (2004), 'Wage and employment decisions of enterprises in downsized industries', WIFO Studies, WIFO, no. 25287, March.

Al-Dajani, H. (2007), 'Women's empowerment: A comparison between non-profit and for-profit approaches in empowering home-based women producers', unpublished PhD thesis, University of Strathclyde, Glasgow.

Al-Dajani, H. and S. Marlow (2010), 'Impact of women's home-based enterprise on family dynamics: Evidence from Jordan', *International Small Business Journal*, **28** (5), 503–24.

Al-Dajani, H. and S. Marlow (2013), 'Empowerment and entrepreneurship: A theoretical framework', *International Journal of Entrepreneurial Behaviour & Research*, **19** (5), 503–24.

Al-Dajani, H., S. Carter, E. Shaw and S. Marlow (2015), 'Entrepreneurship among the displaced and dispossessed: Exploring the limits of emancipatory entrepreneuring', *British Journal of Management*, **26** (4), 713–30.

Aldrich, H. (2009), 'Lost in space, out of time: Why and how we should study organizations comparatively', in B. King, T. Felin and D. Whetten (eds), *Studying Differences Between Organizations: Comparative Approaches to Organizational Research* (Research in the Sociology of Organizations, Vol. 26), Bingley: Emerald Group Publishing Limited, pp. 21–44.

Ali, A.Y.S. and H.A. Mohamud (2013), 'Motivational factors and performance of women entrepreneurs in Somalia', *Journal of Education and Practice*, **4** (17), 47–53.

Alkhaled, S. and K. Berglund (2018), '"And now I'm free": Women's empowerment and emancipation through entrepreneurship in Saudi Arabia and Sweden', *Entrepreneurship & Regional Development*, **30** (7–8), 877–900.

Anisya, T.S. and S.L. Mueller (2000), 'A case for comparative entrepreneurship: Assessing the relevance of culture', *Journal of International Business Studies*, **31** (2), 287–301.

Autio, E., S. Pathak and K. Wennberg (2013), 'Consequences of cultural practices for entrepreneurial behaviours', *Journal of International Business Studies*, **44**, 334–62.

Baker, T. and R.E. Nelson (2005), 'Creating something from nothing: Resource construction through entrepreneurial bricolage', *Administrative Science Quarterly*, **50** (3), 329–66.

Baker, T. and F. Welter (2018), 'Contextual entrepreneurship: An interdisciplinary perspective', *Foundations and Trends® in Entrepreneurship*, **14** (4), 357–426.

Basu, A. and E. Altinay (2002), 'The interaction between culture and entrepreneurship in London's immigrant business', *International Small Business Journal*, **20** (4), 371–93.

Block, J.H., C.O. Fisch and M. Van Praag (2017), 'The Schumpeterian entrepreneur: A review of the empirical evidence on the antecedents, behaviour and consequences of innovative entrepreneurship', *Industry and Innovation*, **24** (1), 61–95.

Block, J.H., R. Thurik and H. Zhou (2013), 'What turns knowledge into innovative products? The role of entrepreneurship and knowledge spillovers', *Journal of Evolutionary Economics*, **23** (4), 693–718.

Boettke, P.J. and C.J. Coyne (2009), 'Context matters: Institutions and entrepreneurship', *Foundation and Trends in Entrepreneurship*, **5** (3), 135–209.

Brush, C., A. Ali, D. Kelley and P. Greene (2017), 'The influence of human capital factors and context of women's entrepreneurship: Which matters more?', *Journal of Business Venturing Insights*, **8** (C), 105–13.

Bugra, A. (2014), 'Revisiting the Wollstonecraft dilemma in the context of conservative liberalism: The case of female employment in Turkey', *Social Politics: International Studies in Gender, State & Society*, **21** (1), 148–66.

Buttner, H.E. and D.P. Moore (1997), 'Women's organizational exodus to entrepreneurship: Self-reported motivations and correlates with success', *Journal of Small Business Management*, **35** (1), 34–46.

Cálas, M.B., L. Smircich and K.A. Bourne (2009), 'Extending the boundaries: Reframing "entrepreneurship as social change" through feminist perspectives', *Academy of Management Review*, **34** (3), 552–69.

Carrasco Miro, G. (2016), *Africa Human Development Report 2016: Accelerating Gender Equality and Women's Empowerment in Africa*, New York: UNDP.

Casale, D. and D. Posel (2005), 'Women and the economy: How far have we come?', *Agenda*, **19** (64), 21–9.

Cinar, K. (2019), 'Women's entrepreneurship in patriarchal societies', in F. Tomos, N. Kumar, N. Clifton and D. Hyams-Ssekasi (eds), *Women Entrepreneurs and Strategic Decision Making in the Global Economy*, Hershey, PA: IGI Global, pp. 79–98.

Coetzee, D. (2001), 'South African education and the ideology of patriarchy', *South African Journal of Education*, **21** (4), 300–304.

Cyr, J. (2016), 'The pitfalls and promise of focus groups as a data collection method', *Sociological Methods & Research*, **45** (2), 231–59.

Davis, R. and J. Thurlow (2010), 'Formal–informal economy linkages and unemployment in South Africa', *South African Journal of Economics*, **78** (4), 437–59.

Essers, C. (2009), 'Reflections on the narrative approach: Dilemmas of power, emotions and social location while constructing life-stories', *Organization*, **16** (2), 163–81.

Fayolle, A., S. Yousafzai, S. Saeed, C. Henry and A. Lindgreen (2015), 'Call for papers. Special issue on Contextual embeddedness of women's entrepreneurship: taking stock and looking ahead', *Entrepreneurship & Regional Development*, **27**, (9–10), 670–74.

Goulding, C. (2005), 'Grounded theory, ethnography and phenomenology: A comparative analysis of three qualitative strategies for marketing research', *European Journal of Marketing*, **39** (3/4), 294–308.

Guiso, L., P. Sapienza and L. Zingales (2006), 'Does culture affect economic outcomes?', *The Journal of Economic Perspectives*, **20** (2), 23–48.

Hall, R.E. and C.I. Jones (1999), 'Why do some countries produce so much more output per worker than others?', *The Quarterly Journal of Economics*, **114** (1), 83–116.

Hartmann, H. (2010), 'Capitalism, patriarchy and job segregation by sex', in J. Goodman (ed.), *Global Perspectives on Gender and Work: Readings and Interpretations*, Plymouth: Rowman & Littlefield, pp. 54–62.

Hayton, J.C., G. George and S.A. Zahra (2002), 'National culture and entrepreneurship: A review of behavioral research', *Entrepreneurship Theory & Practice*, **26** (4), 33–52.

Henderson, J. and S. Weiler (2010), 'Entrepreneurs and job growth: Probing the boundaries of time and space', *Economic Development Quarterly*, **24** (1), 23–32.

Hofstede, G. (1980), *Culture's Consequences: International Differences in Work-related Values*, Beverly Hills: Sage Publications.

Hofstede, G., G.J. Hofstede and M. Minkov (2010), *Cultures and Organizations: Software of the Mind*, 3rd rev. edn, New York: McGraw-Hill.

Horkheimer, M. (1982), 'Egoism and the freedom movement: On the anthropology of the bourgeois era', *Telos*, **1982** (54), 10–60.

Hossain, N. (2012), 'Exports, equity, and empowerment: The effects of readymade garments manufacturing employment on gender equality in Bangladesh. Washington, DC: World Bank.

Hu, X., S. Marlow, A. Zimmermann, L. Martin and R. Frank (2020), 'Understanding opportunities in social entrepreneurship: A critical realist abstraction', *Entrepreneurship Theory & Practice*, **44** (5), 1032–56.

Huault, I., V. Perret and A. Spicer (2014), 'Beyond macro- and micro-emancipation: Rethinking emancipation in organization studies', *Organization*, **21** (1), 22–49.

Inglis, T. (1997), 'Empowerment and emancipation', *Adult Education Quarterly*, **48** (1), 3–17.

Ireland, R.D., M.A. Hitt and D.G. Sirmon (2003), 'A model of strategic entrepreneurship: The construct and its dimensions', *Journal of Management*, **29** (6), 963–89.

Irene, B.N.O. (2016), 'Gender and entrepreneurial success: A cross-cultural study of competencies of female SMEs operators in South Africa', PhD thesis, Cardiff Metropolitan University.

Irene, B.N.O. (2018), 'Women entrepreneurs in South Africa: Maintaining a balance between culture, personal life, and business', in S. Yousafzai, A. Fayolle, A. Lindgreen, C. Henry, S. Saeed and S. Sheikh (eds), *Women Entrepreneurs and the Myth of 'Underperformance': A New Look at Women's Entrepreneurship Research*, Cheltenham, UK and Northampton, MA, USA: Edward Elgar Publishing, pp. 90–106.

Irene, B.N.O. and T. Hussain (2020), 'The accessibility and affordability of education in Sub-Saharan Africa: The debate on low-cost and private higher education institutions', in K. Adeyemo (ed.), *The Education Systems of Africa*, Cham: Springer.

Irene, B.N.O., A.P. Opute and W. Murithi (2019), 'Women entrepreneurs in South Africa: An empirical insight into the factors affecting the oscillation of female SMMEs operators from self to paid employment', presented at the 1st Afripreneur Conference, De Montfort University, May.

Jennings, J.E., P.D. Jennings and M. Sharifian (2016), 'Living the dream? Assessing the "entrepreneurship as emancipation" perspective in a developed region', *Entrepreneurship Theory and Practice*, **40** (1), 81–110.

Kabeer, N. (2012), *Women's Economic Empowerment and Inclusive Growth: Labour Markets and Enterprise Development*. First of the series of reports supported by the UK's Department for International Development (DFID) and the International Development Research Centre (IDRC).

Kabeer, N. (2013), 'The rise of the female breadwinner: Reconfigurations of marriage, motherhood and masculinity in the global economy', in Shirin M. Ray and Georgina Waylen (eds), *New Frontiers in Feminist Political Economy*, New York: Routledge, pp. 62–84.

Kabeer, N. and L. Natali (2013), 'Gender equality and economic growth: Is there a win–win?', *IDS Working Paper 417*, Brighton: Institute of Development Studies.

Kitzinger, J. (1994), 'The methodology of focus groups: The importance of interaction between research participants', *Sociology of Health & Illness*, **16** (1), 103–21.

Laclau, E. (1996), *Emancipation(s)* (reprinted 2007), New York, NY: Verso.

Langowitz, N.S. and M. Minniti (2007), 'The entrepreneurial propensity of women', *Entrepreneurship Theory & Practice*, **31** (3), 341–64.

Lansky, M. (2000), 'Gender, women and all the rest (Part I)', *International Labour Review*, **139** (4), 481–504.

Liu, Y., T. Schøtt and C. Zhang (2019), 'Women's experiences of legitimacy, satisfaction and commitment as entrepreneurs: Embedded in gender hierarchy and networks in private and business spheres', *Entrepreneurship & Regional Development*, **31** (3–4), 293–307.

Lumpkin, G.T. and G.G. Dess (1996), 'Clarifying the entrepreneurial orientation construct and linking it to performance', *Academy of Management Review*, **21** (1), 135–72.

Madriz, E. (2003), 'Focus groups in feminist research', in N.K. Denzin and Y.S. Lincoln (eds), *Collecting and Interpreting Qualitative Materials*, 2nd edn, Thousand Oaks, CA: Sage Publications, pp. 363–88.

Marlow, S. (1997), 'Self-employed women: New opportunities, old challenges?', *Entrepreneurship & Regional Development*, **9** (3), 199–210.

Marlow, S. and A. Martinez Dy (2018), 'Annual review article: Is it time to rethink the gender agenda in entrepreneurship research', *International Small Business Journal*, **36** (1), 3–22.

Marlow, S. and M. McAdam (2013), 'Gender and entrepreneurship: Advancing debate and challenging myths, exploring the mystery of the under-performing female entrepreneur', *International Journal of Entrepreneurial Behaviour & Research*, **19** (1), 114–24.

Marlow, S. and J. Swail (2014), 'Gender, risk and finance: Why can't a woman be more like a man?', *Entrepreneurship & Regional Development*, **26** (1–2), 80–96.

Mathur-Helm, B. (2004), 'Women in management in South Africa', in L. Davidson and R. Burke (eds), *Women in Management Worldwide: Progress and Prospects*, Aldershot: Ashgate Publishing.

Nagra, B. (2018), 'Cultural explanations of patriarchy, race, and everyday lives: Marginalizing and "othering" Muslim women in Canada', *Journal of Muslim Minority Affairs*, **38** (2), 263–79.

Ncanywa, T. (2019), 'Entrepreneurship and development agenda: A case of higher education in South Africa', *Journal of Entrepreneurship Education*, **22** (1), 1–11.

Nchimbi, M.I. and M. Chijoriga (2009), 'Gender and entrepreneurship', in D.R. Olomi (ed.), *African Entrepreneurship and Small Business Development: Context and Process*, Dar es Salaam: Otme Publishers.

North, D.C. (1990), *Institution, Institutional Change and Economic Performance*, Cambridge: Cambridge University Press.

Okeke-Uzodike, O.E. (2019), 'Sustainable women's entrepreneurship: A view from two BRICS Nations', *Journal of International Women's Studies*, **20** (2), 340–58.

Okeke-Uzodike, O.E., U. Okeke-Uzodike and C. Ndinda (2018), 'Women's entrepreneurship in Kwazulu-Natal: A critical review of government intervention politics and programs', *Journal of International Women's Studies*, **19** (5), 147–64.

Patton, M.Q. and M. Cochran (2002), *A Guide to Using Qualitative Research Methodology*, Paris: Medicins Sans Frontiers.

Rindova, V., D. Barry and D.J. Ketchen, Jr (2009), 'Entrepreneuring as emancipation', *Academy of Management Review*, **34** (3), 477–91.

Roos, A. (2019), 'Embeddedness in context: Understanding gender in a female entrepreneurship network', *Entrepreneurship & Regional Development*, **31** (3–4), 279–92.

Sarasvathy, S.D. and S. Venkataraman (2011), 'Entrepreneurship as method: Open questions for an entrepreneurial future', *Entrepreneurship Theory & Practice*, **35** (1), 113–35.

Sarasvathy, S.D., N. Dew, S.R. Velamuri and S. Venkataraman (2003), 'Three views of entrepreneurial opportunity', in Z.J. Acs and D.B. Audretsch (eds), *Handbook of Entrepreneurship Research*, Boston, MA: Springer, pp. 141–60.

Sethi, J. and A. Saxena (2013), *Entrepreneurial Competencies, Motivation, Performance and Rewards*, Darya Ganj, Delhi: Deep and Deep Publications.

Simmons, S.A., J. Wiklund and J. Levie (2014), 'Stigma and business failure: Implications for entrepreneurs' career choices', *Small Business Economics*, **42** (3), 485–505.

Siu, W.S. and E.S. Lo (2013), 'Cultural contingency in the cognitive model of entrepreneurial intention', *Entrepreneurship Theory & Practice*, **37** (2), 147–73.

Smith, J.A. (2004), 'Reflecting on the development of interpretative phenomenological analysis and its contribution to qualitative research in psychology', *Qualitative Research in Psychology*, **1** (1), 39–54.

Smith, J.A. and M. Osborn (2015), 'Interpretative phenomenological analysis as a useful methodology for research on the lived experience of pain', *British Journal of Pain*, **9** (1), 41–2.

Smith-Hunter, A.E. and R.L. Boyd (2004), 'Applying theories of entrepreneurship to a comparative analysis of white and minority women business owners', *Women in Management Review*, **19** (1), 18–28.

Statistics South Africa (StatsSA) (2018). Quarterly Labour Force Survey Quarter 2 2018. Statistical release P0211, Pretoria: Statistics South Africa. Accessed 16 May 2020 at www.statssa.gov.za.

Titi Amayah, A. and M.D. Haque (2017), 'Experiences and challenges of women leaders in Sub-Saharan Africa', *Africa Journal of Management*, **3** (1), 99–127.

Tlaiss, H.A. (2015), 'Entrepreneurial motivations of women: Evidence from the United Arab Emirates', *International Small Business Journal*, **33** (5), 562–81.

Torres, P. and Augusto, M. (2019), 'Cultural configurations and entrepreneurial realisation', *International Journal of Entrepreneurial Behavior & Research*, **25** (1), 112–28.

United Nations (1995), 'Report of the Fourth World Conference on Women', Beijing, 4–15 September United Nations publication, Sales No. E.96.IV.13.

Valliere, D. (2019), 'Refining national culture and entrepreneurship: The role of sub-cultural variation', *Journal of Global Entrepreneurship Research*, **9** (47), 1–22.

Verduijn, K. and C. Essers (2013), 'Questioning dominant entrepreneurship assumptions: The case of female ethnic minority entrepreneurs', *Entrepreneurship & Regional Development*, **25** (7–8), 612–30.

Verduijn, K., P. Dey, D. Tedmanson and C. Essers (2014), 'Emancipation and/or oppression? Conceptualizing dimensions of criticality in entrepreneurship studies', *International Journal of Entrepreneurial Behavior & Research*, **20** (2), 98–107.

Weber, K., K.L. Heinze and M. DeSoucey (2008), 'Forage for thought: Mobilizing codes in the movement for grass-fed meat and dairy products', *Administrative Science Quarterly*, **53** (3), 529–67.

Welter, F. (2011), 'Contextualizing entrepreneurship: Conceptual challenges and ways forward', *Entrepreneurship Theory and Practice*, **35** (1), 165–84.

Welter, F., C. Brush and A. de Bruin (2014), 'The gendering of entrepreneurship context', working paper 01/14. Bonn: IfM Bonn.

World Bank (2012), *World Development Report, 2012. Gender Equality and Development*, Washington, DC: World Bank.

World Economic Forum (2017), *The Global Gender Gap Report 2017*, Geneva. Accessed at http://www3.weforum.org/docs/WEF_GGGR_2017.pdf.

Xheneti, M.S., S. Thapa Karki and A. Madden (2019), 'Negotiating business and family demands within a patriarchal society: The case of women entrepreneurs in the Nepalese context', *Entrepreneurship & Regional Development*, **31** (3–4), 259–78.

Yousafzai, S., A. Fayolle, S. Saeed, C. Henry and A. Lindgreen (2019), 'The contextual embeddedness of women's entrepreneurship: Towards a more informed research agenda', *Entrepreneurship & Regional Development*, **31** (3–4), 167–77.

Zahra, S.A. and M. Wright (2011), 'Entrepreneurship's next act', *Academy of Management Perspectives*, **25** (4), 67–83.

7. Role of socio-cultural factors in shaping entrepreneurial decision and behavior: an Indian perspective

Jasmine Banu, Rupashree Baral, Upasna A. Agarwal and Mansi Rastogi

INTRODUCTION

Entrepreneurship has been widely acknowledged globally for its numerous contributions (Venkatesh et al., 2017). It is the key to the overall economic development of the nations (Bruton et al., 2008; Paul and Sharma, 2013) and has an indispensable role in the eradication of poverty along with home-lessness (Thorpe, 2017). In many countries, more specifically in emerging economies like India, entrepreneurship promotes rural development (Bruton et al., 2008; Paul and Sharma, 2013). Entrepreneurship has also been regarded as a tool for supporting economies by generating employment at all levels (Venkatesh et al., 2017). In all, entrepreneurship offers fuel to the engine of the national economy by providing employment, eradicating poverty, and promoting self-reliance in the country. It is largely observed that both women and men tend to possess adequate entrepreneurial competencies irrespective of their gender. Despite the evidence of the critical role of women entrepreneurs in the innovation, economic growth of a nation and global competitiveness (Shastri et al., 2019), entrepreneurship is still a male-dominated field, and only a few women have made headway in the entrepreneurship domain (Chatterjee et al., 2018; Gupta and Mirchandani, 2018).

The business case for gender diversity and inclusion as a source of competitive advantage is now known widely. For example, the McKinsey Global Report (2018) has documented a positive correlation between gender diversity and EBIT (earnings before interest and taxes) margin and economic profit. Gender-diverse business units report higher employee engagement and higher total return to shareholders and return on invested capital (Catalyst, 2018). However, while research has consistently shown the value that women leaders bring to their companies, women's participation remains scarce in the main workforce in India and more so in the entrepreneurship domain, according to the Sixth Economic Census Report, 2016. According to estimates of the Global Entrepreneurship Monitor (GEM) report, there are only seven women entrepreneurs for every ten men entrepreneurs in India, and this slow growth rate of women-run businesses in India is typically attributed to the societal and cultural factors which hinder women's progress in India (Bosma and Kelley, 2019). The Mastercard Index of Women Entrepreneurs (MIWE, 2019) also reports that women are less likely to be involved in entrepreneurial activities than men due to societal fabric, social norms, and gender bias. The role of gender, education and the culture on entrepreneurial intentions, motivations and behaviors is well documented (Anlesinya et al., 2019; Itani et al., 2011). Though gender does not determine entrepreneurial skills, research suggests that society's culture and norms, along with bias related to gender, limit the decision-making competencies among women, which stops them from flourishing as entrepreneurs (Bastian and Zali, 2016). The existing limited empirical research to examine how entrepreneurial decision-making and behavior are influenced by the national culture (e.g., Thampi et al., 2015; 2018) motivates us to understand women entrepreneurship in India from a cultural perspective.

The source of a rich entrepreneurial mindset in India from time immemorial has been well acknowledged. The Indian entrepreneurial mindset can be traced to the highly enabling socio-economic conditions during 600 BCE and 700 CE (Dana, 2000). The period was characterized by a growing agrarian economy, self-sufficient and reasonably prosperous villages and urban centers, highly developed crafts and specialized small industries, booming internal and international trade and commerce, and patronage of large, stable and centralized empires (Thapar, 1981). In the early days, India's art and craft, silk, and muslin products were traded across the world but, under British rule, Indians had limited scope to showcase their entrepreneurial innovation (Dana, 2000). Despite the competition from British traders, some business communities of India were able to break the barriers and monopoly of British traders by pioneering native trading and modern manufacturing in India by the end of the nineteenth century (Dana, 2000; Gupta and Gupta, 2008). The entrepreneurial potential of Indians could not remain restricted for too long, and the post-independence era witnessed an immense change.

As a result, India saw a focus on micro, small and medium business sectors in the Government's planning and development initiatives with many benefits and tax exemptions (Dana, 2000; Subrahmanya, 2014). This was the time when the enactment and implementation of the Industries (Development and Regulation) Act, 1951, gave much-needed emphasis on the enablement of small businesses as instruments of economic and industrial growth. The Government of India (GOI) established various national-level apex organizations to facilitate the growth of small enterprises. Economic reforms through industrial and trade liberalization in 1991–92 marked the beginning of a new era for industry in India (Singh et al., 2010). The Small Industries Development Bank of India (SIDBI), set up in 1990, introduced the Integrated Infrastructure Development (IID) Scheme in 1994 and also set up the Technology Development and Modernisation Fund Scheme in 1995 for direct assistance to small-scale industries (Ministry of MSME, Annual Report, 2011–2012). In recent years, India has been gradually moving towards a start-up ecosystem. The GOI has initiated several schemes and policies to encourage the entrepreneurship sector (India Skills Report, 2019), reported by the Confederation of Indian Industry (CII). To boost entrepreneurship, in 2014 the GOI created an independent Ministry of Skill Development and Entrepreneurship dedicated to facilitating new businesses. Several initiatives and schemes have been introduced under the aegis of the current Government to promote entrepreneurship in India. Some of them include Start-up India, Aspire, Micro Units Development Refinance Agency (MUDRA) bank in order to boost the growth of small businesses in rural areas, Atal Innovation Mission, eBiz portal, Dairy Processing and Infrastructure Development Fund (DIDF), Support for International Patent Protection in Electronics & Information Technology (SIP-EIT), Software Technology Park (STP) Scheme, Multiplier Grants Scheme (MGS), The Venture Capital Assistance Scheme (VCA), and Credit Guarantee Scheme for Start-ups (CGSS) (Ashwini, 2020).

Although these initiatives have been introduced for entrepreneurial development, representation of women in the entrepreneurial domain is not very encouraging. According to the Census of India Report (2011a), India has 497 million women, which is almost 48 percent of India's total population. Yet it is surprising to state that three in four women in India do not work (Kapil, 2019). Unfortunately, the female labor force participation (FLFP) rate has potentially declined from 34 percent in 2006 to 24.8 percent in 2020, according to a recent study by UNGC (United Nations Global Compact) India (2020). FLFP is one of the lowest in the world, with only nine countries below India, as stated by the Mind the Gap Report (2019). The Economic Survey of India (2018) indicates a gender gap of more than 50 percent in entrepreneurial activities across the nation. While media, as well as scholarly reports, are full of evidence about the growth of individual and organizational entrepreneurship in both urban cities and remote villages (Sinha, 2014), women's participation in the entrepreneurial setup is sparse. The Sixth Economic Census report (2016) highlighted the low presence of women entrepreneurs at the national level, where women constitute only around 14 percent of the total entrepreneurship, that is, 8.05 million out of the total of 58.5 million entrepreneurs. Out of these 8.05 million women entrepreneurs, only two Indian women have been featured in the Most Powerful Women by Forbes (Forbes – Express Web Desk, 2019), namely Roshni Nadar Malhotra, CEO and Executive Director, HCL Enterprise (ranked 54), and Kiran Mazumdar-Shaw, Chairman and MD of Biocon (ranked 64). Despite numerous efforts towards women's development and empowerment, the Employment and Entrepreneurship in India Report (UNDP, 2015) highlighted their lower representation in India. Women entrepreneurs have evolved at a slow rate, with 20 percent of the total registered women-run businesses focusing on a small-scale operation (Bosma and Kelley, 2019). Most of the firms are micro, small and medium enterprises (MSMEs) (Lenka and Agarwal, 2017; Paramanandam and Packirisamy, 2015). As per the 73rd Round of the National Sample Survey Office (NSSO), women in India own 195 proprietary MSMEs for every 1000 MSMEs (Ministry of MSME Annual Report, 2017–18).

One of the explanations for the limited participation of women could be the cultural milieu of India (MIWE, 2019). India is not an egalitarian society. Traditional Indian society was based on the premise of inequality and hierarchical values that permeated every sphere of collective life (Sinha, 2014). Caste and gender discrimination are intrinsic and perpetuating, and even today, most household decisions are taken by a male member in a typical Indian family structure (Batra and Reio, 2016). The combination of family, community, cultural and religious norms of the country has intentionally or unintentionally altered the social fabric of Indian society, inhibiting a girl's literacy, education and occupational mobility (Senapati and Ojha, 2019). Familial commitment and values are deeply entrenched in the culture, and women are expected to take up more family responsibilities than men. For women, the primary experience of self is relational, and the self is organized and developed in the context of important relationships (Surrey, 1991).

In recent decades, the rise of emerging markets, industrialization and globalization, which are inextricably connected to the economic performance of the nation, has led to visible cultural and demographic transformation, creating a conducive environment for women in India (Chatterjee et al., 2018). Urbanization and India's liberalized economy have provided women with access to higher education, jobs, and better opportunities. The society offers an entirely new ecosystem for women's employment, financial independence, and a vital source for innovation (Cho et al., 2020). Hence, women are increasingly entering the workforce. But, even today, in the twenty-first century, familial/societal gender role expectations continue to pose challenges for working women. The societal constructed gender bias views entrepreneurship as a male-dominated profession, and that one should possess masculine traits to survive in the market (Chatterjee et al., 2018; Marlow and McAdam, 2013). Gender stereotype shapes the intention of women to venture into entrepreneurship, and it negatively impacts women's motivations and performance (Prasad et al., 2013). The tradition-bound Indian society silently compels women to pursue their careers without disrupting their family responsibilities (Prasad et al., 2013). From childhood, it is drilled in the impressionable minds of girls that their ultimate success lies in a happy household – managed by them – and their main goal in life is to be an ideal wife and a perfect mother. And when the time comes to make a choice, women, in a Pavlovian sort of way, 'choose' home above career as a conditioned response. This results in withdrawal from a successful career. The societal expectations and the domestic sphere have left them with little power to alter their career paths and pose as deterrents to women's career success (Cho et al., 2020).

Nevertheless, despite several social hurdles, women in some parts of India are making success stories by stepping out of the four walls to join the pool of paid workforce as well as entrepreneurship with high self-esteem (Venkatesh et al., 2017). The coexistence of traditional and modern values across Indian families provides an interesting context in which to study the entry into and growth of women-run businesses and to explain the success factors as well as hindrances in the journey of women's entrepreneurship.

With the above background, this study examines the influence of socio-cultural factors on women entrepreneurs' career choice, growth and performance in the business using a qualitative research design. It intends to address a broad research question: *What is the impact of society and culture on the decision of women to enter entrepreneurship and on their business performance?* We aim to add significantly to the body of knowledge on entrepreneurship by examining the role of individual and cultural factors in shaping entrepreneurial motivations and behaviors among Indian women.

We first present the context of the study, followed by a discussion on the culture and entrepreneurship in India. Then, we delineate the research methodology, the analysis of results, and findings. Finally, we highlight the implications, limitations of the study and outline future research directions.

CULTURE AND VALUES OF INDIAN SOCIETY: MAKING A CASE FOR THE GROWTH AND SUCCESS OF WOMEN'S ENTREPRENEURSHIP

Culture is a holistic idea that is interconnected with significant elements such as beliefs, values and rituals representing the way of life of the people (Tlaiss, 2014). It is a long-term phenomenon that has many layers reflecting the symbols, shared values, norms of the society (Hofstede, 2011; Hofstede and Bond, 1984), interactions, expected behaviors, and choices of the individuals (Thampi et al., 2018). Culture lays the foundation for the human being and shapes their attitudes, behaviors, roles and motivations (Hofstede and Bond, 1984).

The societal value system shapes the behaviors of the groups in specific ways (Hofstede, 2011). Hence, a better understanding of the culture, implicit norms, and social customs is crucial to identify the drivers of women entrepreneurs' career choice and success in a developing country where the growth rate of women's entrepreneurship is still low compared to its counterparts in developed countries. So, to develop an in-depth understanding of women's career choices towards entrepreneurship, particularly in the Indian cultural context, it is necessary to highlight the obvious aspects of culture that directly or indirectly shape women's career decisions. We have used Geert Hofstede's cultural dimensions, that is, Power Distance, Individualism/Collectivism, Masculinity/Femininity, Uncertainty Avoidance, Long/Short-Term Orientation, and Indulgence/Restraint (Hofstede, 2011), to examine the dominant cultural dimensions of India and how they might influence the attitude and behavior of women entrepreneurs. Figure 7.1 is the representation of Indian culture relative to the global culture through the lens of the 6-dimension model of Hofstede.

Here we briefly define the dimensions which are significant to cultural aspects related to entrepreneurial decisions and behaviors among women.

Power distance is the degree of inequality of power between people at higher and lower levels in a hierarchy. In the case of higher levels of power distance, individuals tend to abide by formal codes of conduct, accept a hierarchical order, and seldom disagree with superiors. As per Hofstede (2011), India, with a ranking of 77 compared to a world average of 56 on a scale of 0 to 100, indicates the importance of power and authority and the presence of inequality in Indian society.

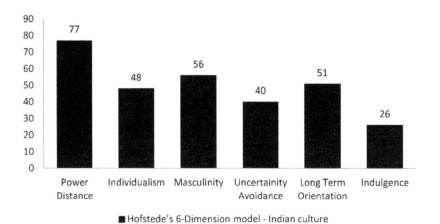

Source: https://geerthofstede.com/research-and-vsm/dimension-data-matrix/.

Figure 7.1   *Hofstede's 6-dimension model representing Indian culture*

Individualism is the degree to which people in a country prefer to act as individuals, and expect to look after themselves, with an emphasis on independence and self-expression; personal goals assume more importance than collective, group-level goals. *Collectivism* emphasizes group conformity and a high preference for interdependency. Collectivist societies give more importance and priority to the group's welfare, goals and interests over personal needs or goals and have a high level of reciprocation. India, with a moderate score of 48 on individualism, is a society reflecting both collectivistic and individualist traits.

Uncertainty avoidance occurs when people feel uncomfortable or threatened by uncertain situations. Those with higher levels of uncertainty avoidance create beliefs and institutional systems to insist on conformity to rules and norms. Individuals or groups with lower levels of uncertainty avoidance tend to take more risks (Jeffrey et al., 2008). India has a score of 40 for uncertainty avoidance compared to the world average of 65. On the lower end of this ranking, the culture may be more open to unstructured ideas and situations where people do not get easily disheartened by failure and strive to be resilient and successful.

Masculinity/femininity determines a preference in society for achievement, heroism and assertiveness versus preference for cooperation, modesty and quality of life. Success, money, position, personal gains and so on are perceived as male values, whereas caring for others and quality of life are considered female values. Individuals in masculine societies are more aggressive, ambitious and competitive, while individuals in feminine societies are relatively more modest, humble and nurturing (Hofstede et al., 2010). Traditional male values (masculinity) are dominant in the Indian culture with a mid-range score of 56, according to Hofstede's framework.

Long-term orientation or pragmatic orientation symbolizes persistence or perseverance, ordering relationships by status and abiding by this order, and thrift. Short-term (also termed as normative) orientation, in contrast, means personal stability or steadiness and respecting one's tradition (Hofstede, 2011). India scores 61 on long-term orientation, showing the preference for perseverance.

Indulgence versus restraint: this dimension is defined as the extent to which people control their desires and impulses. India is a culture of restraint with a score of 26 in the indulgence dimension, that is, individuals are governed by social norms of what is 'good' versus 'bad', and there is a tendency to view indulgence as 'wrong' or not appropriate (Hofstede et al., 2010).

Although Hofstede's cultural dimensions originated from his analysis of country cultures, it has also been used to analyze regional cultures (Hofstede et al., 2010). Recent work done by Thampi et al. (2015; 2018) attempted to bring out the cultural dimensions relevant to Indian society. While they have tried to identify the dominant cultural dimensions of India's society by interacting with experts, they have called for more detailed micro-level studies to explore how and to what extent these cultural attributes influence the performance of small entrepreneurs.

Since data on entrepreneurial ventures in India suggest differences in the number of enterprises owned by women, their enterprise size growth, and performance across states and regions, we assume that cultural factors may be one of the underlying factors for the differences. Entrepreneurs' achievement motivation and risk-taking propensity are found to be significantly related to enterprise performance (Tang and Tang, 2007). These attributes of entrepreneurs are clearly born out of their cultural grooming, and the degree of entrepreneurial activity could be contingent on the cultural environment in which it takes place (Jenniskens et al., 2011). The research objective, therefore, is to understand how and to what extent the cultural values and dimensions influence the entrepreneurial decision and performance of women-owned businesses in the MSME segments across various regions of India.

RESEARCH METHODOLOGY

Approach

This study adopts a qualitative approach to understand the lived experiences of women entrepreneurs, their career choices, the barriers they face in their entrepreneurial journey, and their business performance, and which are socially embedded phenomena behind the entrepreneurial process (Surangi, 2018). A semi-structured interview with open-ended questions helps to recognize the perspectives, thoughts, behaviors, attitudes and perceptions of the respondents (Jamshed, 2014). Hence, we used this method to unveil the journey of women entrepreneurs to understand how cultural values shape their behaviors and growth.

Sample

We have selected a sample of 20 successful women entrepreneurs using purposive sampling, which allowed us to choose information-rich participants (Creswell and Poth, 2016). As Patton (2002) mentioned, purposeful sampling is regarded as the most appropriate sampling technique to select respondents rather than randomly selected, larger samples in qualitative studies. The respondents were contacted using the list obtained from the Regional Joint Director of Industries and Commerce, Guindy, Tamil Nadu, Kerala Start-up Mission (KSM), and through personal contacts. The respondents were from micro, small and medium-sized enterprises representing the manufacturing and service sectors. The selection criteria were deliberately flexible in identifying diverse samples of women entrepreneurs across regions, both in the manufacturing and service sectors, who had been running the business for at least three years. The respondents were experienced and mature enough to share the relevant information related to the study objectives. Data were collected from respondents representing three of the top five states of India, having a significantly higher number of women entrepreneurs. The top five states of India which contribute to women-owned ventures are: Tamil Nadu at 13.51 percent with the largest share, followed by Kerala with 11.35 percent, and by Andhra Pradesh with 10.56 percent, West Bengal at 10.33 percent, and Maharashtra at 8.25 percent. Moreover, Kerala has the highest literacy rate at 93.91 percent, Maharashtra at 82.91 percent, and Tamil Nadu at 82.04 percent (Census of India Report, 2011b). All three states have sustained industrial development growth, good infrastructure, and are preferred investment bases for investors (Sundar, 2009). The sample states have high social collectivism, social reform movements, and political awareness (Thresia, 2014; Venugopalan, 2013; World Bank, 2020), providing a rich context for culture and entrepreneurship studies. The demographic details of the respondents are represented in Table 7.1.

Procedure

The questionnaire was prepared in three languages: English, Hindi and Tamil, for the comfort of the respondents, although most of the respondents were quite conversant with English. As a result, the majority were interviewed in English and in face-to-face interviews at their work locations. The conversations were audio recorded with the consent of the participants. We followed the suggestions of Alvesson (2003) while interviewing the respondents to elicit their lived experiences. All the interviews were transcribed in English immediately after the interviews. The questionnaire and the transcripts were cross-verified by two expert researchers. The interviews lasted between 45 minutes and 90 minutes. The participants could ask questions to clarify their doubts about the study before their participation. The written consent of the participant was obtained before the actual participation. The participants were assured of anonymity and data confidentiality. The respondents could express their views without any intervention. The interview transcripts were shared with the respondents to receive their feedback and to enhance the credibility of the data (Patton, 2002). The data were collected between July 2019 and October 2019.

Table 7.1　　Demographic details of the respondents

Respondent's name	Age	Marital status*, No. of children	Prev. work experience	Educational status	Age of enterprise (years)	Type of enterprise	Nature of enterprise	Sources of funding	Number of employees	Size of business	Nature of business
Ent#1	40	M,1	Yes	Certification courses	9	Manufacturing and service	Sole proprietorship	Bank loan and self	35	Small	Coaching centre and 3D printing
Ent#2	48	M,1	Yes	Master's	5	Service	Sole proprietorship	Bank loan and parents	35	Medium	Restaurant
Ent#3	30	M,2	Yes	Bachelor's	6	Service	Sole proprietorship	Bank loan	10	Medium	Beauty salon
Ent#4	40	M,2	Yes	Master's	3	Service	Sole proprietorship	Husband	3	Medium	Online shipping service forum
Ent#5	44	M,1	Yes	Bachelor's	6	Service	Partnership	Self	40	Small	HR consulting services
Ent#6	42	D,2	Yes	Master's	3	Service	Sole proprietorship	Self	3	Micro	Business consulting
Ent#7	40	M,1	No	Bachelor's	3	Service	Partnership	Husband	8	Small	Hotel
Ent#8	39	M,2	Yes	Bachelor's	4	Service	Sole proprietorship	Bank loan	23	Small	Photo studio
Ent#9	38	M,2	Yes	Master's	2	Service	Sole proprietorship	Father and husband	7	Small	Montessori

Respondent's name	Age	Marital status*, No. of children	Prev. work experience	Educational status	Age of enterprise (years)	Type of enterprise	Nature of enterprise	Sources of funding	Number of employees	Size of business	Nature of business
Ent#10	56	M,2	Yes	Master's	6	Service	Sole proprietorship	Bank loan and husband	8	Small	Fitness studio
Ent#11	48	M,1	No	Bachelor's	5	Service	Sole proprietorship	Bank loan and self	3	Micro	Beauty parlor
Ent#12	25	S	No	Bachelor's	4	Service	Sole proprietorship	Self	7	Small	Event management and marketing
Ent#13	32	S	Yes	Bachelor's	6	Manufacturing and service	Sole proprietorship	Bank loan and self	10	Small	Book publishing and creative designing
Ent#14	43	D	No	Bachelor's	7	Service	Sole proprietorship	Self	10	Small	Restaurant
Ent#15	35	M,1	Yes	Bachelor's	2	Manufacturing	Sole proprietorship	Self	10	Small	Food – salads
Ent#16	45	M,1	No	Bachelor's	13	Manufacturing	Sole proprietorship	Bank loan	60	Small	Bee farming
Ent#17	43	M,2	No	Bachelor's	4	Manufacturing	Sole proprietorship	Husband	8	Small	Textiles

Respondent's name	Age	Marital status*, No. of children	Prev. work experience	Educational status	Age of enterprise (years)	Type of enterprise	Nature of enterprise	Sources of funding	Number of employees	Size of business	Nature of business
Ent#18	38	M,2	No	Master's	4	Service	Sole proprietorship	Husband and father in law	352	Medium	Online tuition
Ent#19	25	D	No	Master's	5	Service	Sole proprietorship	Self	10	Small	Training and development
Ent#20	29	M	No	Bachelor's	6	Manufacturing	Sole proprietorship	Father	10	Small	Footwear

Note: *M: Married; D: Divorced; S: Single.

Analysis

Thematic analysis was followed to code the qualitative data critically and to explore the emerging themes (Braun and Clarke, 2006; Patton, 2002). An inductive approach was adopted to identify the codes and themes based on the content of the data (Gioia et al., 2013). Three researchers, including two faculty and one research scholar, performed the data analysis independently. The outcome was achieved in five stages. In the first stage, the researchers familiarized themselves with the transcripts by listening to the audio, reading transcripts, and by highlighting initial notes. In the second stage, a framework matrix was created in Microsoft Excel to code individual respondents' short sentences or phrases. The data were copied in the codebook in raw form. In the third stage, the researchers identified recurring themes and sub-themes. The themes were reviewed to determine new themes, renamed themes, and interpretations that were mapped in the fourth stage. In the final stage, the write-ups were woven together in narrative form. The data extracts were con-textualized and related to the existing literature. All the steps were repeated until the researchers analyzed the qualitative data meaningfully (Braun and Clarke, 2006).

RESULTS AND DISCUSSION

The interview results were organized under three major themes and several sub-themes around the personal interpretations and explanations as provided by the women entrepreneurs regarding their decisions, support, challenges or barriers faced in the journey of entrepreneurship. The emerged dimensions, sub-themes and themes are represented in Figure 7.2.

   In this section, we outline our findings by showing how salient aspects of the socio-cultural context of India influenced women to take the decision to enter and grow as entrepreneurs. To understand and interpret the results accurately, some pieces of evidence are presented in verbatim quotes.

THE DECISION TO CHOOSE ENTREPRENEURSHIP AS A CAREER

Personal Attributes

Motivation and ability
We found evidence for the existence of both opportunity- and necessity-driven women entrepreneurs based on the descriptions of their motivations to enter entrepreneurship. Six out of 20 respondents said they were pushed into entre-preneurship to supplement the need of the family. Strong motivation, determi-

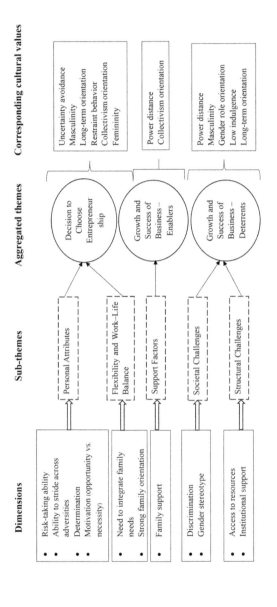

Figure 7.2   Findings: emerged themes and corresponding cultural values

nation, and aspiration to achieve success were the other most cited factors that pushed them into entrepreneurship.

A respondent who owns a Human Resource consulting service said:

> My mom was a cancer patient, and my dad was retired. I could not continue to work in night shifts as things were difficult at home. Nobody was there to take care of my daughter. I felt it was time to quit. To manage the expense, and to take care of my daughter, I decided to try entrepreneurship for six months, where I would have the flexibility to bring her to my office. I know it was not a smart solution, but I was prepared to face any kind of uncertainties. I learned everything in a hard way to become self-reliant. (Ent#5, Kerala)

Results of our analyses corroborate earlier research findings (e.g., Chatterjee et al., 2018; Das, 2000; Goswami et al., 2019; Thampi et al., 2018; Venkatesh et al., 2017) and highlight that the majority of Indian women enter entrepreneurship because of necessity. Since women have to take care of the economic needs of the family, they cannot afford indulgence as a matter of choice, which reflects the low indulgence and high restraint behavior that is predominant in the country. As discussed earlier, India is low on uncertainty avoidance, which was supported by our respondents' cases as well. They continually highlighted their risk-taking propensity, ability, and preparedness to stride through adversities to achieve success.

Need for flexibility and work–life balance

Along with strong determination and the need to do something unique as the biggest drivers in entrepreneurship for most women, the requirement for flexibility and work and family integration were clear indicators to choose entrepreneurship.

A 48-year-old entrepreneur who owns a beauty parlor said:

> The best part of being an entrepreneur is at any time you need not depend on anybody. If you go to an office, you are answerable to so many people. If you need a holiday, you need to ask for permission. But for us, it is on our own. So, you can tell your customers to come after some time if you have an emergency to handle. (Ent#3, Tamil Nadu)

Strong family orientation

Most of the respondents highlighted that the needs of the family come before their businesses or that family is their foremost priority. They preferred the work location to be close to their residences to reduce travel time and help them to attend to family needs along with job responsibilities.

A 30-year-old entrepreneur said:

> I run a beauty salon which is very close to my home. My husband is happy as my job provides the flexibility to accommodate the needs of my family and kids to stay close to them. Elder one goes to school, and the little one stays with me in my office. We all go back home together after 7 pm. My trained employees take care of my clients, so my work does not suffer. (Ent#3, Tamil Nadu)

A 43-year-old respondent who runs a textile company quoted:

> I have established myself as a strong entrepreneur. Most workers are men in my factory; they have accepted a woman as their boss. I have help at home for cooking and take care of other household chores. But I cannot ignore my husband and kids, who are my priorities. I believe the power of a woman is her home. (Ent#17, Maharashtra)

In a society like India, the family plays a central role, especially when it comes to career choices, and the responsibilities and convenience of children/family members cannot be ignored. The strong family orientation, which is the dominant social norm of Indian culture, forces women to integrate the needs of the family with their aspiration to pursue a career such as entrepreneurship. In general, the findings of this study support the earlier claims (e.g., Chatterjee et al., 2018) that women entrepreneurs have a tendency to run their businesses in ways that are geared towards family needs and that do not conflict with their family responsibilities. These findings highlight the prevalence of Hofstede's femininity cultural dimensions, underscoring the preference of people for modesty, cooperation, quality of life, and caring for the weak.

FACTORS ENABLING AND SUPPORTING GROWTH AND SUCCESS OF VENTURES

A further study objective was to identify the support factors or enablers for the success of women entrepreneurs. Analysis of responses heavily highlighted family support as the key to entrepreneurial success.

Societal Factors

Family support
Notably, family support emerged as the biggest driver for the growth and success of ventures as reported by our respondents, evidenced in their responses.

A 40-year-old respondent shared the joy of staying in an extended family system and said:

> At the early stages of my business, I could not help my daughter with her studies, but my mother in law would take complete care of my son and daughter. She took care of the entire family and was very supportive of my career. My sister in law was great support who took care of my son when he was just four months old, and I was going through a tough time in my business. (Ent#4, Tamil Nadu)

One of our respondents, aged 38, who runs online tuition classes, highlighted the pivotal role of the family system in India and said:

> I always keep telling people, if we have elders at home, we can do business better because we learn from their experience. (Ent#18, Maharashtra)

An experienced 38-year-old respondent who owns a Montessori school high-lighted the close ties between the elders of the family and her children and said:

> My in-laws, who are retired, stay at my home. I need not worry about my kids as they take care of them, their studies, and provide them food on time. I can continue with my business with their support. (Ent#9, Tamil Nadu)

A 25-year-old respondent of this study said that the strong moral support of the family was the primary driver of her entrepreneurial journey. She said:

> I come from an orthodox family where girls get married by 18 years. My marriage failed, and I shifted to my parents' place. They motivated me to pursue higher studies and start the business. (Ent#19, Maharashtra)

The respondent aged 56 finds support from her spouse to be crucial since that helps her to reduce her work–family conflict and achieve career satisfaction. She said:

> I own a fitness studio exclusively for women for the past six years. My husband is my mentor. I believe in him as he has the experience, even though he is not into business. Open communication with my spouse helps me to identify my weaknesses. He understands my work commitments and takes care of my daughter. This helps me to cope with my stress and achieve a balance between my family and work. (Ent#10, Tamil Nadu)

A 48-year-old entrepreneur had lost her first business and had to pay back the loan amount to the bank. She was disheartened by the failure of the venture, but it was her husband who motivated her to start again from small beginnings. She said:

> I could handle the stress only because of my husband. He used to say, don't get tensed because of all these. They are part and parcel of life. Right now, you have one more business that you have to lookout, i.e., home. We will do something for this, and you don't need to worry. I think I am here today because of the support of my spouse only. Whatever you do, your children and your husband are the pillars for you. (Ent#3, Tamil Nadu)

The joint family system is an integral part of Indian society and helps strengthen the familial bonding and absorb qualities of accepting others' viewpoints, providing a sense of security (Wennberg et al., 2013). Support of the family (both emotional and moral) was found to be an asset for women entrepreneurs. Having strong family support at home not only allows women to focus on their work but also helps them to have the desired work–family balance. These are reflections of the strong collectivist orientation of Indian families, which were highlighted by our respondents, helping them to pursue their entrepreneurial journey.

FACTORS HINDERING THE GROWTH AND SUCCESS OF WOMEN ENTREPRENEURS

Another study objective was to investigate the culturally embedded challenges faced by women during their entrepreneurial journey. An analysis of the in-depth interviews generated codes relating to access to resources, lack of institutional support, and social factors.

Structural Factors

Access to resources

The biggest barrier in women-run micro-businesses, as reported by our respondents, was access to finance, which is in line with earlier research findings (e.g., Kungwansupaphan and Leihaothabam, 2016; Senapati and Ojha, 2019). Seven of the 20 respondents showed their reluctance to approach financial institutions to borrow money because of the stringent requirements, paperwork, fear of failure of the business, and legality associated with non-payment. When there was a lack of sufficient funding from institutions such as banks, or when women were deterred by the amount of paperwork, they very often relied on their personal savings, support from family and friends to start a venture, or they survived by failing. Most women entrepreneurs in our study reported financial support from their immediate family and some close friends when starting and running the venture. This can be linked to the traditional family-oriented culture of India where seeking help from family members and close relatives is a general practice.

A 40-year-old experienced entrepreneur who initiated her venture with a limited capital amount borrowed from her parents and husband said:

> I borrowed money from my parents and husband. I didn't want to take any loan because it needs a lot of paperwork, and I did not want to go through all those procedural issues. (Ent#4, Tamil Nadu)

A 38-year-old image consultant who had previously gone bankrupt when her business partner ditched her and she could not repay the loan was very apprehensive at the thought of starting it all over again. She said:

> It was because of my mistake to rely on others, and I had to pay for it. Finally, I had to go to bankruptcy. I still do not have the loan paid, which is on my head now. Since the loan is legally in my name, since my partner wanted it in my name, I am accountable for it … I wish someone in the school had taught us the legal issues involved in taking loans, how your credit history could get affected completely. Because of this negative incident, I could never be eligible for a loan or EMI, etc. (Ent#12, Tamil Nadu)

A 48-year-old entrepreneur who obtained a bank loan still faced difficulty at some point in time to pay her workers and relied on the husband's financial support and said:

> My husband used to help me. When I was not able to give the rent, my husband helped, and slowly, when I earned money, I used to repay him. (Ent#3, Chennai)

Another respondent who received an initial investment of 1.2 million rupees for her business from Kerala Start-up Mission (1 million = 10 lakhs in Indian rupees) finds continued investment a challenge for the growth and success of her business. Thus, it is evident that access to finance and sufficient capital is particularly important for the growth of a business. In the event of a lack of financial support from investors, banks and institutions, family support is vital for the growth of women entrepreneurs. Given the collectivist orientation of the culture and the importance given to families and relationships, this finding is not surprising. Earlier studies (e.g., Kothari, 2017) also found that families play a significant and supportive role in the journey of women entrepreneurs.

Prior studies highlight the role of networking in the entrepreneurial process (e.g., Surangi, 2018). Even though our respondents appreciated the role of networking, and a few of them mentioned being part of business network initiatives in their fields, many confined themselves to close personal ties, often ignoring business networks due to lack of time, family responsibilities or a strong desire to balance work and family.

A 34-year-old entrepreneur said:

> Although I knew networking would help, I was into so many things. I did not get enough support from my partner. So marketing was purely through word of mouth, so I had few friends who were referring me to their friends and family. So, there were a few sets of people, every day I did have work, but the work which was coming in was not enough to do even a break-even. Because of the continuous loss, I tried cutting down of employees, I tried getting outflows to work, but after a point, I realized this is going nowhere. I am going to debt every other day. (Ent#12, Tamil Nadu)

A 48-year-old entrepreneur said:

> I don't have time for networking. My role as a mother is vital and packed between home and business. I have acquired all my clients through word of mouth. Moreover, it is less costly and more powerful. (Ent#3, Tamil Nadu)

The findings highlight the feminism aspect of Hofstede's culture dimensions among women entrepreneurs, showing the importance of quality of life and care over achievement and status. They also highlight the strong gender role ideology of Indian society where the roles of women and men are shaped by their gender. Society expects women to be at home and taking care of household chores while the roles of men resonate with that of breadwinner for the family, and men can work hard and are given full support to achieve career success. As was discussed earlier (e.g., Das, 2000), Indian culture emphasizes the family-orientation of society and deep-rooted social norms of inequality in India. The findings also highlight the restraint behavior of women regarding indulging in joy and fun over care and support.

Institutional support

Many of our respondents had received institutional support from their respective states in the form of financial assistance, training, mentoring, and networking support from institutions such as the New Entrepreneur-cum-Enterprise Development Scheme (NEEDS) promoted by the Directorate of Industries and Commerce, Government of Tamil Nadu, Kerala Start-Up Mission, and several private and public sector banks. Despite significant steps and several schemes from the Government to encourage women's entrepreneurship development, several implementation issues and legal complications pose challenges for women entrepreneurs.

A 25-year-old respondent said:

> I was quite frustrated with the response from the private banks. They asked for a male guarantor. The interest rate was very high for me. So, I did not go for a bank loan and sold all my gold and silver to raise the capital fund. (Ent#19, Maharashtra)

The study found criticisms as well as an appreciation for institutional support. The results indicate the discontent among women entrepreneurs regarding the way the business feasibility assessment is done before financing a project by the schemes. In contrast, some respondents revealed their ignorance about the loan schemes, while some received financial support without any criteria of collateral requirement. Eight respondents from Tamil Nadu, who have obtained loan assistance with a subsidy under the New Entrepreneur-cum-Enterprise Development Scheme (NEEDS), were highly appreciative of the institutional support.

A 39-year-old entrepreneur who owns a photo studio said:

> I heard about NEEDS schemes through one of the bank managers. The loan processing team was accommodating. I have availed loan without any collateral. (Ent#8, Tamil Nadu)

Women entrepreneurs are not entitled to any formal benefits such as maternity benefits and child-care facilities as corporate job holders are. They must personally make these arrangements or rely on family members such as their parents, in-laws, or social support such as paid nannies to look after the children.

A 30-year-old respondent and mother of two children said:

> During my second pregnancy, I remember working until the last night. We don't get maternity leave. After delivery, I came back to work in fifteen days, even though it was a C-section. The point is it is your own business, you have to be there. No excuses and no maternity leave. (Ent#3, Tamil Nadu)

The difficulties in getting loans from banks or financial institutions and the inequality in the benefits corporate job holders enjoy compared to women entrepreneurs reflect the high-power distance of Indian culture, reinforcing the prevalence of gender inequality in the society, as is mentioned in earlier studies such as Tlaiss (2014). Another interesting finding is that many respondents were unaware of the existence of loan schemes by financial institutions targeting women entrepreneurs. Insufficient capital substantially impacts the choice of the sector and size of the venture of women entrepreneurs and women entrepreneurs primarily operate micro and small enterprises with low-value products in the retail and services sector (Venkatesh et al., 2017). The hesitation to obtain bank loans because of the fear of being unable to repay them in the event of business failure reflects the long-term orientation of Indian society.

Societal Factors

Social discrimination and gender stereotype

It is never an easy decision for a woman to start a business. Indian families are mostly patriarchal, where parents have a great deal of influence on the education and careers of children. Women need approval and assurance from their parents, if they are unmarried, and from husbands and in-laws, if they are married, to pursue a career of their choice. The respondents in this study highlighted these facts very clearly.

One entrepreneur shared her experience as:

> We are three sisters, and I am the eldest. I have grown up in a strict family. We need to be back home before 6 pm, regardless of any work. We were never permitted to mingle with males other than the family members. My dad often insisted girls should get married immediately after completing their secondary school level. Investing in their education to pursue a higher degree is a waste of money; rather, one must save that money to spend on their marriage. (Ent#12, Tamil Nadu)

One of the respondents who runs an HR consultancy and got divorced early talked about her parents' concern about her raising her children alone without the support of her husband. She said:

> I got married at an early age of 19. After ten years of marriage, I got divorced. As I needed to raise two little girls, my parents wanted me to marry again. I didn't want to get into another trouble. My father was even always averse to my decision to start a business. (Ent#5, Tamil Nadu)

A 40-year-old respondent who owns a coaching center said:

> I am a qualified professional and wanted to resign from my job due to work pressure. I got permission from my husband to resign the job, and he permitted me to sell the jewels which my parents gave me during my marriage. It helped me to pay the rental deposit and buy furniture for my coaching center. (Ent#1, Tamil Nadu)

Although many respondents were not vocal about any social discrimination they faced and spoke more about the support and encouragement they received, a few said the opposite. Women still face a lot of social discrimination, and they often are not allowed to decide things independently and express their views openly.

A 40-year-old respondent said:

> My husband is the decision-maker in the family. I had to seek permission to start this business. As my emotions were never respected, and my views were suppressed in the family, I lacked the confidence to handle my clients initially. However, I learned to make critical decisions in my business. (Ent#7, Kerala)

A few participants shared with us negative perceptions of a few friends, colleagues and customers about their abilities as entrepreneurs. There is a gendered social perception about what products that women-owned businesses 'should' provide, whether women 'can do' certain jobs, and how women have obtained the opportunities if their businesses are successful. For instance, one respondent highlighted the comments she got, especially because she embarked on a male-dominated business. She said:

> I am into the 3-D printing business. But some of my clients always had this question in their minds, who is running the show? The community is probably not ready to accept that I can handle machinery and manage people – their tone changes, 'a lady only' in a demeaning way. I think the public mindset is a hurdle. (Ent#1, Tamil Nadu)

An opportunity-driven entrepreneur who owns a flight and logistics business said:

> Initially, it was very difficult for me to make my family understand what I am doing. From all possible dimensions, I heard only negative comments, and there was no supporting voice from my relatives, but all that I do is I put a smile on my face and move ahead. I don't like to argue and prove them but to let my achievements talk about it. (Ent#4, Tamil Nadu)

A 32-year-old shared her challenges as:

> My parents were old and were a little hesitant to take risks in supporting me financially. I could not risk their savings and never borrowed money from others. But, now, I have obtained a loan from the bank and used a credit card to manage my day-to-day financial challenges concerning business. (Ent#13, Kerala)

A 40-year-old respondent who handles online shipping service forms, being disappointed over the lack of recognition and the behavior of people, said:

> Yes! The opposition was there at the initial stage, people who I met said it is a dominantly male field, even they struggle in this field. In 3–4 months, relatives said, 'Please request your manager to give the money back it will not work.' After six months they said, 'At least now close this business you can't handle it.' They saw me with pity. (Ent#4, Tamil Nadu)

Two of our respondents spoke of the lack of respect for women's work and the sociologically constructed stereotypes, as below:

> When I started a restaurant, my friends thought it is going to be an effortless process because I am a woman. But it does not get any worse or any better. Everybody has

to go through the same bureaucratic procedure. The challenges are the same for everyone, irrespective of gender. (Ent#14, Maharashtra)

More than my parents, my neighbour would ask me why are you coming so late from the office, do you have so much work in the office. (Ent#5, Tamil Nadu)

A 40-year-old respondent who owns a coaching center and 3D printing manufacturing business believed that society often stereotypes women with businesses in the services sector. She said:

The moment I expressed my interest to become an entrepreneur, relatives asked, are you going to sell kurtas and sarees [forms of Indian women's attire]? Are you going to do it alone? You are educated and earning well. Then why are you crazy? It was very irritating, since they felt I am incapable. (Ent#1, Tamil Nadu)

Another respondent, who is 48 years old and owns a beauty parlor, said:

My relatives were showing pity on me saying, 'Oh! Why do you need to run a shop to manage your daily needs? You can think of joining a job …' (Ent#11, Kerala)

A 30-year-old respondent who owns a beauty parlor said:

People said, 'How can a woman be an entrepreneur and be independent? It is risky.' (Ent#3, Tamil Nadu)

These women entrepreneurs' experiences are coherent with the extant literature which shows that women are constrained by the social norms and stereotypes about gender roles and entrepreneurship (Chatterjee et al., 2018; Marlow and McAdam, 2013; Prasad et al., 2013). The findings reflect the challenges and realities embedded in Hofstede's Masculinity and Power Distance cultural dimensions (Hofstede, 2011). Gender stereotypes are still prevalent, society still values masculinity, and there is a power distance acknowledged by women, although they view these features as challenges in the path of their entrepreneurial journey.

But there is a silver lining. There is a positive change in the minds of people and society. Education, modernization and urbanization have shaped the attitudes of families and society to change their perception towards working women. Also, encouraging policies and schemes from the Government has motivated women to join the entrepreneurial community and beat all the challenges. It is very encouraging to see that, irrespective of the challenges, women have been successful in accumulating resources to grow their business, and have been able to show entrepreneurial intent with their dedication, strong motivation and ability to stride across adversities with the support of family.

One of the respondents shared the changing mindset of the family and the society as:

> My parents allowed me to pursue education and follow my passion. I am 30 years old now and eldest in my siblings. I am the role model for my sisters (Ent#3, Kerala)

A 32-year-old entrepreneur who has a book publishing company is not perturbed by the perceptions of people. She said:

> Entrepreneurs have the ability to change any negative thoughts into a positive one; if you become an entrepreneur, you will automatically develop different perspectives and thoughts and look for opportunities out of it and to prove yourself. We don't care about other people like what they think, how they will understand us. We will be sticking to our ideas like how to develop, how to seek for opportunities. That is what gets us going. (Ent#13, Kerala)

Although the literature has shown that gender can play a critical role in entrepreneurship (e.g., Prasad et al., 2013), a woman entrepreneur is not always disadvantaged because of her gender. In our study, many women said that they did not face any societal backlash because of their gender. They were confident of their capability and determined to contribute to society.

One entrepreneur said:

> To be successful, all one needs to know is how to do business, your gender, caste, and religion does not matter, and you can do anything with strong determination and with the help of family support. (Ent#14, Tamil Nadu)

CONCLUSION

This study investigated the influence of culture as represented in family and societal values, beliefs and practices on women entrepreneurs' career choices and their respective business performances using Hofstede's culture topology. It has emerged that, in India, the culture is influential in the growth and success of women-run businesses, highlighting the strong family orientation of Indian culture, pervasive gender inequality, the dominance of masculinity, and widened power distance in the society and extending the same to the entrepreneurship context as well.

While identifying the drivers of entry into the business, it was found that women entrepreneurs were often pushed into entrepreneurship to overcome uncertainty and ambiguity. Women were found to be ready to take risks to ride through the troubled journey of entrepreneurship, which shows a strong determination and resilience to cope with challenges. Any failure in the growth path did not deter them as they considered a failure as part of the entrepreneurial process, and their family the reason to live. Mostly, women reported enjoying entrepreneurship more than a typical nine-to-five corporate job because of the flexibility it provided to integrate work and family, especially to take care of small children.

The driving factor behind the success and growth of business boiled down to strong family support. The presence of a strong collective orientation of Indian society, as mentioned in Hofstede's framework, was evident in the strong emotional and instrumental family support they received. In addition, financial support from family members in times of need helped them to persist and to grow in business. Family support not only provided the required confidence, self-esteem and resilience but also reduced the sense of isolation and work–family imbalance to overcome any challenges in the business journey.

Societal challenges in the entrepreneurial journey were found to have given rise to more necessity-driven than opportunity-driven entrepreneurs in India. Many of these challenges are deeply rooted in Indian society. The patriarchal society in India and cultural norms inhibit women's actions and choices in India. A woman embarks on her journey as an entrepreneur only with a man's approval (be it the father, brother or husband) in the family. A woman abandons her intention to follow a career if she lacks permission from her father when she is single or from her husband when she is married. The initial investment to start a business or start-up capital comes from the support of the father, brother or husband or their approval to use personal savings, including jewelery. This finding highlights the prevailing masculinity and high-power distance dimensions of Indian culture.

Apart from Hofstede's cultural dimensions, our study brings out the marked strong gender role orientation of Indian culture. The social norms and cultural expectations force women to make decisions that would prevent conflict in the family. So often, women use entrepreneurship as an alternative option to gain the required flexibility and autonomy to pursue career aspirations and earn money at the same time as combining family responsibilities successfully. They often work fewer hours, set up their business at home or close to their home to be able to manage the family, which is an implicit gender role expectation in the Indian scenario. They do not mind excluding themselves from the association of personal and professional networks to deal with two important roles of their life: 'work' and 'family'.

IMPLICATIONS OF THE STUDY

The findings highlight the key cultural dimensions of Indian society to explain the intention and behavior of women entrepreneurs. These identified factors may also provide a partial explanation for the low rates of growth of women-run businesses in India. Based on the findings, government initiatives can be customized, keeping in mind the implicit cultural values, to push for more women entrepreneurship in India. For instance, future initiatives could emphasize the status of women as equal partners in society and in domestic spheres, to reduce the dominance of masculine aspects of society. Government and social organizations should work towards creating awareness among people to educate them on the crucial role women entrepreneurs play in employment generation by reducing unemployment and poverty. The economic role of women must be emphasized along with their traditional home-maker or caretaker role. A change in mindset in society is a must for women's growth, prosperity and equality in society.

It was found that most women resist going to financial institutions or banks to obtain loans for their businesses either because they fear their business may not be a success or to avoid the paperwork and procedural hurdles involved. Thus, we recommend that financial institutions help women to obtain loans more easily. An integrative approach of ease of procedures to access capital and capacity-building programs will help women to have equal opportunities with men in society.

The passion, confidence and determination shown by the women entrepreneurs of this study demonstrate not only the strong willpower of women to beat every challenge in their way to progress in their growth path but also the substantial role of education and family upbringing and support. This has implications for the Government to continue the good work of providing important aids for girls' survival and education in India, for example the flagship scheme by the Government of India, 'Beti Bachao, Beti Padhao' (save daughters, educate daughters) in 2015. The benefits of educating girls not only have implications for families' well-being but also have far-reaching impacts within the entire society.

This study makes a significant theoretical contribution to the literature on women entrepreneurship. The United Nations, in 2015, shared a set of goals for the developed and developing nations to address several great challenges, including the growth and development of women. Out of 17 Sustainable Development Goals (SDGs), this study makes a significant contribution to the improvement of women (SDG 5), which are gender-sensitive targets based on culture, social behavior, gender and economies through a rich insight-based qualitative study from a developing and emerging economy perspective. This piece of work not only provides a pervasive socio-cultural scenario of India but also intertwines the socio-cultural fabric, and explicit and inherent cultural values with women's entrepreneurship literature.

LIMITATIONS AND FUTURE RESEARCH DIRECTIONS

This study has a few limitations which are worth mentioning here. First, the scope of the study is limited to the Southern and Western regions of India. Therefore, the findings cannot be generalized to the whole of India as regions do vary in terms of culture within the country. We have included highly educated samples from socially and economically advanced states having a higher number of women-run businesses, like Tamil Nadu, Kerala and Maharashtra, which may not represent the social and economic structure of every other region of India. We have not asked questions about the role of caste, ethnicity and religion and how they affect entrepreneurial attitudes and behaviors, so the study cannot comment on the role of these cultural values and traditions. Earlier studies suggest that all ethnic groups have their own intrinsic social and cultural inheritance which is reflected in their behavior and attitudes (Thampi et al., 2015). Hence, future research must aim to capture these aspects of culture to fully extend our understanding of the connection between culture and women's entrepreneurship. Second, the sample size is limited to 20 women entrepreneurs. Although the primary interest of this study is to contextualize rather than generalize, future studies should consider a larger sample size representing several states with varying cultural values. Third, this study focused only on women entrepreneurs. So, a comparative study exploring the role and impact of culture on the career choice, growth and success of both men and women entrepreneurs would be interesting. Fourth, a cross-cultural study comparing the women entrepreneurs of developing countries would be an interesting future research topic. Finally, this study focused on the impact of cultural values using a qualitative approach. In future research, it may be useful to consider exploring the impact of cultural factors by applying quantitative techniques on a large sample of women entrepreneurs to validate the findings of this study.

There are several studies available to highlight the enormous challenges women entrepreneurs face globally and in India. Also, several studies have underscored the drivers of their entrepreneurial success irrespective of the obvious structural, societal and familial challenges. However, there is a dearth of studies to understand and describe not only the challenges but also their motives and intentions for self-employment and identification of opportunity from a cultural perspective by keeping a strong theoretical framework as the basis for analysis. To better understand the barriers that women entrepreneurs face and how they ride through the wave of challenges with a strong intention to build a thriving enterprise, this study uses Hofstede's typology of cultural values as a base. The important findings of this study reveal that cultural values have a powerful impact on the impediments faced as well as the courage

Women's entrepreneurship and culture

gathered by women entrepreneurs, not only during the process of business formation but also in their path to growth and success.

ACKNOWLEDGEMENT

We would like to thank the Indian Council of Social Science Research (ICSSR) for funding this research (Project No.- IMPRESS/P1424/81/18-19/ICSSR).

REFERENCES

Alvesson, M. (2003), 'Beyond neopositivists, romantics, and localists: A reflexive approach to interviews in organizational research', *The Academy of Management Review*, **28** (1), 13–33.

Anlesinya, A., O.A. Adepoju and U.H. Richter (2019), 'Cultural orientation, perceived support and participation of female students in formal entrepreneurship in the sub-Saharan economy of Ghana', *International Journal of Gender and Entrepreneurship*, **11** (3), 299–322.

Ashwini (2020), 'List of Government Schemes to Support Start-ups in India', accessed 5 August 2020 at https://startuptalky.com/list-of-government-initiatives-for-startups/.

Bastian, B.L. and M.R. Zali (2016), 'Entrepreneurial motives and their antecedents of men and women in North Africa and the Middle East', *Gender in Management*, **31** (7), 456–78.

Batra, R. and T.G. Reio (2016), 'Gender inequality issues in India', *Advances in Developing Human Resources*, **18** (1), 88–101.

Bosma, N. and D. Kelley (2019), 'The Global Entrepreneurship Monitor 2018/2019 Global Report', accessed 5 August 2020 at https://www.gemconsortium.org/report/gem-2018-2019-global-report.

Braun, V. and V. Clarke (2006), 'Using thematic analysis in psychology', *Qualitative Research in Psychology*, **3** (2), 77–101.

Bruton, G.D., D. Ahlstrom and K. Obloj (2008), 'Entrepreneurship in emerging economies: Where are we today and where should the research go in the future', *Entrepreneurship Theory and Practice*, **32** (1), 1–14.

Catalyst (2018), 'Why diversity and inclusion matter: Quick take', accessed 5 August 2020 at https://www.catalyst.org/research/why-diversity-and-inclusion-matter/.

Census of India Report (2011a), *Gender Composition*, accessed 5 August 2020 at https://censusindia.gov.in/2011-prov-results/data_files/mp/06Gender%20Composition.pdf.

Census of India Report (2011b), *State of Literacy*, accessed 5 August 2020 at https://censusindia.gov.in/2011-prov-results/data_files/india/Final_PPT_2011_chapter6.pdf.

Chatterjee, S., G.S. Gupta and P. Upadhyay (2018), 'Empowering women and stimulating development at bottom of pyramid through micro-entrepreneurship', *Management Decision*, **56** (1), 160–74.

Cho, Y., J. Li and S. Chaudhuri (2020), 'Women entrepreneurs in Asia: Eight country studies', *Advances in Developing Human Resources*, **22** (2), 115–23.

Creswell, J.W. and C.N. Poth (2016), *Qualitative Inquiry and Research Design: Choosing Among Five Approaches*, Thousand Oaks, CA: Sage Publications.

Dana, L.P. (2000), 'Creating entrepreneurs in India', *Journal of Small Business Management*, **38** (1), 86.

Das, M. (2000), 'Women entrepreneurs from India: Problems, motivations and success factors', *Journal of Small Business and Entrepreneurship*, **15** (4), 67–81.

Economic Survey of India (2018), accessed 5 August 2020 at https://www.indiabudget .gov.in/budget2019-20/economicsurvey/doc/echapter.pdf.

Forbes – Express Web Desk (2019), 'Forbes names Nirmala Sitharaman as 34th most powerful woman in world, two more Indians in top 100', accessed 5 August 2020 at https://indianexpress.com/article/india/nirmala-sitharaman-forbes-2019-list-of-the -worlds-100-most-powerful-women-roshni-nadar-malhotra-kiran-mazumdar-shaw -6165415/#:~:text=Three%20Indians%20%E2%80%94%20Finance%20Minister %20Nirmala,world%20as%20named%20by.

Gioia, D.A., K.G. Corley and A.L. Hamilton (2013), 'Seeking qualitative rigor in inductive research: Notes on the Gioia methodology', *Organizational Research Methods*, **16** (1), 15–31.

Goswami, K., B. Hazarika and K. Handique (2019), 'Socio-cultural motivation in women's entrepreneurship: Exploring the handloom industry in Assam', *Asian Journal of Women's Studies*, **25** (3), 317–51.

Gupta, K.R. and J.R. Gupta (2008), *Indian Economy*, New Delhi: Atlantic Publishers & Distributors.

Gupta, N. and A. Mirchandani (2018), 'Investigating entrepreneurial success factors of women-owned SMEs in UAE', *Management Decision*, **56** (1), 219–32.

Hofstede, G. (2011), 'Dimensionalizing cultures: The Hofstede model in context', *Online Readings in Psychology and Culture*, **2** (1), 8.

Hofstede, G. and M.H. Bond (1984), 'Hofstede's culture dimensions: An independent validation using Rokeach's value survey', *Journal of Cross-Cultural Psychology*, **15** (4), 417–33.

Hofstede, G., G.J. Hofstede and M. Minkov (2010), *Cultures and Organizations: Software of the Mind*, 3rd edn, New York, NY: McGraw-Hill.

India Skills Report (2019), 'India Skills Report', All India Council for Technical Education (AICTE), accessed 5 August 2020 at https://www.aicte-india.org/sites/ default/files/India%20Skill%20Report-2019.pdf.

Itani, H., Y.M. Sidani and I. Baalbaki (2011), 'United Arab Emirates female entre-preneurs: Motivations and frustrations', *Equality Diversity and Inclusion: An International Journal*, **30** (5), 409–24.

Jamshed, S. (2014), 'Qualitative research method-interviewing and observa-tion', *Journal of Basic and Clinical Pharmacy*, **5** (4), 87–8.

Jeffrey, C., P. Jeffery and R. Jeffery (2008), *Degrees without Freedom? Education, Masculinities and Unemployment in North India*, Stanford, CA: Stanford University Press.

Jenniskens, I., J. Ulijn and S. Tywuschik (2011), 'Cultural capital and European entre-preneurship research: A plea for a paradigm focusing on national, corporate and professional cultural capital', *International Journal of Entrepreneurship and Small Business*, **14** (1), 39–55.

Kapil, S. (2019). 'Women's labor force participation in India among with world's lowest: Oxfam', accessed 5 August 2020 at https://www.downtoearth.org.in/news/ agriculture/women-s-labour-force-participation-in-india-among-the-world-s-lowest -oxfam-63743.

Kothari, T. (2017), 'Women entrepreneurs' path to building venture success: Lessons from India', *South Asian Journal of Business Studies*, **6** (2), 118–41.

Kungwansupaphan, C. and J.K.S. Leihaothabam (2016), 'Capital factors and rural women entrepreneurship development: A perspective of Manipur state, India', *Gender in Management*, **31** (3), 207–21.

Lenka, U. and S. Agarwal (2017), 'Role of women entrepreneurs and NGOs in promoting entrepreneurship: Case studies from Uttarakhand, India', *Journal of Asia Business Studies*, **11** (4), 451–65.

Marlow, S. and M. McAdam (2013), 'Gender and entrepreneurship: Advancing debate and challenging myths; exploring the mystery of the under-performing female entrepreneur', *International Journal of Entrepreneurial Behavior & Research*, **19** (1), 114–24.

Mastercard Index of Women Entrepreneurs (MIWE) (2019), accessed 5 August 2020 at https://newsroom.mastercard.com/wp-content/uploads/2019/11/Mastercard-Index -of-Women-Entrepreneurs-2019.pdf.

McKinsey Global Institute (2018), 'The power of parity: Advancing women's equality in Asia Pacific', accessed 5 August 2020 at https://www.mckinsey.com/featured -insights/gender-equality/the-power-of-parity-advancing-womens-equality-in-asia -pacific.

Mind the Gap Report (2019), 'Mind the gap: The state of employment in India', accessed 5 August 2020 at https://www.oxfamindia.org/sites/default/files/2019-03/ Full Report - Low-Res Version %28Single Pages%29.pdf.

Ministry of MSME (2012), MSME Annual Report, accessed 5 August 2020 at https:// msme.gov.in/sites/default/files/MSME-Annual-Report-2011-12-English_0.pdf.

Ministry of MSME (2017–2018), MSME Annual Report, accessed 5 August 2020 at https://msme.gov.in/sites/default/files/MSME-AR-2017-18-Eng.pdf.

Paramanandam, D.A. and P. Packirisamy (2015), 'An empirical study on the impact of micro enterprises on women empowerment', *Journal of Enterprising Communities: People and Places in the Global Economy*, **9** (4), 298–314.

Patton, M. (2002), *Qualitative Research and Evaluative Methods* (3rd edn), London: Sage Publications.

Paul, M. and A. Sharma (2013), 'Entrepreneurship as a tool for rural development', *Global Journal of Management and Business Studies*, **3** (3), 319–22.

Prasad, V.K., G.M. Naidu, B. Kinnera Murthy, D.E. Winkel and K. Ehrhardt (2013), 'Women entrepreneurs and business venture growth: An examination of the influence of human and social capital resources in an Indian context', *Journal of Small Business & Entrepreneurship*, **26** (4), 341–64.

Senapati, A.K. and K. Ojha (2019), 'Socio-economic empowerment of women through micro-entrepreneurship: Evidence from Odisha, India', *International Journal of Rural Management*, **15** (2), 159–84.

Shastri, S., S. Shastri and A. Pareek (2019), 'Motivations and challenges of women entrepreneurs: Experiences of small businesses in Jaipur city of Rajasthan', *International Journal of Sociology and Social Policy*, **39** (5/6), 338–55.

Singh, R.K., S.K. Garg and S.G. Deshmukh (2010), 'The competitiveness of SMEs in a globalized economy', *Management Research Review*, **33** (1), 54–65.

Sinha, J.B. (2014), *Psycho-social Analysis of the Indian Mindset*, New Delhi: Springer India.

Sixth Economic Census Report (2016), 'All India Report of Sixth Economic Census', New Delhi: Central Statistics Office, accessed 5 August 2020 at https://msme .gov.in/sites/default/files/All%20India%20Report%20of%20Sixth%20Economic %20Census.pdf.

Subrahmanya, M.B. (2014), 'Why does India's economic growth process falter?', *Economic and Political Weekly*, **49** (8), 18–20.

Sundar, S.K.R. (2009), 'Current state and evolution of industrial relations in Maharashtra', Geneva: International Labour Organization, accessed 5 August 2020 at http://goo.gl/JQCf18.

Surangi, H.A.K.N.S. (2018), 'What influences the networking behaviours of female entrepreneurs? A case for the small business tourism sector in Sri Lanka', *International Journal of Gender and Entrepreneurship*, **10** (2), 116–33.

Surrey, J.L. (1991), 'The "self-in-relation": A theory of women's development', in J.V. Jordan, A.G. Kaplan, J.B. Miller, I.R. Stiver, J.L. Surrey (eds), *Women's Growth in Connection. Writings from the Stone Center*, New York: Guilford Press, pp. 51–66.

Tang, J. and Z. Tang (2007), 'The relationship of achievement motivation and risk-taking propensity to new venture performance: A test of the moderating effect of entrepreneurial munificence', *International Journal of Entrepreneurship and Small Business*, **4** (4), 450–72.

Thampi, P.P., A. Jyotishi and R. Bishu (2015), 'Cultural characteristics of small business entrepreneurs in India: Examining the adequacy of Hofstede's framework', *International Journal of Business and Globalisation*, **15** (4), 475–95.

Thampi, P.P., A. Jyotishi and R. Bishu (2018), 'Revisiting Hofstede in the Indian context: Understanding the influence of entrepreneurial culture on performance of micro, small, and medium enterprises', *International Journal of Entrepreneurship and Small Business*, **33** (3), 380–99.

Thapar, R. (1981), 'Ideology and the interpretation of early Indian history', *Social Science Information*, **20** (2), 239–58.

Thorpe, D. (2017), 'The role of entrepreneurship in ending poverty and homelessness', *Forbes*, accessed 5 August 2020 at https://www.forbes.com/sites/devinthorpe/2017/09/12/the-role-of-entrepreneurship-in-ending-poverty-and-homelessness/#50625402653d.

Thresia, C.U. (2014), 'Social inequities and exclusions in Kerala's "Egalitarian" development', *Monthly Review Referencing*, 1 February, accessed 5 August 2020 at https://goo.gl/UKJEFU.

Tlaiss, H.A. (2014), 'Women's entrepreneurship, barriers and culture: Insights from the United Arab Emirates', *The Journal of Entrepreneurship*, **23** (2), 289–320.

UNDP (2015), 'Women's voices: Employment and entrepreneurship in India report', UNDP, accessed 5 August 2020 at https://www.undp.org/content/dam/india/docs/poverty/Womens%20Voices%20Employment%20and%20Entrepreneurship%20In%20India%20Report.pdf.

United Nations Global Compact (2020), 'Female labour-force participation in India declined from 34 pc in 2006 to 24.8 pc in 2020: Study', accessed on 5 August 2020 at https://www.outlookindia.com/newsscroll/female-labourforce-participation-in-india-declined-from-34-pc-in-2006-to-248-pc-in-2020-study/1754272.

Venkatesh, V., J.D. Shaw, T.A. Sykes, S.F. Wamba and M.W. Macharia (2017), 'Networks, technology, and entrepreneurship: A field quasi-experiment among women in rural India', *Academy of Management Journal*, **60**, 1709–40.

Venugopalan, K.V. (2013), 'Industrial relations in the public and private enterprises in Kerala', Mahatma Gandhi University, Department of Commerce and Research Centre', accessed 5 August 2020 at http://goo.gl/3lVb5K.

Wennberg, K., S. Pathak and E. Autio (2013), 'How culture moulds the effects of self-efficacy and fear of failure on entrepreneurship', *Entrepreneurship and Regional Development*, **25** (9–10), 756–80.

World Bank (2020), 'Tamil Nadu – Poverty, growth, and inequality', accessed 5 August 2020 at http://documents.worldbank.org/curated/en/380971504177733539/ Tamil-Nadu-Poverty-growth-and-inequality.

PART III

Culture and self-determination in women's entrepreneurship

8. Mobilising "she power": Chinese women entrepreneurs negotiating cultural and neoliberal contexts

Dongling Zhang and Nancy C. Jurik

INTRODUCTION

Mainland China (henceforth, China) has been glorified as one of the few nations vigorously advocating gender equality in women's self-employment (Au, 2017). In 2019, women owned 25.6 per cent of all businesses in China (MasterCard, 2019). In some industries, including internet start-ups, more than half of new businesses were founded by women (Xinhua, 2015). As China's economy slowed in recent decades (National Bureau of Statistics, 2019), the government began promoting women's self-employment, including microenterprise as a method for driving economic growth. The rising popularity of the term "she economy" acknowledges women's contributions to economic development through consumption and self-employment (Ren, 2019). China's efforts are consistent with a global emphasis on self-employment and microenterprise development programmes (MDP) as a solution to poverty, unemployment and economic stagnation (Chow, 2010). Although the Chinese government links these strategies to women's empowerment, its gender equality discourses are used more to further its programmes than to achieve actual equality (Zhang, 2015). Moreover, Chinese patriarchal family culture and the increasing care burdens due to economic reforms pose significant challenges for women entrepreneurs.

While the popular press is keen to report women free enterprise heroes as evidence of China's rise to global economic power, most women entrepreneurs run microenterprises – businesses with a very small number of employees and limited start-up capital (Chan and Lin, 2014; Wang, 2017). They are typically "pushed" into necessity-based forms of entrepreneurship rather than being motivated or "pulled" toward a perceived attractive business opportunity (Zhang et al., 2006). Push factors include unemployment, layoff, underemployment and work–family care conflicts (Zhang, 2015). Necessity-based women microentrepreneurs who choose self-employment in the face of limited employment opportunities constitute a large but neglected group deserving of greater attention.

Accordingly, we examine the Chinese government's promotion of urban women's self-employment during the post-1978 era and the experiences of self-employed women in small microenterprises in two Chinese cities. We focused on less educated and likely more necessity-based microentrepreneurs. In the next section, we elaborate a contextualised doing entrepreneurship/doing gender approach. It highlights how women simultaneously do gender and entrepreneurship within the Chinese cultural and economic context, drawing on samples from 2010–11 and 2019–20 (Bruni et al., 2005; Jurik et al., 2019; Welter, 2020; West and Zimmerman, 1987). Our approach explicates the daily practices of doing gender and doing business that are informed by and reshape their Chinese context (Welter, 2020). Next, we describe the Chinese context including the history and rationale of the government's advocacy of women's self-employment, and provide a review of Chinese entrepreneurship research. Afterwards, we describe our data and methods, which include interviews and observations of women microentrepreneurs.

Our data focus on women's business experiences and perceptions of government programmes aimed at promoting their self-employment. The interviews elaborate how Chinese women business owners negotiate between norms associated with male-dominated family culture and Western neoliberal values of entrepreneurship. Our findings are important both theoretically and practically. They elucidate how economic and cultural contexts are sites where individual women struggle with structural inequalities. These findings also provide insights for policies to improve the government's support for women's self-employment.

A CONTEXTUALISED DOING ENTREPRENEURSHIP, DOING GENDER APPROACH

Entrepreneurship is typically associated with idealised Western masculinities, which includes aggressive competitiveness, risk-taking, prioritisation of profit, growth, and a single-minded focus on paid work devoid of routine family care responsibilities (Gupta et al., 2009). Prior research has been criticised for "othering" women entrepreneurs, portraying them as deviating from these "core" business values. Findings suggest that relative to men, women are more often pushed into business ownership due to employment barriers, fail because their enterprises fall in low-growth, labour-intensive sectors, and avoid risks that would help their businesses succeed (Ahl and Marlow, 2012; Bruni et al., 2005). Accordingly, much entrepreneurship discourse comprises a gender subtext that subordinates women to Western normative manhood

(Bruni et al., 2005). Feminist approaches explicate the gendered nature of entrepreneurship. Contextual approaches reveal that women entrepreneurs are always embedded within specific socio-economic, political and cultural settings that involve demands and expectations of how they should act (Welter, 2020). Institutional and cultural contexts and the intersecting identities of race, ethnicity, education, family status and social class of entrepreneurs must be considered when examining business motivations and types (Hughes, 2006), views of risk (Humbert and Brindley, 2015), immigrant businesses experiences (Gonzalez-Gonzalez et al., 2011; Webster and Haandrikman, 2017) and entrepreneurial identities (Knight, 2016).

We will explain how a lack of employment opportunities was associated with China's market-oriented reforms, economic recession and the government's efforts to push women into the microenterprise self-employment sectors. We combine feminist contextual-embeddedness and doing entrepreneurship/doing gender approaches to frame our research.

Feminist contextual-embeddedness frameworks emphasise the importance of examining how surrounding environments enable and constrain women's entrepreneurship (Welter, 2020). Institutional contexts, particularly government regulations (e.g., tax, family, childcare policies) have been a frequent focus for contextual research (Jurik et al., 2019). Cultural expectations that paid labour and entrepreneurship are predominantly masculine activities, and the expectations associated with motherhood are significant components of enabling or restrictive contexts (Neergaard and Thrane, 2011). Recently, however, contextual research has begun to explore how contexts are socially constructed and how entrepreneurs "do" (shape) the contexts in which they live and work (Welter, 2020). Research (e.g., Villares-Varela and Essers, 2019; Xheneti et al., 2019) illustrates how women negotiate gender and entrepreneurship in particular contexts so as to reconcile conflicting demands upon them.

The contextual approach complements the doing entrepreneurship/doing gender approach (Bruni et al., 2005; West and Zimmerman, 1987). A hybrid contextual-embeddedness and doing entrepreneurship/doing gender framework examines the simultaneous production of entrepreneurship and gender as intertwined practices both shaped by and shaping a particular social context (Bruni et al., 2005; Welter, 2020). Both entrepreneurship and gender are situated, ever-emergent discursive and material practices, not fixed attributes of individuals. People do entrepreneurship and gender within social interactions, knowing that they are accountable to social norms (West and Zimmerman, 1987). Human agency plays an active role in revising normative expectations about entrepreneurship and gender, but norms still shape and constrain discourse and material practice.

We utilise this hybrid approach to analyse the making/remaking of the Chinese woman entrepreneur as an aggregation of discursive and material practices that are realised through women's daily experiences and actions. A combination of contextual-embeddedness with doing entrepreneurship/ doing gender perspectives permits attention to gendered cultural and economic impediments to Chinese women's earnings and their agency in seeking to overcome and reframe obstacles. We examine the following: first, how the government's efforts to encourage women's entrepreneurship shape women's routine experiences of doing businesses and doing family lives; second, how women negotiate the different and sometimes opposing cultural mandates of China's traditional patriarchal family structure and globalised neoliberal discourses of self-employment and individual responsibility as a solution to economic hardship.

WOMEN AND MICROENTERPRISE: GLOBAL AND CHINESE CONTEXTS

Globally, MDPs have been labelled an effective economic development tool that assists small business owners through lending and training (Dumas, 2010). Advocates claim that lack of credit access is the main reason that people in developing countries like China remain poor (Ding et al., 2018). Leading proponent Muhammad Yunus established the Grameen Bank in Bangladesh in 1983, a bank targeting poor women who operate microenterprises for collateral-free loans. MDPs have been praised and replicated around the world in developing and developed countries. Despite criticisms, advocates claim that MDPs help women exit poverty and become empowered in their families and communities (e.g., Hulme and Mosley, 1996).

The MDP model fits nicely with prevailing neoliberal ideologies defining poverty as an individual problem and shifting responsibility for poverty allevi-ation away from government and employers onto the poor, especially women (Jurik, 2005). However, this strategy for economic empowerment has short-comings in that poor women's microenterprises tend to fall in labour-intensive and competitive sectors with limited profit margins; many are located in regions with scarce resources, such as water and internet access (Scott et al., 2017). Clearly, the nature and success of women's microenterprises are strongly shaped by their country and regional contexts (Welter, 2020).

The rise of China's MDPs and women entrepreneurs is integrally linked to China's integration into global capitalism. The positioning of contemporary China as the world factory in an international division of labour is a product of state power and global capital. These provide the bedrock for the making/ remaking of Chinese women. Thus, it is important to examine how the increasing capitalisation and marketisation of Chinese society has affected Chinese women's lives and self-employment careers.

When the Chinese Communist Party (henceforth, the Party) took power in 1949, Mao envisioned a new China where women could hold up half the sky. The 1954 Constitution promised guarantees of women's equality, and over time, other legislation promised to radically transform women's roles in the family (Hershatter, 2004). However, central to such policies was making women available for the paid labour force (Wang, 2005). The Maoist regime promoted women's entry into wage-work particularly in low-paid sectors, and allocated men to higher-skilled, higher-paying jobs (Hershatter, 2004). Gender has consistently remained a tool used by the Party to legitimise socialist formations/re-formations. For example, during periods of economic recession, local and central governments strongly re-emphasised women's return to family responsibilities (Hooper, 1984).

As the market-oriented reform era unfolded in 1978, the private sector resurfaced after being suppressed for nearly 30 years. Small businesses included small-scale retailing, handcrafts, food and service businesses (Dickson, 2007). Between 1992 and 2004, the number of privately-owned enterprises increased by 35 per cent per year and the Party officially recognised the private sector as important (Zhang, 2005). Growth trends were fuelled by the restructuring of state-owned enterprises (SOEs) in the 1990s. Women accounted for nearly two-thirds of those laid off from SOEs even though they constituted less than 40 per cent of employees (Wang, 2003). Those laid-off, in particular, less-educated women, faced limited re-employment opportunities (e.g., temporary, unskilled low-wage jobs in non-state-owned enterprises) (Solinger, 2002).

China's emphasis on entrepreneurship entailed another wave of Chinese state feminism promoting women's independence through self-employment. The Four-Self Spirit raised at China's Fifth National Women's Congress in 1983 encouraged women to become self-respectful, self-loved, self-disciplined and independent so as to protect their economic well-being and legal rights. These words were repeatedly emphasised in major media outlets and government propaganda (e.g., Sun, 2019). The restructuring of SOEs in the 1990s and the 2008 global economic recession further fuelled China's adoption of microenterprise as a way of keeping pace with capitalist globalisation. MDPs in urban areas were viewed as viable solutions for easing the unrest due to layoffs and the absence of sufficient new employment opportunities. Chinese MDPs were established and operated by local governments. In 1997, Shanghai pioneered the Re-employment Service Centre (RSC) as the prototype for Chinese MDPs (Solinger, 2002). RSCs replaced the SOEs as "trustees" for laid-off and other unemployed persons for up to six years after layoff. RSCs were responsible for providing basic living allowances, paying medical expenses and pensions, facilitating re-employment opportunities, or training and lending for self-employment. However, allowances, stipends and training never lived up to government promises. Simultaneously, declines in support services for family care during economic restructuring increased child- and elder-care demands on women (Chen et al., 2017; Solinger 2002).

By the mid-2000s, the local governments proclaimed success in facilitating re-employment and self-employment and began to discontinue RSCs (Huang, 2005). Following this phaseout, the government initiated other programmes to promote women's entrepreneurship. In 2007, the Chinese Education Ministry coined the term "she-economy" to stress the importance of women consumers to the economy (Ren, 2019). This term was later expanded to boost the "she power" through self-employment. The central and local governments initiated other self-employment support policies, including tax and fee reductions/ exemptions, training, social security benefits and low-cost lending for small business owners having difficulty finding employment (Chen, 2004). The stress on self-help through self-employment is consistent with global neo-liberal solutions to poverty and unemployment, yet these programmes often failed to reach the poorest groups of entrepreneurs (Chen et al., 2017; Chow, 2010).

There were further shifts in support programming during the past decade. The All-China Women's Federation launched the @Her Entrepreneurship Plan (henceforth, the Plan) in 2015 (United Nations Development Programme, 2015). The Plan's mission was to build "an integrated resource platform aimed at mobilising new thinking, new technology and new public-private mechanisms for female entrepreneurship". The Plan provides some services similar to the RSCs but concentrates on helping well-educated women to start internet-focused businesses. This shift prioritised economic development over poverty alleviation objectives.

Government's encouragement of women's entrepreneurship also conflicts with traditional cultural views about women's place in the family. Patriarchal family structures remain prevalent, and women are still viewed as workers secondary in importance to men. According to the Confucian culture, a woman in an ideal Chinese traditional home must demonstrate obedience at every stage of her life: as a child, she is required to obey her father; as a wife, she has to obey her husband; and even as a widow, she should obey her grown son (Tu, 1998). Women are responsible for managing the household and supporting husbands as breadwinners (Wang, 1997). This culture promotes struggles for women balancing paid work and family responsibilities (Xie, 2013). Research also describes a paternalistic culture in Chinese businesses typically headed by men (Sposato, 2019), and the importance of large, heterogeneous networks to business success (Welsh et al., 2013). Together, these cultural contexts pose obstacles to women's entrepreneurship, economic self-sufficiency and gender equality.

Literature on Chinese women's entrepreneurship has focused primarily on economic outcomes and rarely attends to the gendered processes in entrepreneurship (Liu and Zhao, 2019). Several studies focus on rural entrepreneurship (e.g., Ding et al., 2018; Welsh et al., 2013). Even though interest in women's entrepreneurship has increased, there is still little in-depth examination of Chinese women's entrepreneurial experiences or perceptions about government support efforts. Most studies stress revenue and growth as the most important measures of women's entrepreneurial successes (e.g., Sequeira et al., 2016; Welsh et al., 2017). Other research investigates personality and motivation factors in self-employment, focusing on gender differences (e.g., Zhu et al., 2019; Warneck et al., 2012). Survey data suggest that compared to men, women entrepreneurs have smaller families, work longer hours, share decision-making, and have more homogeneous social networks. Women also have fewer profits, limited access to financing and less business longevity (Yu, 2010). Finally, some research examines the institutional dynamics producing Chinese layoffs, MDP practices, and increasing care-work demands for women (Chen et al., 2017; Solinger, 2002; Wang et al., 2019). Given the importance of China as a world economy, its transition to a state-managed, market economy and the presence of over 29 million women entrepreneurs, it is important to research self-employed women's experiences and perceptions (Welsh et al., 2017).

METHODS AND DATA

In this research, we regard participant voices in interviews and observations as offering important insights into how women do entrepreneurship and gender in the new China. We examine narratives of experiences and perceptions about the contexts in which they live. We employ a qualitative methodology including in-depth interviewing and observations.

We adopted a convenience-purposive sampling design. We first contacted acquaintances who were women microentrepreneurs or MDP employees. Contacts and respondents then referred us to additional respondents whom we selected so as to vary the sample demographics listed in Table 8.1. The first wave of interview respondents (n = 49) came from Nanjing and Haikou between 2010 and 2012. They were interviewed face-to-face in their workplaces for periods of one to three hours.

The first author also shadowed 13 willing respondents before or after interviews for approximately one hour each. Shadowing refers to observations of research participants' daily activities (Bruni et al., 2005). Observations focused on the interactions of the respondent with others present in the workplace (e.g., collaboration among business partners, communication with customers, contacts with MDPs and family or other self-employed women). Observational data including conversations and non-verbal language were recorded in detailed notes and triangulated with interview data.

In order to grasp the impact of MDP shifts since the first interview time period, a second wave of seven interviews was conducted in Nanjing between December 2019 and January 2020. We again obtained respondents through acquaintances or participant referrals. Probably in part due to recent US–China tensions, fewer women were willing to speak with a US-based researcher in this second wave (first author). Those who participated differed from the first wave sample: they were older; none had a college education; all were married with children; most were in family-owned businesses.

Interviews for both waves included topics of motives, business experiences, work–life balance, and perceptions of Chinese MDP practices. Interviews were approximately the same length in both waves. Detailed notes were taken for all interviews because respondents were uncomfortable with recording. In our analysis, we list case number in parentheses after respondent quotations. The number before each dash indicates whether the respondent was in interview wave 1 or 2.

Consistent with Charmaz (2006, p. 115), we were "open to what is happening in the field and … willing to grapple with it" to avoid foreclosing analytic possibilities too early. For example, the second wave sample allowed us to garner women's perceptions of newer government programmes focused on women entering internet-oriented businesses.

Consistent with narrative analysis and grounded theory methodology (i.e., Bruni et al., 2005; Charmaz, 2006), we focused on entrepreneur stories about their daily experiences of doing business and family. We asked about the support they received from government and family/friends. We developed a thematic coding scheme (Charmaz, 2006) that included the following: business motivations, opportunities, barriers, family responsibilities, work–family conflict, identities, government support and family/friend support. We next conducted line-by-line open coding to discover unanticipated themes (Charmaz, 2006). During the second coding stage, we noted women's concerns about coordinating the responsibilities of good mothers/wives and successful businesswomen. They confronted conflicting norms associated with past emphasis on employment duties, a newer neoliberal emphasis on women's self-employment and independence, and traditional patriarchal cultural values. Although no city differences emerged, other variations in sample demographics and two time periods allowed for other comparisons and the identification of hypotheses for a grounded theory of Chinese women microentrepreneurs.

Table 8.1   *Research participant demographics*

		Wave 1: 2010–12[a]	Wave 2: 2019–20[a]
Age	20–30	7	0
	31–40	10	0
	41–50	19	2
	51–60	13	4
	61–70	0	1
Marital status	Single	3	0
	Married	46	5
	Divorced	0	1
	Widowed	0	1
Number of Children[b]	0	3[c]	0
	1	40	6
	2	6	1
Education	Elementary	20	2
	Junior High	12	2
	Senior High	10	2
	Vocational	4	1
	College	3	0
Line of business	Bakery	5	2
	Flower shop	7	0
	Laundry	6	2
	Barbershop	5	0
	Convenience store	7	1
	Computer repair	10	0
	Restaurant	9	0
	Produce retailing	0	2
Number of employees	0	39	5
	1–5	7	2
Type of ownership	Self-owned	33	1
	Family-owned	13	6
	Non-family-owned	3	0
Original Household Registration	Urban	26	5
	Rural	23	2
Source of Participant	Acquaintance[d]	2	2
	Referral	47	5

		Wave 1: 2010–12[a]	Wave 2: 2019–20[a]
Location of Fieldwork Site	Nanjing	26	7
	Haikou	23	0

Notes: [a]   The fieldwork was conducted in two waves. The first wave of 49 participants was drawn from Nanjing and Haikou in 2010–2012; a second wave of seven respondents was recruited in Nanjing between December 2019 and January 2020. Nanjing is the capital of Jiangsu province, a heavy industry production centre of East China. Haikou is the capital of Hainan province in the South China Sea, intending to develop into an international tourist resort.
[b]   All married and formerly married respondents have children. The one-child policy was implemented nation-wide in the 1980s and gradually relaxed since 2016. Accordingly, most respondents, especially those with original urban household registration, have one child.
[c]   The only three women with no child in the first wave sample were unmarried, college graduates.
[d]   Acquaintances were either employees of MDPs or self-employed women connected to the MDPs.

FINDINGS

Our findings reveal ways that women construct entrepreneurship, family and gender in the context of China's marketisation, incorporation of neoliberal values, and continued patriarchal family culture. They identify ways that women interpret and define that context in their business and family practices through negotiating the conflicting influences of China's traditional family culture and Western neoliberal values. In doing so, they draw on multiple images of self, family and entrepreneurship. They reference neoliberal, traditional family and gender empowerment imagery to mould their work and care regimes in complicated and sometimes contradictory ways. We observe differences among women with college degrees who were also younger and unmarried when compared with the majority of our sample who were less-educated, older, married and mothers. The complications and variations that emerged underscore the need for a dynamic and contextualised approach to the study of Chinese women entrepreneurs.

Our findings take on additional significance because the fieldwork took place during two periods after the Chinese government incorporated neoliberal-oriented policies for economic development. Doing business, for all the respondents in our sample, means a burden. The goal of becoming a successful entrepreneur has complicated their personal lives and brought them an extra responsibility for both their families and the state's economy. We divide our findings into three sections (see Table 8.2 for exemplary respondent comments under each analytic theme). The first section addresses government incentives and entrepreneurial motivations. The second examines the tensions and support surrounding gendered work and family life. The third section highlights women's moulding of neoliberal and family cultural contexts to achieve business success, a process of both adaptation and resistance.

Table 8.2   Exemplary quotes from the respondents by analytic themes

Government and Push–Pull of Entrepreneurship	Work–Family Tensions & Support	Doing Entrepreneurship/Doing Gender
Push/Necessity: – I am tired of moving from one temporary job to another … [so] compared with paid jobs recommended by the RSC, the only option left is self-employment (1-7). – When I was laid off with nothing left, I clearly knew that was the only choice available (2-1). *Business as Opportunity:* – I do not think the three of us would be able to put up with a fixed 9-to-5 work schedule as our classmates do … [Also,] we equally share every cent of profit that we have made. […so we] earn more than the other classmates doing paid jobs (1-12).	*Lack of Support or Mixed Support:* – Since my husband was not supportive, I was under great pressure when I first started my own business to take care of it and my family (1-33). – My parents believed that even doing a temporary job was better than self-employment… [and this] made me so sad especially in the early stage of my business (2-5). *Support:* – [I was too busy to] make a breakfast for my son and husband, [so] my son took the initiative to do it then … When my husband and I were both busy with our work and could not do lunch or dinner for him, we sent him to my parents and he got along with my parents very well (1-1).	*Prioritising Business by Single Women:* – Due to the Chinese traditional family culture, a woman's life is imperfect without having a family … [but] we all know that a successful self-employed woman in the new century must be independent, create her own life trajectory, and make contributions to the wider society (1-9). *Prioritising Business by Married Women:* – I do not fit the traditional ideal image of a good mother who spends her spare time taking care of and educating her kid … Every individual should be innovative in living a unique life and must make contributions to not only his/her own personal life but also the wider society (1-31).

Government and Push–Pull of Entrepreneurship	Work–Family Tensions & Support	Doing Entrepreneurship/Doing Gender
– Self-employment is where our personal interests intersect (1-9).		– I had to spend most of my time on my business in order to feed the family at the cost of my role as a mom and wife (2-3).
Fulfillment for Necessity Entrepreneurs:	*Family Business:*	*Dissatisfaction w/New Programmes:*
– [I] … gained the greatest sense of job autonomy that I have ever had in my life (1-8).	– Since I was laid off and ran the business with my husband, the time that we spent together has doubled. Despite many conflicts, we have made a business success and a good family life (1-14).	– I have stopped attending any on-line training session because what they discussed is definitely for people with college degrees and it is not related to what I am doing (2-1).
… have more opportunities in both my personal life and work (1-16).	– … My son and daughter-in-law had their first baby, and it was expected that my husband and I were supposed to take care of the kid … In China, the grandchildren should be closer to and taken care of by the grandparents on their father's side … It was a miserable experience to juggle doing business with childcare. I made it with my husband managing the business with me (2-7).	– From what the teacher said, I can tell that the course was tailored to younger generations with an interest in and capabilities of starting their businesses in the high-tech industry which I am not familiar with and not interested in (2-4).
– … finally understand that a window opens when one door closes (1-44).		
– … showed my daughter a good example of what she should do even when her loved ones are not supportive (2-6).		

Government and the Push–Pull of Women's Entrepreneurship

Generally speaking, all 56 interviews in our sample reported that the government's advocacy played a key role in their entry into self-employment. Government restructuring policies and state-operated MDP (i.e., RSC) incentives produced a combination of necessity- and opportunity-based rationales for self-employment. Even necessity-oriented respondents said self-employment had changed their personal lives in positive ways. These narratives elucidate the nuances in women's views of government policies advocating self-employment and the influence of state-operated MDPs on their lives.

On the one hand, necessity-based motives were referenced in most interviews. These factors include post-layoff periods when "the whole family had no idea about when and where the next paycheck will be … [and] the RSC officials always reminded that the assistance is temporary" (1-4).

Laid-off respondents with limited education backgrounds identified the government's promotion of women's entrepreneurship as one of few options or even a last resort. However, financial resources provided by the government were described as helpful in business start-up. A woman in her 40s who opened a small flower shop said: "I actually did not worry too much about start-up capital, because the severance package I got from my previous SOE was sufficient for starting such a small business" (1-31).

In contrast to older women with children, the three younger women with college degrees expressed more opportunity-oriented views of self-employment (1-6; 1-9; 1-12). They planned to start a business together upon graduation to take advantage of China's market reform context. "The government's policies have shown that self-employment is a good route for women to achieve career success … Our parents gave us start-up capital and we just gave it a try" (1-6). They also expected to earn much higher incomes and enjoy more flexible schedules than they would as employees.

Still, even respondents who stressed necessity-based motivations described how self-employment was a turning point in their career and personal lives. The convenience store owner who expressed fear of not having an income (above) also saw self-employment as:

> a new starting point in my personal life and career … It has definitely been a good opportunity to tap into my true potential to take 100 per cent responsibility for whatever I do, ranging from the minutest decision of which brand of salt would be the best fit for the … residents nearby to the broadest of what the self-employed career means to my personal life. (1-4)

Other respondents (e.g., 1-1; 1-5; 1-29) identified opportunities that came from their necessity entrepreneurship. They described gains in resilience and self-confidence from their self-employment experiences.

This section has revealed how government support encouraged respondents to try self-employment. Those who perceived few alternative opportunities viewed entrepreneurship as a necessity, while those with college education were more likely to stress its opportunity. Yet all respondents indicated self-employment had increased their autonomy and self-confidence.

Work and Family: Tensions and Support

Despite the benefits of being their own bosses, respondents also described gender-related hardships in building their businesses. Being your own boss was a gendered concept and respondents associated business adversity with cultural views that men rather than women were breadwinners. A laundry owner who was pleased with her "job autonomy" associated gendered images with her initial lack of confidence and double workday:

> I used to believe that I would work for that SOE until I retire. Before I was laid off in the mid-1990s, I never anticipated that I, as a woman, would be capable of building and running my own business. I firmly believed in the old traditions that men are supposed to be the sole or at least primary breadwinners and women's duties inside the home take precedence over work outside the home. This belief made me almost give up the idea of starting my own business, [but it] has become and will always be part of my career and personal life … Though doing business is a high-stress job, I feel obligated to keep the wife and mother's role which is a pre-condition of a harmonious family life. Doing the two things together does make me feel exhausted very often, but this is not what I can choose or dodge. (1-8)

In this case, traditional gender imagery initially impeded the woman's entrepreneurial career. She ultimately embraced both work and home duties in order to meet the normative expectations of the traditional Chinese family. The resulting double workday exemplifies the intersection of doing entrepreneurship and doing gender (Bruni et al., 2005; Jurik et al., 2019).

Cultural traditions reinforced claims that self-employment was for men but not women. A female flower shop owner (1-33) said her husband believed self-employment was "man's territory", and women were stay-at-home mothers. Some parents opposed their daughters' self-employment. A barber-shop owner said she almost begged on her knees for start-up capital from her parents because they considered self-employment as an option appropriate only for men:

> They finally agreed to lend me money, but seriously warned me not to borrow from anyone else. They expected my business failure and did not want to have anybody

else to share the cost with them … Since then, I have been working very hard to pay them back as not only a good daughter but also a successful businesswoman. (1-25)

Despite the discouragement, this respondent and two others (1-37; 1-46) reported that their families' scepticism inspired their determination to succeed in both family life and self-employment. Ironically, this determination to succeed in both work and family realms reinforced women's embrace of double workdays.

However, women also described ways that families eased their double burden. The flower shop owner described how her parents eased the lack of support from her spouse.

My parents said they would be willing to give me some money if I needed more for start-up capital … However, I knew that they were not rich, so I did not want to use their money. [But] I got their emotional support that I should have gotten from my husband. [Also], my son almost lived with them during the first few years of my business. (1-33)

A woman in her late 40s started her laundry business after being laid off from an SOE. She also detailed getting help with family care from her parents and her son (2-1).

For women in family businesses, balancing was sometimes easier (Welsh et al., 2013). A woman in her mid-60s started a small-size convenience store with her husband after both were laid off (2-7). She discussed how her experiences taking care of her grandson and doing her business were eased because she and her husband worked in the business together (see Table 8.2).

Although China's traditional patriarchal culture posed barriers for women's entrepreneurship, opposition also provided a motivating force for women's determination to succeed even when it meant embracing a double workday. At the same time, it was also clear that some families provided extensive support for women's enterprises both in family businesses and in sole-proprietorships. This section has revealed how patriarchal culture was influential, but could also be reshaped by women entrepreneurs and their families. Although some families were unsupportive, others helped ease the double burden of work and family. Next, we discuss how women drew on both family and neoliberal contexts to do entrepreneurship and gender in contemporary China.

Doing Entrepreneurship/Doing Gender in China: Incorporation and Resistance

This section focuses on Chinese women's incorporation of traditional family culture and neoliberal values into their entrepreneurial and gender identities. We also discuss women's response to government shifts in MDP mission in our second wave sample. As women entrepreneurs constructed their approach, they sometimes accommodated traditional gender identities and/or the principles espoused by MDP staff regarding independence, resilience and business success. At other times, their narratives rejected such principles, including the new MDPs promising to help them. Our findings illustrate how human agents shape structural contexts, their own life experiences, and ongoing social identities.

Some women drew on MDP discourse about prioritising business responsibilities even if that meant devoting less time to motherhood and personal life. The three business owners with college degrees (1-6; 1-9; 1-12) agreed that the best strategy to handle their parents' pressure to marry was to commit themselves to work (see Table 8.2).

Several married respondents also challenged patriarchal family norms. An owner of a computer repair shop describes how RSC officials encouraged her to stress the importance of business success for her family:

> Despite the progress that I made in my self-employed career, I always feel regretful and guilty for not being a good mother and wife ... [However,] as many RSC officials and other self-employed sisters said, to give up part of personal life for the sake of my self-employed career is a pre-requisite for being a successful businesswoman ... My family members would understand my sacrifice and take pride in what I am doing once they realise the value of my business success to my family and the society as a whole. (1-44)

This emphasis on making sacrifices for business success and the long-run importance of the business to families was a recurrent interview theme. In such cases, women do business and do gender in ways that challenge traditional patriarchal family culture. The references to women's self-employment contributions to the wider society dovetail nicely with government objectives for the "she economy". Taken together, these comments might be viewed as evidence of the oppressive power of the neoliberal values espoused by MDP officials and self-employed peers (e.g., independence, toughness, sacrificing family for work). Yet, such discourse also provided women with a space to ease often-oppressive patriarchal cultures.

Women did not always readily acquiesce to government and MDP/RSC discourses. In the first wave interviews, respondents often referenced their unwillingness to take business loans from the RSCs. For instance, another barber owner said: "I trust my family members more than programme staff, so I would borrow money only from my parents or other relatives if I have to" (1-37). Similarly, others (1-25) said they preferred loans from family whenever possible because those were the sources they trusted over government.

The second wave interview sample was comprised solely of less educated women who were mothers. By 2019, the RSC-style MDPs had ended, and the new programmes by the @Her Entrepreneurship Plan were disconnected from SOEs. Despite new programme promises to serve anyone interested in starting a business, our seven respondents uniformly reported that many promises went unfulfilled, and, moreover, that the programme's focus did not include them:

> Though the contact person introduced numerous community services they planned to provide, I have never seen many of them actually being supplied ... I came across a piece of news saying that a similar programme in Sichuan [a province in south-west China] had provided women entrepreneurs with low-cost day-care services. I believe that this is a highly demanded community service ... but unfortunately it is not the case here ... Compared with the old services, the new services are all internet-related... [They] are all about how to do business in a high-tech industry and therefore are not a fit for me and other similar under-educated middle-age women. (2-3)

The Chinese government emphasis shifted toward internet-oriented businesses that would be led by educated entrepreneurs and spur greater economic development for the nation. Our second wave respondents did not fit the internet business profile. "If I was 20 years younger, I would probably take advantage of the on-line platform and look for an investor" (2-6). In response to this lack of fit, the respondents carved out their own approach. One of them (a middle-aged laundry owner) blended traditional family cultural values and her view of women's place in the family with her business goals:

> I started this laundry not for the purpose of becoming super rich. Family is always at the very top of my priority list. As a [Chinese] traditional woman, to become a good wife and a mother is the most important thing in my life ... Nevertheless, I am not saying I would like to become a housewife and wait to be fed by my husband. You see, 15 years ago, I followed the government's call to start my own business after being laid off. Now I am following the government's new call to use the instant messaging phone app to expand my business on-line and even try the mobile payment app to better accommodate newly emerging customer demands. However, this is already the most that I can do. The on-line e-commerce courses that I attended were all about entering a lucrative, high-tech business. I would never try it at the cost of the economic well-being of my family. Both my husband and son need a stable family and my current business is central to that. (2-1)

Although she followed some government suggestions, this respondent also formulated her own response to the multiple pressures she faced, thereby shaping her particular business context.

While enduring hardships and challenges incurred by family demands, government-induced layoffs and declining safety-net support, self-employed women leveraged Western neoliberal values about work and business to address pressures from China's traditional patriarchal family culture. They negotiated between these different cultural settings, trying to earn livelihoods amidst gender inequality and economic marginalisation. Consistent with arguments from the doing entrepreneurship/doing gender and contextual-embeddedness literature (Bruni et al., 2005; West and Zimmerman, 1987), human agency both references and shapes the cultural norms and context for doing business and gender in contemporary China.

CONCLUSION

Consistent with the critics (e.g., Jurik, 2019; Shakya and Rankin, 2008) who question the empowerment potential of MDP models, we suggest that the Chinese government's interest in promoting women's entrepreneurship is not primarily about gender equality but is actually a revised strategy for expropriating women's productive potential to promote party legitimacy and economic growth.

Yet our findings also illustrate how self-employed Chinese women did entrepreneurship and gender in ways that negotiated among conflicting cultural influences of China's traditional family structure, government mandates and Western neoliberal values. Women constructed a context in which they could do business and economically support themselves and their families, even in the face of the increasing marginalisation of less educated, laid-off women by Chinese MDPs. Consistent with arguments by Fraser (2011), our participants' experiences indicate that government, traditional family culture, and neoliberal marketisation offered both opportunities and barriers for Chinese women's empowerment in this process.

Our findings can fill a gap in the existing literature by demonstrating how low-income Chinese women microentrepreneurs use culture to challenge economic exploitation and gender subordination. Our respondent narratives illustrate the interaction between structure and human agency and, more specifically, the active role that human agency can play in social identity construction.

Theoretically, our research provides an example of how a hybrid contextualised doing entrepreneurship/doing gender approach is useful in understanding the dynamic and complex combination of structure and agency in social life. Although our sample is not generalisable to all Chinese urban women entrepreneurs, each analytic section summarises grounded theory findings that can be utilised to formulate hypotheses for future research. Also, the limited size of our follow-up sample and our sole focus on urban women entrepreneurs suggest that future research should turn towards a larger population of Chinese women entrepreneurs in both urban and rural areas. In this way, new studies can contribute to further improvement of China's nationwide self-employment agenda.

Practically, our findings suggest that the approach for small business assistance in the newer Chinese MDPs is leaving behind a population of willing entrepreneurs who still need business support. Older, less educated women described feelings of exclusion from the internet-centric programme now offered. They also described promises of safety-net services that have not been met. The central and local governments must attend to these unmet needs and develop new approaches that go beyond the current economic development-centric focus. Programmes should be more sensitive to the socio-cultural dimensions of women's experiences in doing their businesses, family and personal lives. For some women, self-employment may not be feasible, and thus better assistance in seeking decent employment opportunities is needed (Solinger, 2002). For all women and men alike, the promised social service and care work assistance programmes must be implemented. Only then can women's entrepreneurship offer enhanced life opportunities instead of simply furthering gender inequality and exploitation.

REFERENCES

Ahl, H. and S. Marlow (2012), 'Exploring the dynamics of gender, feminism and entrepreneurship: Advancing debate to escape a dead end?', *Organization*, **19** (5), 543–62.

Au, N. (2017), 'To make China's female entrepreneurs count, let's go beyond just counting them', accessed 17 April 2020 at asiafoundation.org/2017/12/13/make-chinas-female-entrepreneurs-count-lets-go-beyond-just-counting/.

Bruni, A., S. Gherardi and B. Poggio (2005), *Gender and Entrepreneurship: An Ethnographical Approach*, New York: Routledge.

Chan, S. and J. Lin (2014), 'Financing of micro and small enterprises in China: An exploratory study', *Structural Change*, **22**, 431–46.

Charmaz, Kathy (2006), *Constructing Grounded Theory: A Practical Guide Through Qualitative Analysis*, Thousand Oaks, CA: Sage.

Chen, M., J. Hao and M. Baird (2017), 'China: The reconfiguring of women, work and care', in Marian Baird, Michele Ford and Elizabeth Hill (eds), *Women, Work and Care in the Asia-Pacific*, London, UK and New York, USA: Routledge, pp. 41–55.

Chen, X. (2004), 'Different modes of Chinese women's entry into entrepreneurship', accessed 27 April 2020 at www.china.com.cn/zhuanti2005/txt/2004-09/23/content_5666551.htm.

Chow, Gregory (2010), *Interpreting China's Economy*, Hackensack, NJ: World Scientific Publishing Company.

Dickson, Bruce (2007), 'Integrating wealth and power in China: The Communist Party's embrace of the private sector', *The China Quarterly*, **192**, 827–54.

Ding, H., C. Qin and K. Shi (2018), 'Who benefit from government-led microfinance projects? Evidence from rural China', *Journal of Comparative Economics*, **46** (4), 1253–72.

Dumas, Colette (2010), 'Achieving economic self-sufficiency through microenterprise training: Outcome-based evidence from the center for women and enterprise', in Joseph Munoz (ed.), *Contemporary Microenterprise: Concepts and*

Cases, Cheltenham, UK and Northampton, MA, USA: Edward Elgar Publishing, pp. 260–75.

Fraser, Nancy (2011), 'Marketization, social protection, emancipation', in Craig Calhoun and Georgi Derluguian (eds), *Business as Usual*, New York: New York University Press, pp. 137–58.

Gonzalez-Gonzalez, J., F. Bretones, V. Zarco and A. Rodriguez (2011), 'Women, immigration and entrepreneurship in Spain: A confluence of debates in the face of a complex reality', *Women's Studies International Forum*, **34** (5), 360–70.

Gupta, V., D. Turban, A. Wasti and A. Sikdar (2009), 'The role of gender stereotypes in perceptions of entrepreneurs and intentions to become an entrepreneur', *Entrepreneurship Theory and Practice*, **33** (2), 397–417.

Hershatter, Gail (2004), 'State of the field: Women in China's long twentieth century', *The Journal of Asian Studies*, **63** (4), 991–1065.

Hooper, Beverly (1984), 'China's modernization: Are young women going to lose out?', *Modern China*, **10** (3), 317–43.

Huang, Z. (2005), 'The Re-employment Service Centers will be closed at the end of the year', accessed 16 April 2020 at http://news.sohu.com/20050411/n225128125 .shtml.

Hughes, Kevin (2006), 'Exploring motivation and success among Canadian women entrepreneurs', *Journal of Small Business & Entrepreneurship*, **19** (2), 107–20.

Hulme, D. and P. Mosley (1996), *Finance Against Poverty*, London: Routledge.

Humbert, A. and C. Brindley (2015), 'Challenging the concept of risk in relation to women's entrepreneurship', *Gender in Management*, **30** (1), 2–25.

Jurik, Nancy (2005), *Bootstrap Dreams: U.S. Microenterprise Development in an Era of Welfare Reform*, Ithaca, NY: Cornell University Press.

Jurik, Nancy (2019), 'Les contradictions du développement de la microentreprise: L'expérience des américaine' ['The contradictions of microenterprise development: The US experience'] in Nicolas Rebière (ed.), *Quel Rôle pour la Microfinance en Europe en Période d'Austérité? [What is the Role of Microfinance in Europe: Impacts and Issues]*, Bordeaux, France: Presses Universitaires de Bordeaux, pp. 227–49.

Jurik, N.C., A. Křížková, M. Pospíšilová and G. Cavender (2019), 'Blending, credit, context: Doing business, family and gender in Czech and US copreneurships', *International Small Business Journal*, **37** (4), 317–42.

Knight, Melanie (2016), 'Race-ing, classing and gendering racialized women's participation in entrepreneurship', *Gender, Work & Organization*, **23** (3), 310–27.

Liu, J. and X. Zhao (2019), 'Is there a gap on female entrepreneurship research in China and worldwide', paper presented at the 5th International Conference on Economics, Business, Finance and Management, Shenzhen, China, 6–8 June.

MasterCard (2019), 'MasterCard index of women entrepreneurs 2019', accessed 16 April 2020 at newsroom.mastercard.com/wp-content/uploads/2019/11/Mastercard -Index-of-Women-Entrepreneurs-2019.pdf.

National Bureau of Statistics of China (2019), 'The audit report for the GDP in the third quarter of 2019', accessed 17 April 2020 at www.stats.gov.cn/tjsj/zxfb/201910/ t20191018_1703498.html.

Neergaard, H. and C. Thrane (2011), 'The Nordic welfare model: Barrier or facilitator of women's entrepreneurship in Denmark?', *International Journal of Gender and Entrepreneurship*, **3** (2), 88–104.

Ren, X. (2019), 'She economy makes rapid strides', accessed 1 November 2019 at www.chinadaily.com.cn/a/201903/08/WS5c81a82da3106c65c34ed6bf.html.

Scott, L., C. Dolan, M. Johnstone-Louis, K. Sugden and M. Wu (2017), 'Enterprise and inequality: A study of Avon in South Africa', *Entrepreneurship Theory and Practice*, **36** (3), 543–68.

Sequeira, J., Z. Wang and J. Peyrefitte (2016), 'Challenges to new venture creation and paths to venture success: Stories from Japanese and Chinese women entrepreneurs', *Journal of Business Diversity*, **16** (1), 42–59.

Shakya, Y. and K. Rankin (2008), 'The politics of subversion in development practice: An exploration of microfinance in Nepal and Vietnam', *Journal of Development Studies*, **44** (8), 1214–35.

Solinger, Dorothy (2002), 'Labour market reform and the plight of the laid-off proletariat', *The China Quarterly*, **170** (June), 304–26.

Sposato, Martin (2019), 'Understanding paternalistic leadership: How to work with Chinese leaders', *Development and Learning in Organizations*, **33** (6), 19–21.

Sun, Q. (2019), 'Using the Four-self Spirit to live a perfect life', accessed 6 April 2020 at http://www.pkuef.org/info/1175/5123.htm.

Tu, Weiming (1998), 'Probing the Three Bonds and the Five Relationships in Confucian Humanism', in George De Vos and Walter Slote (eds), *Confucianism and the Family*, New York: State University of New York Press, pp. 121–36.

United Nations Development Programme (2015), '@Her Plan: A resource generating platform for female entrepreneurship', accessed 16 April 2020 at www.cn.undp.org/content/china/en/home/presscenter/articles/2015/06/-her-entrepreneurship-plan--a-resource-generating-platform-for-f.html.

Villares-Varela, M. and C. Essers (2019), 'Women in the migrant economy: A positional approach to contextualize gendered transnational trajectories', *Entrepreneurship & Regional Development*, **31** (3–4), 213–25.

Wang, D. (2017), 'Chinese women's Fortune report of 2017', accessed 16 April 2020 at http://i8.hexunimg.cn/hxsps/2017/whitepaper.pdf.

Wang, J., Y. Li and D. Long (2019), 'Gender gap in entrepreneurial growth ambition: The role of culturally contingent perceptions of the institutional environment in China', *International Journal of Entrepreneurial Behavior & Research*, **25** (6), 1283–307.

Wang, Zheng (1997), 'Maoism, feminism and the UN Conference on Women: Women's studies research in contemporary China', *Journal of Women's History*, **8** (4), 126–52.

Wang, Zheng (2003), 'Gender, employment and women's resistance', in Elizabeth Perry and Mark Selden (eds), *Chinese Society: Change, Conflict and Resistance*, London, UK and New York, USA: Routledge, pp. 162–90.

Wang, Zheng (2005), 'State feminism? Gender and socialist state formation in Maoist China', *Feminist Studies*, **31** (3), 519–51.

Warneck, T., L. Hernandez and N. Nunn (2012), 'Female entrepreneurship in China: Opportunity or necessity-based?', *Student–Faculty Collaborative Research Publications*, **23.**

Webster, N. and K. Haandrikman (2017), 'Thai women entrepreneurs in Sweden: Critical perspectives on migrant small businesses', *Women's Studies International Forum*, **60** (January–February), 17–27.

Welsh, D., E. Kaciak, E. Memili and Q. Zhou (2017), 'Work–family balance and marketing capabilities as determinants of Chinese women entrepreneurs' firm performance', *Journal of Global Marketing*, **30** (3), 174–91.

Welsh, H., J. Munoz, S. Deng and P. Raven (2013), 'Microenterprise performance and microenterprise zones in China', *Management Decision*, **51** (1), 25–40.

Welter, Friederike (2020), 'Contexts and gender: Looking back and thinking forward', *International Journal of Gender and Entrepreneurship*, **12** (1), 27–38.

West, C. and D. Zimmerman (1987), 'Doing gender', *Gender & Society*, **1** (2), 125–51.

Xheneti, M., S. Karki and A. Madden (2019), 'Negotiating business and family demands within a patriarchal society: The case of women entrepreneurs in the Nepalese context', *Entrepreneurship & Regional Development*, **31** (3–4), 259–87.

Xie, Yu (2013), 'Gender and family in contemporary China', Population Studies Center Research Report No. 13-808, University of Michigan.

Xinhua (2015), 'Female entrepreneurs account for one quarter in China: White paper', accessed 17 April 2020 at www.chinadaily.com.cn/china/2015-09/22/content _21947630.htm.

Yu, E. (2010), 'Are women entrepreneurs more likely to share power than men entrepreneurs in decision-making?' *International Journal of Business and Management*, **6** (4), 111–19.

Zhang, D. (2015), 'Holding up half the sky: A feminist investigation into the making of the Chinese urban female entrepreneur', Doctoral dissertation, Arizona State University. ProQuest Dissertations Publishing.

Zhang, Houyi (2005), 'Kuaisu Chengzhang de Zhongguo Siying Qiyeshu Jieceng' ['The rapid growth of China's private entrepreneurs'], in Chinese Academy of Social Sciences (eds), *2005 Nian: Zhongguo Shehui Xingshi Fenxi yu Yuce [Blue Book of China's Society 2005: Analysis and Forecast of China's. Social Development]*, Beijing: Shehui Kexue Wenxian Chubanshe.

Zhang, J., L.X. Zhang, S. Rozelle and S. Boucher (2006), 'Self-employment with Chinese-characteristics: The forgotten engine of rural China's growth', *Contemporary Economic Policy*, **24** (3), 446–58.

Zhu, L., O. Kara and X. Zhu (2019), 'A comparative study of women entrepreneurship in transitional economies: The case of China and Vietnam', *Journal of Entrepreneurship in Emerging Economies*, **11** (1), 66–80.

9. Women in copreneurial businesses in the socio-cultural context of Iran

Zahra Arasti, Laleh Sadeghi and Maryam Saeedian

INTRODUCTION

Family businesses are the most prevalent forms of businesses in the world (Lien et al., 2016; Oudah et al., 2018) accounting for more than half of the GDP, 60 percent of new employment, and 65 percent of wages paid (Pieper et al., 2013). 'Entrepreneurial couples' is not a new phenomenon (Webb, 2015). It is the specific subset of family businesses, which means firms owned and managed by a couple (Othman et al., 2016). A unique form of family businesses includes 'copreneurial' businesses in which couples own, manage, operate the business together and commit themselves to it (Othman et al., 2016). They are essential drivers of the gross domestic product (GDP) and contribute to socioeconomic development (Al-Dajani et al., 2014; López et al., 2018; Vieira, 2018) and sustainability (Oudah et al., 2018). Eighty percent of businesses in the world are family-owned, of which one-third are copreneurial businesses (Dyer et al., 2013; Amubode et al., 2016). The study on family businesses is expanding because of the vital role of family businesses in the economy of countries and due to the considerable loss that may arise from failing to foster this type of business in society (Irandust et al., 2014). The number of copreneurial businesses in the world is increasing more than other types of businesses (Wu et al., 2010; Kaul, 2014; Othman et al., 2016). However, despite their importance in the economy and their advantages in terms of productivity (Dahl et al., 2015), their survival rate is only meagre (Nicholson, 2008).

Copreneurship has been studied from different points of view: male versus female entrepreneurs where boundaries and roles, decision-making and influence are addressed (Eisele, 2011); motivating factors for couples' engagement in copreneurship businesses (Othman et al., 2016); pros and cons of copreneurship (Vyas, 2018); social and psychological aspects of copreneurship (Nelton, 1996); work–family conflict (Peregrino-Dartey, 2018); communication between spouses (Lundberg, 1994); factors influencing the effectiveness of a copreneurial business (Farrington et al., 2011); influence of selected demographic variables on the success of copreneurship such as age, gender and education (Eybers et al., 2010); and women's experience in copreneurial tourism businesses (Bensemann and Hall, 2010). However, many theoretical and scientific questions in this regard have not been solved yet. The marriage–work balance is one of the most critical challenges in copreneurial businesses (Farrington et al., 2011; Venter et al., 2012; Randerson et al., 2015), because the growth, survival and success of these businesses are primarily linked with the relationships in the family. Couples share their work and life with each other (Helmle et al., 2014), and shape their businesses in light of the socio-economic environments, family cultures and their mindsets (Saber, 2014). Therefore, copreneurship is highly dependent on the specific context in which it occurs, including cultural, family and domestic settings (Welter, 2011).

Some studies also argue that copreneurship is a gendered process, which is influenced by social norms within a specific context (Deacon et al., 2014; Okello, 2018). Copreneurial businesses in all forms provide an intriguing context for studying the work–family balance from a gender perspective (Franco and Piceti, 2020). Throughout history, women as one of the two main pillars of the family have played a significant role in family businesses. This role has been highlighted in many studies in the field of business and economics, yet it has been largely overlooked in official statistics and surveys on family businesses (Marshack, 1994; Rodríguez-Modroño et al., 2017), due to the masculine structure of entrepreneurship in the society, where the role of women is marginalized (Kirkwood and Tootell, 2008). On the other hand, social norms and beliefs place more significant pressure on women entrepreneurs in developed and developing countries, sometimes leading to exacerbated work–family conflict (Rehman and Roomi, 2012). In Iran, with prevailing gender ideologies that are rooted in social norms and the patriarchal culture, business activities by women are affected by cultural factors (Mortazavi et al., 2009; Arasti and Bahmani, 2017) and some religious misunderstandings limit women's ability to start and develop their businesses (Bastian et al., 2018).

Previous studies have emphasized the impact of 'external field' factors on copreneurial businesses, including 'culture' (Farrington et al., 2011; Helmle et al., 2011; Welter, 2011; Pospíšilová, 2018), especially the need to study copreneurial businesses across different cultures. However, there is still a lack of research on copreneurial businesses in different settings. In addition, how culture affects copreneurial businesses is a neglected research area in the entrepreneurship literature. We maintain that institutional theory has proven useful in entrepreneurship and provides a theoretical lens through which researchers can identify and examine issues such as culture, legal environments, tradition, and so on (Bruton et al., 2010). Considering the gendered nature of all institutions (Brush et al., 2019) and more significant pressure of social norms and beliefs on women entrepreneurs (Hechavarría and Ingram, 2019) in developed and developing countries (Rehman and Roomi, 2012), our chapter attempts to investigate the socio-cultural context of copreneurial businesses in a different setting of a developing country based on institutional theory. First, our findings contribute to the entrepreneurship research, especially in the domain of family businesses, by deepening the knowledge about the socio-cultural context of copreneurial businesses. Second, they shed light on women's entrepreneurship literature and women in copreneurial businesses, where there is only very limited research. Third, this chapter is an application of institutional theory in the entrepreneurship literature. Institutional theory has been used in different domains of entrepreneurship (for example academic entrepreneurship, women's entrepreneurship, and social entrepreneurship). The present study is the first attempt to apply institutional theory in the context of copreneurial businesses. Finally, this chapter applies institutional theory in a developing country, Iran, in a different social setting, hence shedding light on the 'hidden' aspects of institutional theory.

THEORETICAL BACKGROUNDS

In this chapter, we apply institutional theory to deepen our understanding about the effect of the socio-cultural context of Iran on women in copreneurial businesses. An institution constitutes the foundation of social life with formal and informal rules that define the context within which individuals and corporations operate and interact with each other (Campbell, 2004). Institutional theory is a popular theoretical foundation for different domains (for example sociology, the organizational theory, political sciences, economics, etc.) outlined by Scott (2008) in his well-known formulation of three categories of institutional forces: regulative, normative and cultural-cognitive institutions (Bruton et al., 2010). Institutional theory argues that institutions set boundaries for individual behaviors and actions (Welter and Smallbone, 2010). The application of institutional theory in entrepreneurship goes back to a work by Shane and Foo (1999) which explores success in franchises (Bruton et al., 2010). The dissatisfaction with theories that venerate efficiency but downplay social forces as motives of organizational action lead to more application of the institutional perspective in entrepreneurship research. From the institutional perspective, more attention is given to the rules, norms and beliefs that influence organizations and their members, which can vary widely across countries and cultures. Thus, we could develop a more thorough understanding of entrepreneurship research and practice by recognizing what has been institutionalized, that is, which activities, beliefs and attitudes have or have not come to adopt a taken-for-granted or rule-like status, hence fostering or limiting entrepreneurship in a given environment (Bruton et al., 2010).

Regulative, normative and cultural-cognitive institutions (Scott, 2008) influence, directly and indirectly, the desirability and feasibility of entrepreneurship as a career choice (Welter et al., 2014). Any rules which directly influence the costs of setting up a business (for example market entry and exit) are related to regulative institutions. In addition, they are related to policies that have an indirect influence on the desirability and feasibility of entrepreneurship, such as the labor market and tax policies (Welter et al., 2014). Normative and cultural-cognitive institutions, labeled as informal institutions by North (1990), are non-written rules for value-driven actions and behaviors (Scott, 2008). There are uncodified values (which are preferred or considered proper) and norms (how things are to be done consistent with those values) (Yousafzai et al., 2015). Not only do normative institutions influence the desirability of entrepreneurship, since they define acceptable roles for individuals in a society or group, but they also influence the entrepreneurship feasibility by, for example, measuring access to resources (Welter et al., 2014). Cultural-cognitive institutions reflect the interpretation of normative institutions and the shared understanding of individuals as 'the way we do things' (Scott, 2008). Therefore, they also influence the desirability of entrepreneurship, as entrepreneurial intentions are affected by individual cognitions (Welter et al., 2014).

Many studies have pointed out the influence of informal institution on entrepreneurship (Javadian and Singh, 2012; Aramand, 2013; Şeşen and Pruett, 2014; Tlaiss, 2014). Generally, entrepreneurship is influenced by social parameters such as the family, domestic duties, cultures and backgrounds (Shelton, 2006). A wide range of studies support the argument that cultural values influence entrepreneurial behavior. The aggregate level of entrepreneurial activity is uncertain and heavily influenced by culture (Urban, 2007). Of course, cultural issues affect female more than male entrepreneurs (Hechavarría and Ingram, 2019). 'Hidden' institutional constraints, such as the labor market institutions or the roles the society ascribes to women, and the difficulties female entrepreneurs (perceive to) face in engaging in entrepreneurship and growing their businesses could be identified using institutional theory (Brush et al., 2009). Thus, this chapter focuses on socio-cultural issues that could affect women in copreneurial businesses. Therefore, the two next sections present the effect of informal institutions on women's entrepreneurship and copreneurship.

Informal Institutions in Women's Entrepreneurship

All institutions have a gendered nature (Brush et al., 2019). Promotion and expansion of women's entrepreneurial ventures, unlike men's, are highly influenced by the cultural variables of the society. Researchers use institutional theory to address the external contexts that shape women's entrepreneurial activities (Yousafzai et al., 2015). According to institutional theory, formal and informal institutions governing a society can affect the growth or lack of growth of entrepreneurial activities (Welter et al., 2014). In a society, normative institutions determine norms, acceptable roles, and common behaviors for individuals, which significantly affect the desirability of entrepreneurship for women (Ahl, 2006; Baughan et al., 2006; Martinez and Aldrich, 2014). Cultural factors affect the rate of engagement in entrepreneurship by women through influencing the goals and perceptions of the individuals in a society (Hechavarría and Ingram, 2019). Various studies on the subject of women's employment (Yildirim and Aycan, 2008; Moghadam, 2009; Taghizadeh et al., 2017), especially women's entrepreneurship, have frequently emphasized the impact of gender variables as a concept that poses a cultural burden on the rate of entrepreneurship, particularly the rate of women's entrepreneurship (Mungai and Ogot, 2012; Shinnar et al., 2012; Brush et al., 2019). In other words, gender inequality denotes a lack of equal access to social opportunities for men and women. One of these conditions is the creation of businesses and entrepreneurial enterprises by women. Bruni et al. (2004) believe that the concept of entrepreneurship itself includes a gender subtitle. Thus, women who are interested in entrepreneurship are required to follow seemingly neutral values, while men are required to follow the 'entrepreneurial' masculinity. This has been explained by applying the masculinity–femininity dimension in Hofstede's definition of culture. According to Hofstede's model, 'masculinity represents a society in which social gender roles are clear and distinct: Men are supposed to be assertive, tough, and focused on material success; women are supposed to be more modest, tender, and concerned with the quality of life'. 'Femininity stands for a society in which social gender roles overlap: Both men and women are supposed to be modest, tender, and concerned with the quality of life'. Rubio-Banon and Esteban-Lloret (2016) believe that one of the main variables of women's entrepreneurship is related to the assignment of gender roles, which can be shown in terms of the patriarchal–feminist dimension of Hofstede (2003). Rubio-Banon and Esteban-Lloret (2016) argued that cultures with a unique value on the scale of masculinity have many gender differences, which can be used to predict the highest level of entrepreneurship. However, in cases where female values are predominant, women are more likely to be employed by firms. They have also shown that women in patriarchal societies effectively reduce their participation in entrepreneurial activities when they feel distant from the events in their society, that is, they are less able to create a company.

Many studies (Crespo, 2017; Bastian et al., 2018; Hosseinzadeh and Kazemi, 2018) have introduced culture and its related components as barriers to women's entrepreneurship. Some of these studies have been conducted in the context of Islamic countries, and they have shown the impact of cultural factors as an obstacle to women's entrepreneurship that could hinder access to capital and family support for women entrepreneurs (Tlaiss, 2014). More specifically, women's ability to access social, cultural, human and financial capital is limited by constructed and learned ideas (Gatewood et al., 2003; Marlow and Patton, 2005; Gupta et al., 2009). Conformity to gender-role stereotypes is essential to secure resources, such as capital, access to potential suppliers and customers, and mentorship. Usually, suppliers often decide to support and provide resources under the influence of existing stereotypes. Therefore, women who intend to engage in entrepreneurship may be at a disadvantage when they do not fit the prevalent stereotypes (Gupta et al., 2009).

Although a lot of research points to the hindering role of socio-cultural context on women's entrepreneurship, some studies demonstrate its positive effect. For example, Aramand (2013) believes that the Mongolian nomadic culture of adventurism, the secular culture of feminism and the Asian culture of collectivism have key parts in encouraging and supporting women toward success in their entrepreneurial efforts. Basu and Altinay (2002) showed that culture as represented in family traditions is linked to strong family ties which could influence job incentives, the nature of the jobs chosen, and women's participation in business.

Cultural influences on women's entrepreneurship are less evident at the society level, but much more pronounced at the family level, which draws attention to the close links between cultural, social and cognitive embeddedness (Welter and Smallbone, 2010). Some researchers in Islamic cultures argue that disagreements in the family could stall the development of women-owned businesses (Roomi and Parrot, 2008; Itani et al., 2011) that is mainly rooted in traditional beliefs or misinterpretation of religious principles (for example the freedom to leave home or meeting with strangers) (Roomi, 2013). Based on current social norms, household activities are traditionally considered among the responsibilities of women. Thus, women are more likely to experience work–family conflict than their male counterparts (Wu et al., 2019). According to Naidu and Chand (2017), of the 17 gender inequality barriers faced by women entrepreneurs, five stem directly from social norms at the level of society: societal expectations where women's primary role includes childcare and domestic household duties, discrimination, and negative attitudes toward women; while the barriers at the family level are problems related to childcare and family commitments. In this chapter, we focus on the socio-cultural issues pertaining to women in copreneurial businesses at both the society and the family levels.

Informal Institutions in Copreneurship

The term 'copreneurs' was first used by Barnett and Barnett in 1988 for couples who have joint ownership of a business and share its related commitments and responsibilities (Muske et al., 2009). Copreneurship is based on trust, equality, sharing and intimacy between partners and reflects a lifestyle that incorporates both work and personal worlds (Barnett and Barnett, 1988). Muske et al. (2002) provide a comprehensive list of criteria for copreneurial businesses based on definitions from 1971 to 1993, including shared entrepreneurial ventures, ownership, commitments, responsibilities, management, shared risks, equality, intertwined worlds, and partnerships. In copreneurial firms, there is an interaction between the professional and personal lives of a couple (Helmle et al., 2014). Copreneurial businesses are fascinating examples of communication and interdependence in intimate relationships and business partnerships, or love and work (Marshack, 1993; Franco and Piceti, 2020).

The literature on copreneurial business highlights four main concerns associated with this type of business venture: (1) the dual relationship theme; (2) emphasis on saving the marriage; (3) coping with a dual relationship; and (4) the role of gender and the division of labor (Cole and Johnson, 2007). Many studies have emphasized the importance of culture in copreneurial businesses (Farrington et al., 2011; Helmle et al., 2011; Welter, 2011; Pospíšilová, 2018). However, one of the issues neglected in previous research is the socio-cultural issues of copreneurship. The related literature highlights the impact of culture through the work–family conflict on the success of copreneurship (Wu et al., 2010; Franco and Piceti, 2020).

At the family level, the balance between marriage and working relationships is one of the most critical challenges in copreneurial businesses (Farrington et al., 2011; Venter et al., 2012; Randerson et al., 2015), because the growth, survival and success of these businesses are primarily related to family relationships. This type of business is unique because of the overlap and synergy between the work–family systems. The combination of these two systems with different approaches could result in conflict, thus reducing the business effectiveness (Schuman et al., 2010; Venter et al., 2012). When couples are committed to fulfilling their multiple roles, they can meet the competitive demands of both their family and work. Otherwise, tension may occur, especially when a copreneurial woman needs more time for her job and her work interferes with her family roles (Wu et al., 2010). In the business literature, it has been argued that women are more likely to suffer from work–family conflict than men, due to the family responsibilities that are mostly borne by women (Shelton, 2006; Walker et al., 2008; Rehman and Roomi, 2012).

At the society level, couples shape their businesses under the influence of the socio-economic environment, family cultures and their mindsets (Saber, 2014). Culture in the copreneurial business research is anchored in the dynamics of marriage within a business context (Bell, 2008; Machek and Hnilica, 2015). Accordingly, the couple's decision to start a joint copreneurial enterprise and to operate and develop it, is influenced by their common 'values and visions', meaning that culture as a macro element overshadows all the organizational dimensions of copreneurship (Eisele, 2011).

On the other hand, throughout history, women as one of the two main pillars of the family have played a significant tacit role in family businesses. This role has been highlighted in many studies in the field of business and economics. However, their role in family businesses has been largely overlooked in official statistics and surveys (Marshack, 1994; Rodríguez-Modroño et al., 2017). Using a comparative method, Jurik et al. (2019) examined men and women in copreneurial businesses in two different cultures: the Czech Republic (CR) and the United States (US) (diverse in terms of entrepreneurial history, norms and policies). Their research showed that the CR men claimed to be the leader of the business. However, the US men referred to popular discourses about shared decision-making and teamwork. None of the US men described themselves as a boss; rather, they stressed that they made crucial decisions together with their spouses. A few US women referred to their husbands as business leaders, and a few US men and women called the woman a business leader. The leadership designation by US copreneurs was more closely related to who started the business. In a study by Deacon et al. (2014), they found that copreneurs share the ownership and responsibilities in their lives and business by displaying equality in their parts (which may be different, but appear to be equally valued). The US men gave women equal credit. In both countries, women are held accountable for domestic responsibilities. Women focused more on business, childcare and housework, while men were more concerned with business. In family jobs, work–family-related patterns may be influenced by cultural dimensions such as the degree of power and collectivism (Helmle et al., 2011). In some traditional societies, such as Pakistan, women's entrepreneurial activities are affected by cultural and social elements, such as the need for women to obey their husbands. Overall, family responsibilities in a patriarchal society challenge women entrepreneurs in achieving a work–family balance. However, in cases where women entrepreneurs have the support of their husbands and families, the work–family conflict declines (Rehman and Roomi, 2012). In developed Western countries, work–family conflict arises from lack of family and spouse support, but in developing countries such as

India, women benefit from extended family support in childcare and face less conflict (Hill et al., 2004).

Considering the dependence of women's entrepreneurial activity on normative support (Hechavarría and Ingram, 2019), and the importance of context in copreneurial businesses (Welter, 2011), the next section describes the socio-cultural context of Iran, particularly from the women's entrepreneurship perspective.

CONTEXT

Shinnar et al. (2012) emphasized the importance of the impact of contextual differences on the rate of entrepreneurial activities. Entrepreneurship research in the last two decades supports the institutional differences that lead to country-level variations in the development of entrepreneurial framework conditions (Yousafzai et al., 2015). National history, institutional policies, and gender norms are the result of differences that affect entrepreneurship and, most likely, women's entrepreneurship (Jurik et al., 2019). In different countries, women's entrepreneurial activities depend on normative support (Hechavarría and Ingram, 2019), while copreneurial businesses are highly dependent on the context in which they occur, including family, cultural and domestic backgrounds (Welter, 2011). Each country's cultural contexts can lead to new findings in terms of effective factors in the success of copreneurship (Farrington et al., 2011).

Iran's GDP estimate for the period of 2019/20 stood at US$463 billion, with a population of 82.8 million. Hydrocarbon, agriculture, services sectors, as well as manufacturing and financial services are among the aspects that shape its economy. Iran stands second in the world with its natural gas reserves and fourth with its proven crude oil reserves. Economic activity and government revenues largely rely on oil revenues and hence they are volatile. Unemployment rates of 8.9 percent and 17.3 percent for men and women respectively, imply the existence of gender gaps in the labor market. Moreover, the labor force participation rate had a slight decline to 44.3 percent in the December quarter 2019, owing to a drop in the female labor force participation rate to approximately 17.5 percent (World Bank, 2020). Also, women's unemployment rate is higher for young women (40.3 percent compared with 23.8 percent for men) and graduated women (28.2 percent compared with 13.5 percent for men) (Statistical Centre of Iran, 2018). Women entrepreneurs do not seem to enjoy an appropriate business environment in Iran. Despite increased entrepreneurial activity by women, its rate is almost 7 percent with a Female/Male TEA (Total Entrepreneurial Activity) Ratio of 0.5. This is while six countries show roughly equal TEA rates between women and men, including Indonesia, Thailand and Panama as well as Qatar, Madagascar and

Angola in MENA countries (Bosma and Kelley, 2018). Furthermore, according to the World Economic Forum (2018), Iran is among the countries with a high gender gap in the economic ranking among 149 countries. It ranks 143 in terms of women's economic participation, and 106 in terms of leadership positions (Modarresi et al., 2017). The environment for entrepreneurial activity in Iran is not very favorable for men either. Based on a GEM report (Global Entrepreneurship Monitor), only 40 percent of Iranian surveyed adults mentioned entrepreneurship as a right career choice (Bosma and Kelley, 2018).

On the other hand, many studies on women entrepreneurs in Iran have demonstrated social and cultural factors as obstacles to the promotion of women's entrepreneurship. For example, Gelard (2005) and Arasti and Bahmani (2017) showed that environmental factors in Iran (including economic, cultural, political and technological variables) do not support women's entrepreneurship.

At the society level, with prevailing gender ideologies that stem from social norms and a patriarchal culture, some misunderstandings have limited Iranian women's ability to start and develop their businesses (Bastian et al., 2018). Traditionally, the man is considered the breadwinner of the house; therefore, women's participation in the labor market and women's economic activities are viewed as unnecessary (Rafatjah and Kheirkhah, 2012). The Iranian traditional culture follows stereotypes that tend to view women as weak. Thus, Iranian women face many problems in a culture with a dominant gender ideology and prevalent gender stereotypes when they intend to start a business. Importantly, to achieve their business goals they need to redouble their efforts to combat gender stereotypes (Javadian and Singh, 2012). The most important cultural barriers faced by women entrepreneurs in Iran are stereotyped beliefs about women, inequalities in the content of textbooks, and inadequate teachings about women's abilities. These stereotyped beliefs shape the mentality of the society toward women and their abilities, negatively affecting women's entrepreneurship (Hosseinzadeh and Kazemi, 2018). Arasti et al. (2012a; 2012b) reported that because of the stereotypes about women in Iran, they must work harder to prove their competency as business owners to customers, suppliers and other stakeholders in the business world. Stereotypes and gender-based discrimination can affect women's economic activities, directly or indirectly. Some of the stereotypes elaborated by women entrepreneurs in the previous studies (Arasti et al., 2012a) are as follows: 'Women are not good enough for managing large businesses', 'Women's minds are limited', 'Women are emotional', 'It is best if women could leave their work when necessary because family should be their priority'. These socio-cultural norms and values also complicate the growth and development of women's businesses due to the society's uncertainty about women's ability. These include hiring the right workforce, finding a business partner, financing, finding an investor, and getting a loan (Arasti et al., 2012a; 2012b). Gender labels that indicate a kind of inequality between men and women are communicated through family teachings, education systems, stereotypes, role expectations, and the labor relations governing women at work. This is how their identity is shaped, that is, how they perceive themselves as women, how they evaluate themselves, and what actions and behaviors they perceive themselves to be capable of and willing to do. They, in turn, shape the motivations, interests and inner forces, and finally the psychology and personality of women. Due to gender inequality, many of the capabilities required for entrepreneurship – such as a determination to change and innovate, leadership power, and risk-taking – are less cultivated in women. This reduces the likelihood of women becoming entrepreneurs (Javaheri and Ghozati, 2004).

At the family level, the primary responsibility of a woman is to the family. Traditionally and as prescribed by society, a woman needs her husband's consent to work outside the home. Accordingly, women in Iran usually prefer family responsibilities, and it is often difficult for them to perform family and job roles at the same time (Taghizadeh et al., 2017). Many studies have mentioned the multiple roles of women in society. They have three simultaneous roles: spouse, parent and worker, each of which has a set of different expectations. Maintaining a balance between work and family will increase mutual conflict within roles and endanger women's health. Additionally, the feelings of guilt and anxiety, resulting from the mindset that they have not been able to cope well with family responsibilities, is one of the main causes of damage to women's mental health (Javaheri and Ghozati, 2004). A study conducted on 20 Iranian entrepreneur women shows that in the course of their entrepreneurial responsibilities, these individuals have faced the problem of taking care of children and the opposition of their spouses or family members (Saber, 2006). Thus, these problems decrease the likelihood of happiness among women, but after a while they engage with new problems, try to change the existing situation, and make it productive, which is necessary for entrepreneurship. Another study on the male and female statistical population about women's employment has had interesting results. With regard to the most important issues and barriers to women's employment, the managers interviewed mentioned family problems (negative attitudes toward women's employment) and lack of cooperation from their husbands. Interestingly, the male managers pointed to cultural problems (negative attitudes toward women's employment and lack of cooperation at home). Another interesting point in this study is that a quarter of the female managers considered employment to improve women's health and mental well-being, while men did not mention this at all. Instead, a quarter of men raised the possibility of conflict at home if their wives were employed. Also, for both male and especially female managers, the most important negative effect of women's employment is not taking care of children (Rafatjah and Kheirkhah, 2012).

Many studies show that Iranian women encounter different socio-cultural barriers to starting and developing their businesses (Gelard, 2005; Arasti et al., 2012a; 2012b; Javadian and Singh, 2012; Hosseinzadeh and Kazemi, 2018) and that they disapprove of the general gender stereotypes that lead to gender inequality and some restrictions on women's daily lives (Rafatjah, 2012). On the other hand, some recent studies have shown that Iran has experienced structural changes in recent decades (Modarresi et al., 2017). Social and cultural improvement of Iranian families in recent years has shaped the successful patterns of women's business in Iran. Considerable cultural and social change has taken place in recent decades, significantly reducing the gender stereotypes among people and social institutions (Rafatjah, 2012). Due to these socio-cultural changes, we have witnessed higher levels of education and higher admission rates to universities among girls, an increase in the average age of marriage, transformation of the family structure from large to nuclear, and reduction of the household size, which may lead to a rapid increase in women's participation in the coming years (Rafatjah and Kheirkhah, 2012). More women with university education could bring more self-confidence to their fellow women and raise greater awareness of women's rights, both in the family and society.

A review of the literature indicates a research opportunity in the field of copreneurial businesses to investigate the role of culture in 'families' (for example values, goals and commitment) and its link to the enterprise success and sustainability (Eisele, 2011). It appears that the entrepreneurship literature has not examined copreneurial businesses in different settings; therefore, this study is the first attempt to look at women in copreneurial businesses in the societal context of Iran and it aims to illustrate the influence of the socio-cultural context on women in copreneurial businesses, in general.

METHODOLOGY

Research Approach

In gender-related entrepreneurship research, qualitative research approaches such as biographies, case studies and discourse analyses are appropriate (Henry et al., 2016). In this research, we examined the role of culture in copreneurship by employing a qualitative research method, whereby we conducted in-depth interviews with women engaged in copreneurial businesses.

Sample and Data Collection

The study sample consists of couples (married men and women living together) in small (less than 50 people as defined by the Iranian Ministry of Industry, Mine & Trade, 2015), early-stage (under 42 months as specified by Bosma and Kelley, 2018) copreneurial businesses in the service sector in Tehran, the capital of Iran. Lack of consistency in the definitions of copreneurship has made it challenging to identify copreneur couples in large databases that include numerous types of family businesses (Muske et al., 2002). In this study, copreneurial businesses (as defined by Muske et al., 2002) are businesses in which couples shared the ownership, commitments, responsibilities, management, risks, intertwined worlds, and partnerships of an entrepreneurial venture.

Previous studies have mostly interviewed couples together or separately (Jurik et al., 2019). The emphasis in these studies has been largely the role of gender on copreneurial businesses and their goal has been to explore the gender dimension of these types of businesses or the complex relationships within copreneurial businesses (Deacon et al., 2014). Therefore, they needed to gather data from wives and husbands. However, we focused on and interviewed only women in copreneurial businesses, and we were interested in their perceptions of the socio-cultural context.

As there is no database of copreneurial businesses in Iran, we used the snowball sampling method to incorporate the criteria defined earlier, that is, couples in small early-stage copreneurial businesses in the service sector in Tehran. Initially, we identified 30 women in copreneurial businesses based on their interest in the research and because we had easier access to them. We gathered the research data through interviews with women entrepreneurs, which continued until the theoretical saturation of data was reached. In total, we conducted 14 semi-structured, face-to-face interviews and each interview lasted about two hours. We undertook purposeful sampling, prolonged engagement, as well as disciplined subjectivity strategies to evaluate the validity of the research. We formulated the interview questions based on the 5W1H technique about the role of socio-cultural factors on copreneurial businesses. This technique helps us to cover all aspects of copreneurial businesses in a socio-cultural context with women entrepreneurs. The main questions were: 'What: What happened and what are its dimensions?'; 'Where: Where did the event take place?'; 'When: When did the event take place?'; 'Who: Who was involved in creating this event?'; 'Why: What were the reasons or purposes for the phenomenon?'; and 'How: How and under what circumstances did this event occur?' (Ikeda et al., 1998).

We revised the initial questions after two pretest interviews by two experts in women's entrepreneurship. However, we also included additional questions

Table 9.1   *Participants' information*

Interviewee code	Business activity	Age of business	Number of employees	Interviewee's age	Interviewee's education
#1	Restaurant	3	5	32	PhD
#2	Restaurant	3	7	27	Master's degree
#3	Wedding services	3	14	31	Bachelor's degree
#4	Travel agency	3	10	32	Bachelor's degree
#5	Wedding services	2	15	28	Master's degree
#6	Gemstone designer	2	4	35	PhD
#7	Wedding services	3	25	32	Master's degree
#8	Cooking training	3	5	28	Bachelor's degree
#9	Financial advisory	2	3	35	Master's degree
#10	Travel agency	1	2	33	Master's degree
#11	Restaurant	3	3	30	Bachelor's degree
#12	Tourism	1	2	33	Master's degree
#13	Wedding services	2	15	34	PhD
#14	Restaurant	1	10	32	Bachelor's degree

after the preliminary data analysis. Next, we transcribed and analyzed all the interviews. We used the same protocols for each interview to assess the reliability requirements, hence development of a unified database. Table 9.1 illustrates the demographic information of the participants.

Data Analysis

In this research, we conducted a thematic analysis, which is a method for identifying, analyzing, organizing, describing and reporting themes found within a dataset (Braun and Clarke, 2006). According to Nowell et al. (2017), it is a linear, six-phased method, and it is in fact an iterative and reflective process that develops over time and involves a constant moving back and forward between phases. The analytic process can consist of six phases (Braun and Clarke, 2006), including familiarization with the data, generating succinct codes, generating initial themes, reviewing themes, defining and naming themes, and contextualizing the analysis in relation to existing literature. As a result of the thematic analysis on the 14 interviews, we identified six themes at the two levels, which will be presented in the next section.

FINDINGS

This section demonstrates the research findings on the effect of the socio-cultural context of Iran on women in copreneurial businesses. As can be seen in the literature, the socio-cultural context can affect women's entrepreneurial activity at the two levels of society and the family. Therefore, the research findings are premised on these two levels.

At the Society Level

At the society level, the findings involve three themes. The first theme illustrates how society approves of the couples in their businesses and the presence of women in these types of businesses. The second theme highlights how society views the position of women in a business and whether society accepts women in management or leadership positions. Finally, the third theme presents how society views women with regard to their duties at home and what is expected of them.

Businesses by couples

This theme shows how people in society view business couples. Almost all participants highlighted the positive view of society about their business activity as a couple. Apparently, Iranian society accepts this new form of business by couples, and women as a pillar of this type of business.

A 32-year-old woman entrepreneur in the food industry said:

> I was always afraid the society would not believe in us, but it was not that way at all; they always welcome us as husband and wife in our business.

In addition, a 35-year-old woman in the financial advisory sector pointed out:

> Wherever we go, once they understand that we are husband and wife and we work together, they welcome us, and this gives us energy.

Women as leaders in copreneurial businesses

Generally, traditional society does not accept women in some positions. In this study, most informants complained that society did not accept them in managerial or leadership positions.

A 27-year-old woman in the food industry said:

> When we talk about our business in the family or among friends, they say that you are better off than your husband. He is the business leader who manages business affairs, not you!

Another 30-year-old informant in the food industry said:

> Although my husband and I are both in business, most people think that they should address my husband for business affairs, because they don't take me seriously in business.

Societal expectations about women's duties

In our study, most women emphasized the importance of society's view on what is expected of women and their roles in society. They believed that women still have a traditional role in Iranian society, a belief that impedes the presence of women in entrepreneurial activities.

A 32-year-old woman in the service sector commented:

> My husband's parents were upset about my engagement in a copreneurial business and wanted me to concentrate more on my life rather than my business.

Another 28-year-old woman in the service sector said:

> On occasion, my husband's parents asked us to have children. Perhaps, they think I'm so busy with my work.

Women entrepreneurs in this study complained about the traditional attitudes toward women, which have not changed in accordance with other changes in the Iranian society.

A 32-year-old woman in the airline industry said:

> We have a traditional society with traditional attitudes. In this day and age, there are people who have the same attitudes their mothers had.

Another woman in wedding services pointed out:

> Our society has not yet managed to pass through the traditional attitudes about women. It's a critical issue, and it should be discussed.

At the Family Level

At the family level, our findings revolve around three themes. The first theme illustrates how the relationship is between couples as a business team. The second theme presents how the relationship is between entrepreneurial couples in life, and the third theme presents work–family conflicts.

Entrepreneurial couples at work
Many informants in this study asserted that they managed their businesses through shared decision-making and team working. They highlighted their managerial roles in their businesses.

A 32-year-old woman in the food industry elaborated on this point:

> We do not have an authoritative leadership style in our business. It is hard to say who the manager in our business is. We discuss everything, we consult, and we do everything together.

Another 33-year-old informant in the airline industry said:

> We consult each other about all business matters. We are also partners in managing our business.

Entrepreneurial couples in life
The informants contended that there was a good relationship between couples in their copreneurial businesses.

> We enjoy being together because of our special type of business. We live and work together, so we are always together, and it is a pleasure for us. (28-year-old in the field of confectionery training)

> My husband always supports me, and this encourages me even more. (32-year-old in educational services)

> My husband understands me and sympathizes with me. My happiness is important to him. (32-year-old in the airline services)

Work–family conflict
We have outlined the positive and negative examples for this theme. On the negative side, some informants complained about the uneven share of duties and responsibilities that they had as women in life and business.

A 32-year-old woman in the food industry remarked:

> I didn't have enough time for myself. I was confused; my work conflicted with my family.

Another 34-year-old in wedding services stated:

> It was tough for me. I was at the same time a wife, an employee, and a business owner. I had all the roles together.

A 32-year-old woman in the service sector said:

> At the beginning of my work, I couldn't maintain a balance between my work and family, and everything messed up.

Of course, on the positive side, women entrepreneurs came up with solutions for maintaining the work–family balance through planning.

A 32-year-old woman in wedding services noted:

> Many things can be learned over time. For example, after a while, I realized that it was nice to be able to separate work from one's personal life.

A 35-year-old in the financial advisory sector said:

> It's better to set your boundaries and not take family matters to work and vice versa. Of course, it is easier said than done!

DISCUSSION

Summary

This research examined the question: How does the socio-cultural context affect women in their copreneurial businesses? This study investigated the Iranian context, a social setting rarely examined, through the lens of institutional theory. Findings show that the socio-cultural context could be influential at two levels.

At the society level, we talked about society's acceptance of couples in copreneurial business and especially the presence of women in these types of businesses. It was revealed that copreneurial businesses have received excellent emotional support from society. Positive views toward copreneurship encourage and support individuals to create copreneurial businesses. The narratives also indicate approval of women in these businesses. It could be that the traditional Iranian society prefers women who work with their family in the workplace. Therefore, from society's point of view, a copreneurial business that gives woman the possibility of working with her husband is the best type of business for women entrepreneurs.

Another reason could be the high rate of unemployment for women, especially young educated women, and also the recent adverse economy which has left many young couples working together to cope with the situation. Nowadays, in big cities men need not be the only breadwinner in the family as it was in the time of their fathers and grandfathers. This has probably resulted in more acceptances of women working as employees or employers.

The question is, however, how far can this go? Does Iranian society accept women in management positions? According to the findings, the answer is negative. Many people in this traditional society do not accept women in managerial positions. We can see that women are not allowed in leadership positions in many societies (Yeganeh and May, 2011; Kuhlmann et al., 2017; Madsen and Scribner, 2017). For example, Czech men and women are more likely to credit men with business leadership (Jurik et al., 2019).

In the Iranian context, this may be for two reasons: first there is a gender-rooted belief that shapes society's mentality and expectations of women and their abilities and this affects women's entrepreneurship (Hosseinzadeh and Kazemi, 2018). Arasti et al. (2012a) found that society believes women are not good enough to lead large businesses. In fact, society does not yet believe in managerial competencies of women. Another reason is that society is concerned that women may not be able to fulfill their traditional duties and responsibilities should they be occupied with business leadership.

The women in our study contended that their responsibilities as mothers and wives traditionally take a higher priority than their employment and business – a tradition which is rooted in gender expectations and gender roles in society. Studies on Iranian growth-oriented women entrepreneurs (Arasti et al., 2012a; 2012b) stressed the perceptions of women entrepreneurs about stereotypes and gender discrimination in Iranian society, which directly or indirectly affect the business activity of women. Even in non-Islamic countries, we can see these traditional beliefs. A widely-held Czech view is that men are the breadwinners and women are the keepers of home and family. Furthermore, Hamilton (2006) points out that men's role in entrepreneurship stems from traditional assumptions where the man is a business manager who enjoys the visibility and success in business, while the woman is the manager of the household and is always committed to household roles and has limited participation in business. Welter et al. (2014) also asserted that patriarchal cultures, where traditional norms prevail, conflict with Western modernity. Therefore, women from such a culture are restricted to conventional business sectors, home-bound and low-growth activities.

At the family level, the situation is different. Findings show that the relationship between couples in copreneurial businesses is based on honesty and trust. Our research findings are consistent with the study by Deacon et al. (2014) and Jurik et al. (2019) who observed that copreneurs share ownership and their responsibilities in their lives as well as business by practicing equality in their roles. In general, trust and reasonable expectations, shared vision and companionship could help a couple to run their copreneurial business effectively and efficiently (Machek and Hnilica, 2015). Thus, the decision-making process can be shorter and more effective (Deacon et al., 2014).

Moreover, it seems that men in copreneurial businesses have confidence in the managerial role of women or have at least learned to deal with this situation. This is likely to be due to the recent change in attitude in society as mentioned by other Iranian researchers (Rafatjah, 2012; Rafatjah and Kherkhah, 2012; Modarresi et al., 2017). Young men are more receptive to women working. They support women more than their fathers and grand-fathers. Also, young women in Iranian society are more educated and more experienced and have more self-confidence. As noted, our sample consisted of young educated women aged from 28 to 35. Furthermore, today, there are many more role models of successful women entrepreneurs even in traditionally masculine-based businesses (for example international transit). Role models could increase the desirability and feasibility of entrepreneurial activity by women. In sum, all these elements reinforce the position of women in the family. They have become aware of their rights and seek them from their families.

This change in family structure is even more pronounced compared to a previous study on highly educated Iranian women entrepreneurs (Arasti and Akbarijokar, 2006), where a larger number of men did not accept their wives as business leaders; therefore, women had no choice but to relinquish the business leadership to their husbands. However, now 14 years later, we have found that the majority of women in our study received great support in their entrepreneurial activities from their husbands, and that men were more receptive to the idea of their wives in managerial positions.

Our research findings presented a positive and negative side to this issue. Although young educated women are stronger in the present family structure, there has not been significant change regarding their responsibilities in house-hold duties. Many women entrepreneurs in our study talked about the burden of work–family responsibilities, and they complained of household duties that are traditionally assumed to be women's responsibilities. They experience significant family–work conflict, and it is too difficult for them to be a mother, a wife, and an entrepreneur at the same time. Overall, married women in Iran do not have enough time and energy to perform their work and family duties simultaneously, and this triggers anxiety, discomfort and restlessness in women (Taghizadeh et al., 2017).

It could be for this reason that Iranian women have entered the public sphere and have contributed to the economic expenditure of the family, but their spouses are not yet willing to take responsibility for household duties (Rafatjah, 2012). So a common strategy of women entrepreneurs to achieve a balance between business and family lives is to keep their business small, because they know they would have more conflict if they grew their businesses.

Nevertheless, in copreneurial businesses managing work–family conflict is not easy and needs strategies like personal coping with planning, effective communication, delegating, and asking others for help (Peregrino-Dartey, 2018). In our study, some women entrepreneurs could maintain a balance between work and family by receiving more collaboration from their husbands in doing household duties and by setting boundaries and separating their work from their personal lives.

Contribution to Theory and Research

Our first contribution is to the family business literature. Copreneurial businesses are a unique form of family business, which have not been investigated in all their different aspects. One of these overlooked aspects is the influence of environmental factors on copreneurial businesses. However, copreneurship is highly dependent on the specific context in which it occurs, including the cultural, family and domestic settings (Welter, 2011). Our research investigated the socio-cultural context of copreneurial businesses and shed light on this neglected area. The study findings point to the specific context of the family, that is, the relationship between entrepreneurial couples in life and work. In addition, now, we know more about how socio-cultural environments and family cultures influence copreneurial businesses.

The second contribution is to women's entrepreneurship literature. Women become interested in copreneurial businesses for different reasons. The literature on women in copreneurial business is, however, very scarce and we did not find any research about what women have experienced in this type of business. Copreneurial businesses in all forms provide an intriguing context for studying the work–family balance from a gender perspective (Franco and Piceti, 2020). Throughout history, women as one of the two main pillars of the family have played a significant role in family businesses. This role has been highlighted in many studies in the field of business and economics, yet it has been largely overlooked in official statistics and surveys on family businesses (Marshack, 1994; Rodríguez-Modroño et al., 2017), due to the masculine structure of entrepreneurship in society, where the role of women is marginalized (Kirkwood and Tootell, 2008). Our research contributes to this area by defining the leadership position of women in copreneurial businesses and the work–family conflict that they may experience.

The third contribution is the application of institutional theory in the entrepreneurship literature. Institutional theory in entrepreneurship literature has grown significantly over the last decades but entrepreneurship research has looked at institutional influences primarily based on state and market logics, and entrepreneurship research, therefore, has a limited understanding of how other institutional logics (professional, family, religious, corporate and community) influence and interact in the entrepreneurial process (Su et al., 2017). In the family business literature, there are some studies investigating how

family firms are influenced by or may influence formal and informal institutions in their institutional context (Soleimanof et al., 2018); however, our
research is the first attempt to apply institutional theory in the context of copreneurial businesses, thus describing the influence of informal institutions at the
two levels of society and the family on women in copreneurial businesses.

And finally, the fourth contribution is the application of institutional
theory in a developing country with a different social setting. Much of the
research which has used institutional theory in entrepreneurship has been
done in Western developed countries. However, some previous studies have
underlined the importance of research on the role of 'external field' factors on
copreneurial business, including 'culture' (Farrington et al., 2011; Helmle et
al., 2011; Welter, 2011), and particularly the need to study copreneurial businesses within different cultures. This research investigated the context of Iran
in its unique socio-cultural setting, which differs from the developed Western
countries, and from other Islamic countries. Moreover, the research findings
shed light on 'hidden' aspects of institutional theory.

Implications

Our first implication is for policymakers. We suggest that policies be set up
to overcome the socio-cultural challenges of women to increase the feasibility
of creating copreneurial businesses. Women in entrepreneurial functions are
generally under-represented; therefore, those who aim to perform such functions could find role models among a network of mothers, parents and female
friends (Max and Ballereau, 2013). In addition, role models would be able to
increase the desirability and feasibility of entrepreneurial activity. Policies
and programs are also in place to address some of the subcultures that restrict
women's entrepreneurship. The media can play a crucial role in changing
a society's view about women and their abilities as business owners/managers
by introducing successful couples in copreneurial businesses as role models.
The media make use of rare resources to introduce students and audiences to
entrepreneurial role models on television, in the classroom and in the press
(Bosma et al., 2011). Additionally, mass media messages on entrepreneurship
could impact the career decisions that young people may make (Byrne et al.,
2019).

The second implication is for educators. Work–family conflict has a considerable effect on business performance (Welsh et al., 2017), and women give
high priority to work–family balance (Panda, 2018). They know that work–
family balance is not a 'universal formula' but an 'individual model' developed by themselves (Cesaroni et al., 2018), and the country context is related
to work–family conflict and related personal problems (Kaciak and Welsh,
2020). We suggest that specific training programs are defined to help women

in copreneurial businesses to achieve a work–family balance. Furthermore, training couples with time management skills and division of tasks in business and at home could pave the way towards leading a better life and business.

Finally, the third implication pertains to women entrepreneurs. Cultural measures to address inequality and gender discrimination are essential; nevertheless, women should not passively wait for change, but should work to change the status quo (Javaheri and Ghozati, 2004). Realistic acceptance of gender differences between men and women, avoidance of unnecessary comparisons that reduce self-esteem, confidence in their talents and abilities, purposefulness and choice of rational programs not only change the psychological structure of women's personality, but also change the attitudes of others toward women.

Limitations and Future Research Directions

In this research, we held interviews, so social desirability bias poses a threat to the data analysis and the validity of the data; future research could investigate this subject by triangulation of data. Another limitation of this research is the small size of our sample. Future studies could investigate using a quantitative study on a larger sample in different sectors and from various geographic areas to allow the findings to be generalized. Moreover, this study has only captured the experience of women in copreneurial businesses. Admittedly, the opinions and perceptions of the two sides in a relationship about the type of relationship could cause the results to vary (Deacon et al., 2014). Thus, we suggest that in future research, data be collected from both men and women for a more comprehensive analysis.

CONCLUSION

This research investigated the role of the socio-cultural context of Iran on women in copreneurial businesses by conducting a qualitative study with a sample of 14 women entrepreneurs engaged in small, early-stage copreneurial businesses in the service sector in Tehran, Iran. We presented the results through the lens of institutional theory at the two levels of society and the family. At the society level, the results showed that Iranian society is receptive to the presence of a woman in business, though at the side of her husband but not yet as a business leader. Iranian society still gives priority to the household and motherhood roles of women. At the family level the situation is very different. The relationship between entrepreneurial couples is based on cooperation and support. But at the same time, women suffer from dual duties at work and in the home. Hence, they ask for a greater contribution by their husbands to housework to achieve a balance between work and family.

In contrast to previous studies that showed a very dark version of Iranian society and family in relation to the status of women in businesses, our study shows a gradual change, with considerable difference at the two levels of society and the family. The new generation of Iranians respects women's rights more than before. In our study sample, which consisted of individuals aged from 28 to 35, the husbands were more receptive to women working and respected women's rights more than their fathers and grandfathers. On the other hand, at the society level, although young women are more educated and more experienced and have more self-confidence, they have experienced many challenges in their businesses. But, the growing number of successful businesswomen shows that the younger generation, particularly the young and educated women entrepreneurs, have learned to 'escape the traditional gender norms' and can redefine the traditional gender roles in society. Therefore, the younger generation is changing fast and has the will and impetus to bring about change in society.

REFERENCES

Ahl, H. (2006), 'Why research on women entrepreneurs needs new directions', *Entrepreneurship Theory and Practice*, **30**(5), 595–621.

Al-Dajani, H., Bika, Z., Collins, L. and Swail, J. (2014), 'Gender and family business: New theoretical directions', *International Journal of Gender and Entrepreneurship*, **6**(3), 218–30.

Amubode, A.A., Rauf-Lawal, H.M. and Owodiong-Idemeko, B.M. (2016), 'Attitude of couples and marriageable singles in establishing joint fashion business', *Journal of Management and Sustainability*, **6**(1), 192–205.

Aramand, M. (2013), 'Women entrepreneurship in Mongolia: The role of culture on entrepreneurial motivation', *Equality, Diversity and Inclusion: An International Journal*, **32**(1), 68–82.

Arasti, Zahra and Akbarijokar, Mohammadreza (2006), 'Iranian women entrepreneurs: The effective socio cultural structures of business start-up', *Women in Development and Politics (Women's Research)*, **4**(1–2), 93–119.

Arasti, Z. and Bahmani, N. (2017), 'Women's entrepreneurship in Iran', in S. Rezaei, L.-P. Dana and V. Ramadani (eds), *Iranian Entrepreneurship Deciphering the Entrepreneurial Ecosystem in Iran and in the Iranian Diaspora*, Cham: Springer, pp. 109–17.

Arasti, Z., Rezayee, S.O., Zarei, B. and Shariat Panahi, S. (2012a), 'A qualitative study on environmental factors affecting Iranian women entrepreneurs' growth orientation', *Journal of Management and Strategy*, **3**(2), 39.

Arasti, Z., Valinejad, M., Maleki Karam Abad, M. and Mobaraki, M. (2012b), 'Women entrepreneurs' motivations and its role in business growth', *Women's Studies* [motaleat-i zanan], **11**(1), 71–92 [in Persian].

Barnett, F. and Barnett, S. (1988), *Working Together: Entrepreneurial Couples*, Berkeley, CA: Ten Speed Press.

Bastian, B.L., Sidani, Y.M. and El Amine, Y. (2018), 'Women entrepreneurship in the Middle East and North Africa: A review of knowledge areas and research gaps', *Gender in Management: An International Journal*, **33**(1), 14–29.

Basu, A. and Altinay, E. (2002), 'The interaction between culture and entrepreneurship in London's immigrant business', *International Small Business Journal*, **20**(4), 371–93.

Baughan, C., Chua, B. and Neupert, K.E. (2006), 'The normative context for women's participation in entrepreneurship: A multi-country study', *Entrepreneurship, Theory & Practice*, **30**(5), 687–708.

Bell, S.E. (2008), 'Couples' perceptions of operating a family business together', Doctoral dissertation, ProQuest.

Bensemann, J. and Hall, C.M. (2010), 'Copreneurship in rural tourism: Exploring women's experiences', *International Journal of Gender and Entrepreneurship*, **2**(3), 228–44.

Bosma, N. and Kelley, D. (2018), 'Global Entrepreneurship Monitor report', GEM Global Report 2017–2018, London: Global Entreprenurship Research Association.

Bosma, Niels, Hessels, Jolanda, Schutjens, Veronique, van Praag, Mirjam and Verheul, Ingrid (2011), 'Entrepreneurship and role models', Tinbergen Institute Discussion Paper, No. 11-061/3, Tinbergen Institute, Amsterdam and Rotterdam.

Braun, V. and Clarke, V. (2006), 'Using thematic analysis in psychology', *Qualitative Research in Psychology*, **3**(2), 77–101.

Bruni, A., Gherardi, S. and Poggio, B. (2004), 'Doing gender, doing entrepreneurship: An ethnographic account of intertwined practices', *Gender, Work & Organization*, **11**(4), 406–29.

Brush, C.G., De Bruin, A. and Welter, F. (2009), 'A gender-aware framework for women's entrepreneurship', *International Journal of Gender and Entrepreneurship*, **1**(1), 8–24.

Brush, C., Edelman, L.F., Manolova, T. and Welter, F. (2019), 'A gendered look at entrepreneurship ecosystems', *Small Business Economics*, **53**(2), 393–408.

Bruton, G.D., Ahlstrom, D. and Li, H.L. (2010), 'Institutional theory and entrepreneurship: Where are we now and where do we need to move in the future?', *Entrepreneurship Theory and Practice*, **34**(3), 421–40.

Byrne, Janice, Fattoum, Salma and Diaz Garcia, Maria Cristina (2019), 'Role models and women entrepreneurs: Entrepreneurial superwoman has her say', *Journal of Small Business Management*, Wiley, **57**(1), 154–84.

Campbell, J.L. (2004), *Institutional Change and Globalization*, Princeton, NJ: Princeton University Press.

Cesaroni, F.M., Pediconi, M. and Sentuti, A. (2018), 'It's always a women's problem! Micro-entrepreneurs, work–family balance and economic crisis', *Administrative Sciences*, **8**(4), 1–16.

Cole, P.M. and Johnson, K. (2007), 'An exploration of successful copreneurial relationships postdivorce', *Family Business Review*, **20**(3), 185–98.

Crespo, N.F. (2017), 'Cross-cultural differences in the entrepreneurial activity of men and women: A fuzzy-set approach', *Gender in Management: An International Journal*, **32**(4), 281–99.

Dahl, M.S., Van Praag, M. and Thompson, P. (2015), 'Entrepreneurial couples', in *Academy of Management Proceedings*, **2015**(1), p. 14776, Briarcliff Manor, NY: Academy of Management.

Deacon, J., Harris, J.A. and Worth, L. (2014), 'Who leads? Fresh insights into roles and responsibilities in a heterosexual copreneurial business', *International Journal of Gender and Entrepreneurship*, **6**(3), 317–35.

Dyer, W.G., Dyer, W.J. and Gardner, R.G. (2013), 'Should my spouse be my partner? Preliminary evidence from the panel study of income dynamics', *Family Business Review*, **26**(1), 68–80.

Eisele, P. (2011), 'Copreneurial sustainability: Optimizing structures in small and medium US enterprises', thesis, RMIT University.

Eybers, C., Farrington, S., Venter, E. and Boshoff, C. (2010), 'The influence of selected demographic variables on the success of copreneurships', in Proceedings of the Southern Africa Institute for Management Scientist (SAIMS) Conference 2010, pp. 1–26.

Farrington, S., Venter, E., Eybers, C. and Boshoff, C. (2011), 'Task-based factors influencing the successful functioning of copreneurial businesses in South Africa', *South African Journal of Economic and Management Sciences*, **14**(1), 24–46.

Franco, M. and Piceti, P. (2020), 'Family dynamics and gender perspective influencing copreneurship practices: A qualitative analysis in the Brazilian context', *International Journal of Entrepreneurial Behavior & Research*, **26**(1), 14–33.

Gatewood, E.J., Carter, N.M., Brush, C.G., Greene, P.G. and Hart, M.M. (2003), 'Women entrepreneurs, their ventures, and the venture capital industry: An annotated bibliography', Stockholm: ESBRI.

Gelard, P. (2005), 'Key factors influence on Iranian women entrepreneurs', *Women Studies*, **3**(1), 101–123 [in Persian].

Gupta, V.K., Turban, D.B., Wasti, S.A. and Sikdar, A. (2009), 'The role of gender stereotypes in perceptions of entrepreneurs and intentions to become an entrepreneur', *Entrepreneurship Theory and Practice*, **33**(2), 397–417.

Hamilton, E. (2006), 'Whose story is it anyway? Narrative accounts of the role of women in founding and establishing family businesses', *International Small Business Journal*, **24**(3), 253–71.

Hechavarría, D.M. and Ingram, A.E. (2019), 'Entrepreneurial ecosystem conditions and gendered national-level entrepreneurial activity: A 14-year panel study of GEM', *Small Business Economics*, **53**(2), 431–58.

Helmle, J.R., Botero, I.C. and Seibold, D.R. (2014), 'Factors that influence perceptions of work–life balance in owners of copreneurial firms', *Journal of Family Business Management*, **4**(2), 110–32.

Helmle, J.R., Seibold, D.R. and Afifi, T.D. (2011), 'Work and family in copreneurial family businesses extending and integrating communication research', *Annals of the International Communication Association*, **35**(1), 51–91.

Henry, C., Foss, L. and Ahl, H. (2016), 'Gender and entrepreneurship research: A review of methodological approaches', *International Small Business Journal*, **34**(3), 217–41.

Hill, Jeffrey E., Yang, C., Hawkins, A.J. and Ferris, M. (2004), 'A cross-cultural test of the work–family interface in 48 countries', *Journal of Marriage and Family*, **66**(5), 1300–316.

Hofstede, G. (2003). 'What is culture? A reply to Baskerville', *Accounting, Organizations and Society*, **28**(7–8), 811–13.

Hosseinzadeh, M. and Kazemi, A. (2018), 'Identification of barriers and strategies to improve women's entrepreneurship system using hard and soft operation research methodologies', *Industrial Management Journal*, **10**(4), 503–524.

Ikeda, T., Okumura, A. and Muraki, K. (1998), 'Information classification and navigation based on 5W1H of the target information', in *Proceedings of the 17th International Conference on Computational linguistics*, Vol. 1, pp. 571–7.

Irandust, A., Ghavamipour, M., Ebrahimnejad, R. and Hoseinpour, D. (2014), 'Key factors affecting the success of family businesses in Iran and prioritization', *Journal of Entrepreneurship Development*, **6**(2), 55–74 [in Persian].

Iranian Ministry of Industry, Mine & Trade (2015), *Statistics of the Iranian Ministry of Industry, Mine and Trade*. https://mimt.gov.ir/en/index.php.

Itani, H., Sidani, Y.M. and Baalbaki, I. (2011), 'United Arab Emirates female entrepreneurs: Motivations and frustrations', *Equality, Diversity, and Inclusion: An International Journal*, **30**(5), 409–24.

Javadian, G. and Singh, R.P. (2012), 'Examining successful Iranian women entrepreneurs: An exploratory study', *Gender in Management: An International Journal*, **27**(3), 148–64.

Javaheri, F. and Ghozati, S. (2004), 'Barriers to women's entrepreneurship: Influence of gender inequality on women entrepreneurship in Iran', *Journal of Sociology*, **5**(2), 161–78.

Jurik, N.C., Křížková, A., Pospíšilová, M. and Cavender, G. (2019), 'Blending, credit, context: Doing business, family, and gender in Czech and US copreneurships', *International Small Business Journal*, **37**(4), 317–42.

Kaciak, E. and Welsh, H.B. (2020), 'Women entrepreneurs and work–life interface: The impact of sustainable economies on success', *Journal of Business Research*, 112, 281–90.

Kaul, B.A. (2014), 'Goal congruity within copreneurial partners: An exploration of family business continuance', Doctoral dissertation, North Dakota State University.

Kirkwood, J. and Tootell, B. (2008), 'Is entrepreneurship the answer to achieving work–family balance?', *Journal of Management & Organization*, **14**(3), 285–302.

Kuhlmann, E., Ovseiko, P.V., Kurmeyer, C., Gutiérrez-Lobos, K., Steinböck, S., von Knorring, M. and Brommels, M. (2017), 'Closing the gender leadership gap: A multi-centre cross-country comparison of women in management and leadership in academic health centres in the European Union', *Human Resources for Health*, **15**(1).

Lien, Y.C., Teng, C.C. and Li, S. (2016), 'Institutional reforms and the effects of family control on corporate governance', *Family Business Review*, **29**(2), 174–88.

López, M.C.P., Miranda, M.E.G., Argente-Linares, E. and López-Sánchez, L. (2018), 'The internationalisation of Spanish family firms through business groups: Factors affecting the profitability, and the moderating effect of the family nature of the Spanish business', *Revista de Contabilidad-Spanish Accounting Review*, **21**(1), 82–90.

Lundberg, C.C. (1994), 'Unraveling communications among family members', *Family Business Review*, **7**(1), 29–37.

Machek, O. and Hnilica, J. (2015), 'Copreneurship and its impact on financial characteristics of companies', *Ekonomicky Casopis*, **63**(2), 152–66.

Madsen, S.R. and Scribner, R.T. (2017), 'A perspective on gender in management: The need for strategic cross-cultural scholarship on women in management and leadership', *Cross Cultural & Strategic Management*, 24, 231–50.

Marlow, S. and Patton, D. (2005), 'All credit to men? Entrepreneurship, finance, and gender', *Entrepreneurship Theory and Practice*, **29**(6), 717–35.

Marshack, K.J. (1993), 'Coentrepreneurial couples: A literature review on boundaries and transitions among copreneurs', *Family Business Review*, **6**(4), 355–69.

Marshack, K.J. (1994), 'Copreneurs and dual-career couples: Are they different?', *Entrepreneurship Theory and Practice*, **19**(1), 49–69.

Martinez, M. and Aldrich, H. (2014), 'Sociological theories applied to family businesses', in L. Melin, M. Nordqvist and P. Sharma (eds), *The Sage Handbook of Family Business*, London: Sage Publications, pp. 83–99.

Max, S. and Ballereau, V. (2013), 'Theorizing about gender and entrepreneurship: Bridging the gap with social psychology', *International Journal of Gender and Entrepreneurship*, **5**(1), 97–110.

Modarresi, M., Arasti, Z., Talebi, K. and Farasatkhah, M. (2017), 'Growth barriers of women-owned home-based businesses in Iran: An exploratory study', *Gender in Management: An International Journal*, **32**(4), 244–67.

Moghadam, F.E. (2009), 'Undercounting women's work in Iran', *Iranian Studies*, **42**(1), 81–95.

Mortazavi, S., Pedhiwala, N., Shafiro, M. and Hammer, L.B. (2009), 'Work–family conflict related to culture and gender', *Community, Work & Family*, **12**(2), 251–73.

Mungai, E.N. and Ogot, M. (2012), 'Gender, culture and entrepreneurship in Kenya', *International Business Research*, **5**(5), 175.

Muske, G., Fitzgerald, M.A. and Kim, J.E. (2002), 'Copreneurs as family businesses: Evaluating the differences by industry type', paper presented at the United States Association for Small Business and Entrepreneurship annual conference, Reno, NV.

Muske, G., Fitzgerald, M.A., Haynes, G., Black, M., Chin, L., MacClure, R. and Mashburn, A. (2009), 'The intermingling of family and business financial resources: Understanding the copreneurial couple', *Journal of Financial Counseling and Planning*, **20**(2), 27.

Naidu, S. and Chand, A. (2017), 'National culture, gender inequality and women's success in micro, small and medium enterprises', *Social Indicators Research*, **130**(2), 647–64.

Nelton, S. (1996), *In Love and in Business: How Entrepreneurial Couples are Changing the Rules of Business and Marriage*, New York: Wiley.

Nicholson, N. (2008), 'Evolutionary psychology and family business: A new synthesis for theory, research, and practice', *Family Business Review*, **21**(1), 103–18.

North, D.C. (1990), *Institutions, Institutional Change and Economic Performance*, New York: Cambridge University Press.

Nowell, L.S., Norris, J.M., White, D.E. and Moules, N.J. (2017), 'Thematic analysis: Striving to *Meet the Trustworthiness Criteria*', *International Journal of Qualitative Methods*, **16**(1), 1–13.

Okello, I. (2018), 'Gender dynamics between intimate-partner business owners: A case study of copreneur and solo entrepreneur spouses in Uganda', Master's thesis, Dalhouse University.

Othman, N., Mohamed, S. and Suradi, S. (2016), 'Motivating factors of couple involvement in copreneurship businesses in Malaysia', *International Journal of Social, Behavioral, Educational, Economic, Business and Industrial Engineering*, **10**(1), 256–9.

Oudah, M., Jabeen, F. and Dixon, C. (2018), 'Determinants linked to family business sustainability in the UAE: An AHP approach', *Sustainability*, **10**(1), 246.

Panda, Swati (2018), 'Constraints faced by women entrepreneurs in developing countries: Review and ranking', *Gender in Management: An International Journal*, **33**(4), 315–31.

Peregrino-Dartey, E. (2018), 'Copreneurs' coping strategies for work–family conflict', Ph.D. thesis, Walden University.

Pieper, T.M., Astrachan, J.H. and Manners, G.E. (2013), 'Conflict in family business: Common metaphors and suggestions for intervention', *Family Relations*, **62**(3), 490–500.

Pospíšilová, M. (2018), 'Cultural repertoires of the division of labour market and family responsibilities between Slovak entrepreneurial couples and their gendered nature', in U. Hytti, R. Blackburn and S. Tegtmeier (eds), *The Dynamics of Entrepreneurial Contexts*, Cheltenham, UK and Northampton, MA, USA: Edward Elgar Publishing.

Rafatjah, M. (2012), 'Changing gender stereotypes in Iran', *International Journal of Women's Research*, **1**(1), 61–75.

Rafatjah, M. and Kheirkhah, F. (2012), 'The issues and challenges of women's employment in Iran from the view point of working managers', *Quarterly Journal of Socio-cultural Development Studies*, **1**(2), 130–56.

Randerson, K., Bettinelli, C., Fayolle, A. and Anderson, A. (2015), 'Family entrepreneurship as a field of research: Exploring its contours and contents', *Journal of Family Business Strategy*, **6**(3), 143–54.

Rehman, S. and Roomi, Azam M. (2012), 'Gender and work–life balance: A phenomenological study of women entrepreneurs in Pakistan', *Journal of Small Business and Enterprise Development*, **19**(2), 209–28.

Rodríguez-Modroño, P., Muñoz, L.G. and Agenjo-Calderón, A. (2017), 'The hidden work of women in small family firms in Southern Spain', *Journal of Evolutionary Studies in Business*, **2**(1), 66–87.

Roomi, M.A. (2013), 'Entrepreneurial capital, social values and Islamic traditions: Exploring the growth of women-owned enterprises in Pakistan', *International Small Business Journal*, **31**(2), 175–91.

Roomi, M.A. and Parrott, G. (2008), 'Barriers to development and progression of women entrepreneurs in Pakistan', *The Journal of Entrepreneurship*, **17**(1), 59–72.

Rubio-Banon, A. and Esteban-Lloret, N. (2016), 'Cultural factors and gender role in female entrepreneurship', *Suma de Negocios*, **7**(15), 9–17.

Saber, F. (2006), *The Ways to Women's Entrepreneurship Development*, 3rd edn, Tehran: Intellectuals and Women's Studies [In Persian].

Saber, F. (2014), 'Women's entrepreneurship', *Internal Journal of the Women Entrepreneur Manager Association* [In Persian].

Schuman, A., Stutz, S. and Ward, J.L. (2010), 'Which to choose: Family or business?', in *Family Business as Paradox*, London: Palgrave Macmillan.

Scott, W.R. (2008), *Institutions and Organizations: Ideas and Interests*, Thousand Oaks, CA: Sage Publications.

Şeşen, H. and Pruett, M. (2014), 'Nascent entrepreneurs: Gender, culture, and perceptions', *Journal of Women's Entrepreneurship and Education*, 3–4, 1–21.

Shane, S. and Foo, M.D. (1999), 'New firm survival: Institutional explanations for new franchisor mortality', *Management Science*, **45**(2), 142–59.

Shelton, L.M. (2006), 'Female entrepreneurs, work–family conflict, and venture performance: New insights into the work–family interface', *Journal of Small Business Management*, **44**(2), 285–97.

Shinnar, R.S., Giacomin, O. and Janssen, F. (2012), 'Entrepreneurial perceptions and intentions: The role of gender and culture', *Entrepreneurship Theory and Practice*, **36**(3), 465–93.

Soleimanof, S., Rutherford, M.W. and Webb, J.W. (2018), 'The intersection of family firms and institutional contexts: A review and agenda for future research', *Family Business Review*, **31**(1), 32–53.

Statistical Center of Iran (2018), National Population and Housing Census, 20 August, accessed at: https://www.amar.org.ir/english.

Su, Jing, Zhai, Qinghua and Karlsson, Tomas (2017), 'Beyond red tape and fools: Institutional theory in entrepreneurship research, 1992–2014', *Entrepreneurship Theory and Practice*, **41**(4), 505–31.

Taghizadeh, Z., Ebadi, A., Mohammadi, E., Pourreza, A., Kazemnejad, A. and Bagherzadeh, R. (2017), 'Individual consequences of having work and family roles simultaneously in Iranian married women', *Women & Health*, **57**(1), 52–68.

Tlaiss, H.A. (2014), 'Women's entrepreneurship, barriers and culture: Insights from the United Arab Emirates', *The Journal of Entrepreneurship*, **23**(2), 289–320.

Urban, B. (2007), 'A framework for understanding the role of culture in entrepreneurship', *Acta Commercii*, **7**(1), 82–95.

Venter, E., Farrington, S.M. and Boshoff, C. (2012), 'Relational-based factors influencing successful copreneurships', *Management Dynamics. Journal of the Southern African Institute for Management Scientists*, **21**(4), 14–30.

Vieira, E.S. (2018), 'Board of directors characteristics and performance in family firms and under the crisis', *Corporate Governance. International Journal of Business in Society*, **18**(1), 119–42.

Vyas, M. (2018), 'Copreneurs: pros and cons', *Paripex – Indian Journal of Research*, **6**(10).

Walker, E., Wang, C. and Redmond, J. (2008), 'Women and work–life balance: Is home-based business ownership the solution?', *Equal Opportunities Internaitonal*, **27**(3), 258–75.

Webb, J.P.S. (2015), 'African American and White copreneurs: Comparing education, marriage, business success, and longevity', Doctoral dissertation, Capella University.

Welsh, D.H., Kaciak, E., Memili, E. and Zhou, Q. (2017), 'Work–family balance and marketing capabilities as determinants of Chinese women entrepreneurs' firm performance', *Journal of Global Marketing*, **30**(3), 174–91.

Welter, F. (2011), 'Contextualizing entrepreneurship – Conceptual challenges and ways forward', *Entrepreneurship Theory and Practice*, **35**(1), 165–84.

Welter, F. and Smallbone, D. (2010), 'The embeddedness of women's entrepreneurship in a transition context', in C.G. Brush, A. de Bruin, E.J. Gatewood and C. Henry (eds), *Women Entrepreneurs and the Global Environment for Growth: A Research Perspective*, Cheltenham, UK and Northampton, MA, USA: Edward Elgar Publishing, pp. 96–117.

Welter, F., Brush, C. and De Bruin, A. (2014), 'The gendering of entrepreneurship context', Working Paper No. 01/14, Bonn: Institut für Mittelstandsforschung.

World Bank (2020), *The World Bank Annual Report 2020*, Washington, DC: World Bank Group.

World Economic Forum (2018), The Global Gender Gap Report, 10th anniversary edn, Geneva, accessed September 2017 at: www.weforum.org.

Wu, J., Li, Y. and Zhang, D. (2019), 'Identifying women's entrepreneurial barriers and empowering female entrepreneurship worldwide: A fuzzy-set QCA approach', *International Entrepreneurship and Management Journal*, **15**(3), 905–28.

Wu, M., Chang, C.C. and Zhuang, W.L. (2010), 'Relationships of work–family conflict with business and marriage outcomes in Taiwanese copreneurial women', *The International Journal of Human Resource Management*, **21**(5), 742–53.

Yeganeh, H. and May, D. (2011), 'Cultural values and gender gap: A cross-national analysis', *Gender in Management: An International Journal*, **26**(2), 106–21.

Yildirim, D. and Aycan, Z. (2008), 'Nurses' work demands and work–family conflict: A questionnaire survey', *International Journal of Nursing Studies*, **45**(9), 1366–78.
Yousafzai, S.Y., Saeed, S. and Muffatto, M. (2015), 'Institutional theory and contextual embeddedness of women's entrepreneurial leadership: Evidence from 92 countries', *Journal of Small Business Management*, **53**(3), 587–604.

Index

and women's agency 50–51
and collectivism 69, 81, 82
contextual embeddedness 109
contextualizing 91
creating opportunities for 99–101
and culturally-endorsed
self-protective leadership
ideals 73, 80, 82–3
and culture
effects on embeddedness of 5–8
in MENA region 23–4, 38
relationship between 2–3, 201
and self-determination 11–12
in South Africa 111–13,
130–131
and culture practices 70–72, 82, 83
in Ethiopia 92–104
importance of 1
in India
institutions 159–60
making case for growth and
success 144–7
informal institutions in 200–202
in Iran
gender-rooted belief affecting
214
policies in place to address
restrictions 217
social and cultural factors as
obstacles to 205
in MENA region 23–4, 36, 37–8, 40
as pivotal for economic development
35, 36
prevalence of 1–2, 88

push–pull of
factors 174–5
and government 184–7
relationship to culture 2–3
in South Africa
context 118–19
and culture 111–13, 130–131
and emancipation 111–19
and empowerment 113–14
study limitations 133
theoretical framework 117–18
women's self-employment
and absence of uncertainty
avoidance 73
as act of institutional disintegration
69, 72, 80
analysis of 77–80, 82
in China
background and context 174–5
doing entrepreneurship/doing
gender 175–7, 188–91
findings 183–91
methods and data 180–183
microenterprise 177–80
study conclusions 191–2
countries' scores 75, 80
and culturally endorsed leadership
ideals 72–3
relationship to collectivism 68–70,
76, 81, 82
and self-protective leadership ideals
69–70, 73, 82
work–life balance 11, 154, 181
see also family–work balance